"*Flour Power* is a master class in bread baking from one of the most gifted and grounded teachers around. Tara takes you from field to flour, painting a gorgeous and informed portrait of how to bake like the artist you are."
—Josey Baker, owner of Josey Baker Bread bakery, author of *Josey Baker Bread*, and co-owner of San Francisco's the Mill

"Tara Jensen is a natural teacher. *Flour Power* is not only full of everyday and special occasion recipes; it is jam-packed with the knowledge you need to become an intuitive baker. *Flour Power* is a little bread angel on your shoulder encouraging you through a variety of grains, techniques, bakes, and meals."
—Abra Berens, author of *Ruffage* and *Grist*

"With *Flour Power*, Tara Jensen brings her baking classroom into our homes. Her gift as both instructor and baker is evident on each page as she guides us through the science and alchemy of baking. *Flour Power* is accessible to the novice baker and a gift to skilled ones, providing a valuable contribution to the baker's canon."
—Jennifer Lapidus, founder of Carolina Ground Mill and author of *Southern Ground: Reclaiming Flavor Through Stone-Milled Flour*

"A passionate love letter to sourdough. Tara truly is a master of her craft and we are all so fortunate to learn from her. Devour this book as fast as you can and get to baking. Bread wisdom like this doesn't come around that often."
—Sean Brock, chef and owner of Audrey and June in Nashville and author of *Heritage* and *South*

"I was luck[...] workshop [...] beautiful and delicious sourdough loaves. Tara taught us about flour (we even milled our own), sourdough starter, and, of course, bread making. Reading *Flour Power* is like being back in that workshop. You'll learn so much about making magnificent bread—it's like Tara is holding your hands throughout."
—Klancy Miller, founder of *For the Culture* and author of *Cooking Solo: The Joy of Cooking for Yourself*

"Tara Jensen is an effortless and inspiring teacher. In *Flour Power*, she not only expertly guides readers through baking science and techniques but also passes along the everyday wisdom of how to incorporate baking bread into your life. Tara's undeniable expertise, signature creativity, and floury fingerprints are all over these beautiful pages."
—Erin Jeanne McDowell, author of *The Book on Pie*

"Tara inspires me to bake. She brings together simple ingredients with integrity to bake our way through life's hardest moments. *Flour Power* has all the tools to conquer our sourdough fears in the comfort of our home kitchens. I am lucky she is one of my closest friends and my writing confidante—my baked goods and life are better for it."
—Melissa M. Martin, author of *Mosquito Supper Club*

FLOUR
POWER

THE PRACTICE AND PURSUIT OF BAKING SOURDOUGH BREAD

FLOUR POWER

TARA JENSEN

FOREWORD BY CLAIRE SAFFITZ

Photographs by
Johnny Autry and Charlotte Autry

Illustrations by Jan Buchczik

Clarkson Potter/Publishers
New York

TO VIOLET RYE

Contents

133 Desem

193 Rye

▼ Rye, Spelt, and Anise Loaf (page 218)

251 Extra Credit

294 Resources

296 Acknowledgments

298 Index

Foreword

I FIRST MET TARA JENSEN IN 2016 on the thirty-fifth floor of the World Trade Center in New York City. I was then a food editor at *Bon Appétit* magazine, and Tara, who had recently been featured in the magazine, was in town to teach a weekend workshop on sourdough bread making in the magazine's test kitchen. I "volunteered" to help run the event, but really, after seeing Tara's gorgeous breads and having read her profile, I was dying to learn from her. The fifteen or so students (mostly home bakers but also a professional or two) and I stood rapt as Tara walked us through the fundamentals of sourdough, from wheat categorization to natural fermentation to maintaining a starter. While letting handfuls of a gold-tinged flour (freshly milled in Brooklyn for the workshop) fall through her fingers, she explained the anatomy of a wheat berry using a hand-drawn diagram (much like the illustrated one on page 19). Then she said, "Think of grain as fresh produce."

Her words hit me like a sack of flour. Even as a cooking professional and baker, I was accustomed to thinking of flour as a pantry ingredient, as I think most people are. But Tara's passion for heirloom and ancient grains, and the singular flavors, textures, and aromas they bring to bread, awakened me. Wheat comes from the earth, and the variety, where and how it's grown, and how it's milled, all matter deeply. What I learned in Tara's workshop forever shifted my perspective on grains, flour, and the food we eat in general. I am certain that this beautiful book, written in Tara's kind but authoritative voice, will initiate a similar shift for you.

Tara's a natural teacher, and this book reads as if she's at the bench next to you, patiently articulating the core concepts and techniques of bread making, as well as the joys and rhythms of the craft. *Flour Power* teaches us how to select and use ingredients with integrity, but it's not dogmatic. While she encourages the use of stone-milled whole wheat flours, Tara makes plenty of space for white flour you can buy from the supermarket and explains how good bread is possible with both (and often a blend). It's rigorous but not rigid, honest but understanding.

This book covers the basics, like how to use a digital scale in a way that any novice would be able to follow. Tara has a keen sense of scope throughout, presenting all the information in easy-to-digest parcels so nothing about the process feels overwhelming or unmanageable. At the same time, I admire and appreciate Tara's willingness to delve into more complex concepts like desired dough temperature and baker's percentages. She demystifies these parts of the process that I, as a longtime hobbyist sourdough baker, still find inscrutable, like knowing when my bread is proofed (according to Tara, I'm still under proofing it—I'm sure she's right). For bakers of any skill level, the definitions and explanatory notes are sure to become frequent references, even when baking a recipe from a different source.

The first three chapters of the book, Learning About Flour, Fermenting Flour, and Methods for Bread Making, lay the groundwork for the "formulas" (a term, Tara explains, that is preferable to "recipe" when it comes to bread, as they're not fixed) that come later. Because processes like gluten development and fermentation rely on so many factors, the formulas give time ranges and use temperature as a reliable guide. They also provide timing "snapshots," so you know when to begin, and they note frequent stopping points to help bakers plan and work around busy schedules (Tara wrote the book as a new mom, so trust that she understands the need for flexibility). The breads themselves come in many forms and are a mix of age-old and modern, incorporating ancient and heirloom grains but also fruit, fresh herbs, seeds, and spices. I cannot wait to bake every single one (especially some of the dark, craggy rye breads).

The subtitle of this book, *The Practice and Pursuit of Baking Sourdough Bread*, pinpoints what we all stand to gain from Tara's work. If we approach bread baking as she encourages, with an open and curious mind, it becomes a sustaining act that builds confidence, reduces anxiety, and develops intuition, as well as an avenue for constant exploration and learning. It's a journey, even a lifelong one if you choose, and *Flour Power* will set you firmly on that journey and be there to support you every step of the way.

—**Claire Saffitz,** *New York Times* **bestselling author of** *Dessert Person*

Introduction

IF I HAD TO PICK A STARTING POINT for where I am now, sitting at my kitchen table in Virginia, I'd lead you back in time to a moment in 2001 when I walked into the Morning Glory Bakery, a tiny bakery in coastal Maine. There I found a woman wearing all black, with long dark hair, arms covered in tattoos, listening to Patti Smith. I asked for a job and she looked over my shoulder to see my girlfriend waiting in our Subaru out front. She glanced back at me and told me to come in the next day at 6:00 a.m.

The closest I got to touching bread was toasting bagels, but the place was packed with people who danced to the beat of a different drum. There were midwives, punk rockers, musicians, and artists scattered about, cramming jelly biscuits, hummus sandwiches, and buttered baguettes into their mouths. Growing up the oddball in a small, rural town in Maine, I found the cast of characters that paraded through the door soothing.

At the counter, stacked high with hot loaves, we'd talk about babies, women's rights, the government, the environment, the latest music, astrological signs, and who was dating whom. We'd plan protests, birthday parties, and bike rides and end the day mopping to incredibly loud Morrissey. Impeccable attention to ingredients, ovens, and agriculture would all come later, stemming from this root of safety and comfort in a chosen family.

In 2004 I graduated college and found myself filling out an application on a snowy winter's day at Red Hen Baking Company, a sizable bakery in central Vermont. I exaggerated my previous experience to get in the door, and it was there I was introduced to my new best friends: a wooden peel, a deck oven, a loader, a dough divider, a mixer, a water meter, and tubs upon tubs of delicious, supple artisan bread dough.

The mechanics of producing up to two thousand loaves a day were fascinating. I moved through the stations of shaping, mixing, and baking like a journeyman earning badges. My confidence grew alongside my skill (and biceps, too). There are few other times in my life that I've felt

as powerful as those moments when I would pull back the canvas belt, watch twenty loaves slip onto a hot deck, and rush to hit the steam button, only to swirl behind me and grab another twenty loaves to slash and load. And yet, when everything was shut off and only the hum of the walk-in could be heard, I felt a whisper. *This wasn't the only way to make bread.*

Two years later I loaded up my 1982 Volvo and went to work at Farm and Sparrow, a bakery tucked away in the mountains of western North Carolina. Yet again I found myself in a fake-it-till-you-bake-it scenario. Forget deck ovens and dough dividers. Here, I chopped wood, started fires, and made bread with my blood, sweat, and tears. Catapulted into the world of small-scale grain growing, fresh flour, wood-fired ovens, and wet doughs, I barely kept my chin above water.

There, low to the ground, head spinning, I found what I was looking for: bread made like a good wine, appreciated without any bells or whistles and discussed in terms of vintages and microbial profiles. I began working with freshly milled flour (no big fifty-pound bags of white stuff) and a gentle, diving arm mixer that replicated human kneading. The idea of turning on a machine and whipping bread into shape was horrifying in my new paradigm.

Those special years working with a small group of talented people making extremely good bread were wonderful, but they were also painful. I grew a small plot of wheat for the first time. I learned how to source wood and chop it to the right sizes and amounts to sustain a bread oven. I made

friends with fire. I learned about prestige and the James Beard Foundation Awards and what it was like to have to block off fanatical customers at the farmers' market. I was introduced to chefs and the back door of restaurants and late nights filled with drinking that would predictably end at the Waffle House. I learned what it was like to be called "the best."

I also learned there is a real danger to tying your worth to how the bread comes out any given day and that it's harsh to make fun of people who like sandwich bread. I learned that having extreme values can be lonely. I grew tired and isolated.

After watching my mentors burn bright and then burn out, I realized I didn't want to own a large-scale bakery. I didn't have any interest in a storefront or retail location, didn't have any excitement about hiring staff, and didn't want to spend my time on the computer with spreadsheets, so in 2012, when I began my own bakery—Smoke Signals (named after the smoke from the chimney of a twenty-year-old Alan Scott oven)—I sold only at farmers' markets and made only as much as I could with my own two hands. While the solitary life of wood-fire baking suited me, it didn't represent all of me. Knowing that I didn't want to expand production, I turned to the original source of joy I found in bakeries: other people. I began leading classes from the bakery, taking what I learned in the professional world and sharing it with home bakers.

In 2015, I led a small group of local women through the ins and outs of making an apple pie from scratch, and eventually I expanded to classes on sourdough bread and other baked goods, such as croissants and rye bread. I liked preparing and writing the materials. I liked setting up baking stations with all the fun tools, and I thoroughly enjoyed the sparkle of fulfillment in someone's eyes as their creations emerged from the oven. Watching new and curious bakers gain confidence and skill completely hooked me into teaching. I've been teaching folks how to bake ever since, and it has never ceased to be rewarding.

Most of my bread baking, for now, takes place at home with a toddler underfoot. Home is an incredibly important and often underrated place of work and life. Home is where most of us live, love, cook, make families, cry, listen to music, and play with our dogs. Home is a place of experimentation, discovery, science, and craft. I bake from home now, using either my mobile wood-fired oven or the beastly electric oven in our kitchen. I bake for myself as a form of therapy, I bake to participate in a larger cultural movement, and I bake to remember it in my bones.

The recipes (or formulas, if that's how you like to talk) in this book are a blend of my deepest love for my different "baking parents" and styles that raised me. They incorporate my respect for the technical and professional along with my need to continually find a spiritually fulfilling existence. They honor the comfort of a busy, warm bakery and carry a torch for the kinds of innovation that come from going rogue. Think of each loaf as someone I've shaped a baguette next to, panned up some rye bread alongside, or chopped kindling with. Get to know them. They make good company.

Learning About Flour

WITH ALL THE TRANSFORMATIONS that occur to the wheat berry to make bread, it's often lost that the toast you're enjoying began life as a collection of grass seeds waving in the wind. Good bread starts with good soil, which is why I like to focus on purchasing flour from mills that source from farms using regenerative growing practices, organic pest and weed control, and crop rotation. These elements let me know that the health of our collective home, Mother Earth, was at the forefront of the process each step of the way.

Baking bread with well-made flour offers us a chance to express and taste terroir: the unique flavor that comes from a specific blend of climate, growing methods, and preparation. Just as winemakers talk about the soil and topography a specific grape variety was grown in, so too can we, as bakers, enjoy grains and flour with interesting characteristics and qualities. Let's start at the heart of it all: the components of the wheat berry.

"BREAD SPEAK"

Learning to bake can be as intimidating as learning a foreign language. To make matters worse, bakers have slang words and abbreviations—and one word can mean several things. Here are some basics to get you started talking (and thinking) like a pro.

Autolyse: a resting period of just the flour and water that occurs at the beginning of bread making

Bâtard: a "football" looking, oval loaf that's proofed in an oblong basket

Cereal grain: an agricultural grass grown for the edible seed, such as wheat, rye, and barley

Crumb: the interior of a loaf of bread that may be holey, dense (or tight), or in between

Crust: the exterior of a loaf of bread

Discard: the portion of your starter (white, desem, or rye) that is removed when you refresh it

Extraction rate: how much of the whole wheat berry is left after it's milled

Fermentation: in the case of sourdough, we're talking about yeast and lactobacilli consuming simple sugars and producing alcohol, acids, and gas

Flour: grain crushed into a powder, which can have various levels of coarseness and contain various parts of the berry (endosperm, germ, and the bran—more on that on the opposite page)

Fresh flour: flour less than a week old or, at its very best, flour that's only hours old (fresh flour is exciting!)

Gluten: two proteins, gliadin and glutenin, that form a long chain—the chain is called gluten

Hydration: the amount of water, in relation to the flour, in a starter or dough

Lactobacilli: acid-tolerant bacteria that eat sugars and make lactic and acetic acids

Leaven: a scaled-up portion of starter with more flour and water, needed for a big batch of dough or doughs that require a larger amount of starter than you might have on hand

Loaf: a sandwich-style bread baked in a rectangular pan

Protein level: the amount of gluten a dough will develop and, hence, how strong it will be

Round: a dough that is shaped in a round and proofed in a round basket

Starter: a mix of flour and water that houses natural yeast and lactobacilli, used to flavor and leaven bread

Stone ground: flour made by being crushed between two stones

White flour: standard, fine, white, industrial flour found at the supermarket (no judging)

Yeast: a fungus that eats sugar and produces alcohol and gas

THE WHEAT BERRY—
ANATOMY LESSON

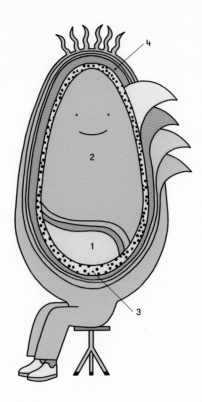

I LIKE TO THINK about the wheat berry like an egg, with the germ as the yolk, the endosperm as the white, and the bran as the shell.

GERM: The germ is by far the most nutritious part and makes up 2% of the overall weight of the berry. It's high in vitamin E and trace minerals, and with moisture and heat, a taproot will burst from the germ and life begins!

ENDOSPERM: The endosperm is the largest portion of the berry at approximately 75% of the overall weight. The endosperm is a storehouse of starch and protein. If you've ever broken open a sprouted wheat berry, you can see a milky portion that feels like mashed potatoes. That's the endosperm. Couched in this substance are gliadin and glutenin, the two proteins necessary for making gluten. Gliadin gives dough extensibility and glutenin provides elasticity.

ALEURONE LAYER: Transitioning between the bran and the endosperm is the aleurone layer, a sheath where enzymes and lactic acid bacteria live. The enzyme amylase works on unknitting simple sugars, while the bacteria create the right levels of acidity for proper growth. Bread dough made with bran included will show higher signs of activity because it contains this extra dose of enzymes and microbes.

BRAN: The bran is 14% of the berry and is made of layers of cellulose and fiber. It protects the endosperm and absorbs water. In flour, bran provides color, texture, and fiber. In wheat, phytic acid, which helps the plant store phosphorus, is found in high volume in the bran. Phytic acid binds with trace minerals, so when we eat unfermented whole grains, such as supermarket whole wheat bread that isn't sourdough, our bodies don't get the full benefit of the calcium, iron, and zinc. In sourdough, the fermentation via the lactic acid bacteria breaks it down, unlocking the total nutrition.

ABOVE
(1) Germ (2) endosperm (3) aleurone layer
(4) bran

THE SIX BASIC WHEAT CLASSIFICATIONS

HARD OR SOFT
PROTEIN LEVEL

Hard wheats are high in protein (10% to 14%) and have enough gluten to trap gas well, making them structurally suitable for hearth-style artisan bread loaves, bagels, and pizza. Softer wheats are lower in protein (9% to 11%) and the gluten they develop is fragile, allowing gas to potentially escape a dough. This makes soft wheat best suited for cakes, cookies, and pan breads. Besides having different levels of protein, the bran of hard wheat and soft wheat each responds differently to being milled, particularly in a stone mill. Hard wheat shatters, making tiny, sharp freckles in the flour that are difficult to remove, whereas the bran of a soft wheat comes off in large portions, making it easy to sift out.

To decide if you want a high- or low-protein flour, or a blend of the two, think about the final qualities of what you're making: does the dough (or batter) need to trap gas well for a strong rise, like in a bâtard with high volume and an open crumb, or does the gas need to pass out of the batter, like in a muffin where air pockets are unwanted or a sandwich loaf where you want all the jam to stay put? Harder grains will hold the gas in, weaker grains will let it out.

RED OR WHITE
DEFINES HUE, FLAVOR, AND PROTEIN LEVEL

When teasing out the difference in color and flavor between red and white wheats, it's helpful to borrow from the wine world and imagine them as red and white grapes. Breads made with red wheats will ferment easily, rise well, and, like wine made with red grapes, have a rosy depth of color and a peppery, nutty, somewhat bitter taste. In contrast, breads made with white wheats will ferment slowly, benefit from rising in a pan, and, like wine made with white grapes, showcase a golden or honey-colored hue and a light flavor.

WINTER OR SPRING
INDICATES PLANTING AND HARVESTING TIMES AND PROTEIN LEVEL

Winter wheats are planted in the fall and harvested in the early summer. Spring wheats are planted in the spring and harvested in the early fall. In general, spring wheats tend to have a higher level of protein and a pronounced elasticity. Breads made from spring wheats do well baked on the hearth and have an excellent rise in the oven. Winter wheats are starchier and structurally delicate. Doughs made from winter wheats do well with cold bulk fermentation (see page 52) to add strength and can benefit from being baked in pans.

> **RYE TIME!** Rye is not wheat! Although similarly composed, rye berries have little to none of the required proteins needed to create gluten. They do have more bran, fiber, and sugars than wheat, making rye flour fragile and quick to ferment. Rye flour may have up to five different grades, textures, and colors depending on the milling style. (For more on rye breads, see the Rye chapter that begins on page 193.)

OTHER KEY CLASSIFICATIONS

Impacts of the Green Revolution (1960–1970)

The Green Revolution was an agricultural campaign to eliminate famine in developing countries by replacing regional varieties of rice and wheat with high-yielding modern varieties. Along with patented new seeds also came new equipment and synthetic pesticides and fertilizers. American wheat breeder Norman Borlog developed some of the first strains of dwarf wheat used: short stalky wheat less prone to lodging (falling over) in the field, making it easy to mechanically harvest. Dwarf wheats are also high yielding, with massive seed heads atop a two-foot stalk. Dwarf wheat became the poster child for ending hunger, and Borlong went on to win the Nobel Peace Prize in 1970. In subsequent years, his work, and the Green Revolution, has been criticized for profiting major biotech corporations, like Monsanto, at the expense of farmers and their communities, and for producing cereal grains with little nutritional value or cultural relevancy.

ANCIENT

"Ancient" describes grains that have remained minimally unchanged for hundreds of years (or millennia), such as einkorn, teff, barley, spelt, emmer, and pseudo cereals like quinoa and buckwheat.

HEIRLOOM OR HERITAGE

Heirloom, or heritage, wheats are too young to be ancient and too old to be modern (mid-1800s to 1960s). These wheats have been passed down from our great-great-grandparents to our grandparents and now to us, sometimes only by the handful (literally). Like heirloom tomatoes or apples, these wheats may have interesting family or place-based names, such as Red Fife, and are often grown on a small scale with special care. Although unique, heirloom wheats are typically selected with predictability, ease of harvesting and milling, and baking performance in mind. Flavor and cultural relevancy also play important roles, balanced by what's good for the farmer, miller, and baker.

LANDRACE

Landrace wheats have been minimally unchanged since domestication and have a wide genetic background, making them highly adaptable. From field to field, even just a few miles apart, landrace grains show wide variation in germination, height, color, and berry size, due to the diversity in the gene pool. This inherent quirkiness (unpredictability) is their strength and value: Drought or mold might impact one field but not another. A great example of a landrace grain is Turkey Red, the wheat I plant in my yard each fall. In a single plot, the color and size of the wheat berries vary, and it behaves differently in different yards, and yet still it grows well!

MODERN

Strictly speaking, modern wheats are wheats that have been bred and developed post-1960. Though the term *modern* can take on a negative context when used to describe industrially farmed, semi-dwarf wheats born out of the Green Revolution (see Impacts of the Green Revolution [1960–1970], at left), there are certainly varieties of wheat being bred and grown today with taste, cultural importance, and soil health in mind.

TASTE THE GRAINBOW

IT'S A GREAT TIME to be a baker! Today many high-quality flours can be delivered right to your doorstep. (See Resources, page 294.) The chart at right is a listing of what I like to keep on hand and what you will want to stock up on to bake from this book.

VARIETY	TYPE	TASTE	USE
Bloody Butcher Corn	Heirloom, Dent Corn	Fruity, buttery, creamy	Corn bread, hominy, tortillas
Buckwheat	Ancient	Slight bitterness, earthy, dirt	Noodles, flatbreads, pancakes
Danko Rye	Heirloom, Winter	Grassy, green, beet-like	Rye bread and pastry
Einkorn	Ancient	Toasted hay, malty	Bread and pastry
Kamut	Ancient, Hard, Red, Winter	Toasted corn sweetness	Bread, pasta, crackers
Oats	Ancient	Milky, toasty, creamy	Porridge, breakfast cereal, breads
Red Fife	Heirloom, Hard, Red, Winter	Herbaceous, cinnamon	Artisan hearth loaves
Sonora	Heirloom, Soft, White, Winter	Vanilla, almond, potato	Noodles, rolls, flatbreads, tortillas
Spelt	Ancient	Nutty, floral, honey-sweet	Bread and pastry
Turkey Red	Heirloom, Landrace, Hard, Red, Winter	Peppery, robust, bold	Artisan hearth loaves
Wrens Abruzzi Rye	Heirloom, Winter	Fresh cider, mossy, black tea	Rye bread and pastry

OPPOSITE FROM LEFT TO RIGHT
Kamut, Oats, Buckwheat, Spelt, White Wheat, Hopi Blue Corn, Rye, Emmer, Einkorn

HOW FLOUR IS MADE

Harvesting Wheat at Home

When the berry-laden head of the wheat grass nods toward the earth, then it's time to harvest. I use a scythe or sickle (or even a sharp pair of scissors!) to mow down my "bread patches" (little plots of wheat I plant in my yard specifically to make a loaf of sourdough bread from). Once the tall grass is cut, I bind portions together into shocks and store the shocks somewhere out of the elements, such as in a barn or a garage, for a few weeks. During this time the grass will fully dehydrate, and the berries will separate easily from the brittle heads.

Returning to the wheat once it's dry, I thrust the heads of the stalks into a pillowcase and beat the case with a rolling pin to separate the wheat berries from the chaff. This process is called threshing. In a larger plot of wheat, threshing is done in the field with a combine that cuts the wheat and separates it immediately. (Technology really can be wonderful!)

After the wheat berries have broken free, I stand on a ladder with a box fan and a bucket below, and I turn the pillowcase over. The light chaff and husks fly away, while the heavy amber berries clank into the waiting bucket. (This is by far one of my favorite sounds.)

I store my haul, which is often not more than a few cups, in an airtight container and excitedly await the next step: grinding the berries into flour. My tiny harvest will be milled in a tabletop mill at home (see page 40). Most flour today is either roller milled or stone milled (stone ground), with each style of milling having its own set of pros and cons.

ROLLER MILLED FLOUR

Roller milling wheat involves feeding the wheat from a hopper through a series of cylindrical, vertical steel rollers. The initial roller—the "breaker"—shatters the berry into pieces for efficient separation. Shaken and sorted, the germ is removed, and the bran is sifted out on the first pass. The remaining starchy center (endosperm) is then ground to a fine texture through another set of four or five "reduction rollers" to make flour. This process makes a uniform flour that is shelf-stable, since all the oily germ has been removed.

Some mills stop there, while others go on to further treat the flour. You may also find roller milled flour that is bleached and bromated. Bleaching makes flour lighter and softer by denaturing the proteins. Whitening the flour also allows the miller to hide discrepancies and create a uniform flour from a blend of wheats. Bromated flour is treated with potassium bromate to improve elasticity and rise. Banned in many countries, the FDA discourages use of this possible carcinogen, yet some mills continue to use it with the attitude that small amounts leave no trace in the final bread.

Roller milled flour may also be enriched with vital minerals and nutrients, such as B vitamins (including folic acid), calcium, iron, and fiber, which are added back into the flour at the end. There must be enough minerals and nutrients present for flour to be classified as food by the FDA. Sadly, without a dose added back at the end, much of the flour you find on the supermarket shelf wouldn't classify as food! Similarly, bran may be added back in to create "whole wheat" flour.

Finally, a small amount of malt (traditionally barley malt in the form of an enzyme-rich powder) may be added to stabilize fermentation, boost color, and improve flavor. Malting is utilized by millers in both roller milled and stone ground scenarios. It's the least aggressive of these alterations and additions.

Despite the drawbacks (heavy processing, lack of nutrition, uniform color and texture), roller milled flour still has a place in my mixing bowl. This level of insurance—that the flour will ferment in a certain amount of time and get a great rise in the oven—is like

> *Stone mills mill at low temperatures to ensure the germ is never heated or spoiled.*

riding a bike with the training wheels on. Roller milled flour is also readily available in any grocery store and at a lower price point than custom stone ground flours, two factors that can't be ignored when trying to make bread for your family. The roller milled flour I use is organic and never bleached, brominated, or enriched. It can be malted or not.

STONE GROUND FLOUR

I pivot toward stone ground flour for nutrition, freshness, and terroir. In a stone mill, the wheat is fed from the hopper into a small opening in the center of two large stones. The bottom stone, or bed stone, has furrows (ridges carved in the stone) running in a pattern like spokes from the center of a wheel. The top stone, or runner stone, swiftly moves over the bed stone, breaking the wheat berries upon entry and milling them into flour as they journey from the center of the stones to the edges. The germ oil penetrates the flour as it makes its way across the stone. At the edge, the flour falls off and is collected and directed toward either a chute on the front of the mill or a flour elevator on the side that carries it to a sifter (also called a bolter).

Stone mills mill at low temperatures to ensure the germ is never heated or spoiled in the process, so it's still in the flour when you bake with it. And because the flour is crushed rather than shattered, tiny freckles of the bran and the aleurone layer (see page 19) are often present in stone ground flour, even with some of the bran removed. The combination of germ and bran makes stone ground flour a truly *living* ingredient. Best yet, nothing needs to be added for it to be considered food.

Flour purchased from a stone mill may be blended from different farms, or it may be "single-origin" from a specific farm on a certain piece of land. Either way, you can expect changes in the flour from year to year. I find this exciting, and I love getting the first of a year's harvest from the mill: It connects me with the seasons and my senses. There is no autopilot when working with freshly milled, stone ground flour.

What really sets stone ground flour apart is flavor! Freshly milled flour has no competition when it comes to complex taste and captivating aromas.

THIRSTY FLOUR

The large stones of a stone mill break down the starches in the wheat berry differently than the rollers in a roller mill, directly affecting the texture of the flour and the way it absorbs water. Stone ground flour tends to be grittier, and it may absorb water at a slower rate than roller milled flour, but it can also hold more of it. This means careful attention must be paid to make sure stone ground flour is properly hydrated.

MAKING FLOUR AT HOME

FLOUR SHOULD BE COLORFUL! Color in flour comes from the hue of the grain and how much bran is included in the flour. Both stone mills and roller mills offer flour from various grains with different extraction rates. The extraction rate (how much of the original berry is left) will be presented on the bag of flour as a number ranging from 00 to 100. For example: A 75 flour will have about 25% of the bran and larger particles removed. It's almost impossible to make completely white flour on a stone mill, so even if you purchase a 00 flour from a stone mill—meaning the finest and most bran-free the mill can make—it will have *some* bran content. As you explore the spectrum from whole grain to sifted, you'll notice bran makes flour darker, or tan in color, so don't be surprised by a new look to your baked goods.

HOME-MILLED FLOUR

Flour milled at home is the freshest of the fresh (see Tabletop Mill, page 40, for more info)! Like grinding coffee while the water boils or cracking pepper over a just-plated salad, flour ground from wheat berries at home will have the strongest aromas, oils, and flavors.

The stones in an electric tabletop mill are *very* small and typically made of self-sharpening composite materials. Because the stones are so small, the cracked-open wheat berry doesn't spend much time passing from the center to the edge, and this can make a gritty flour that is slow to absorb water *and* very thirsty.

To get the right texture in bread doughs made from flour milled at home, add water to the dough in increments over time, until the dough feels supple and extensible. I do this by double hydrating with an autolyse, meaning I mix the majority of the water and flour together, allow the flour to hydrate, and then add the rest of the water when I mix in the starter and salt. If the dough still feels stiff as time goes on, I may smear a bit of extra water on the table during the folding process. (For more on double hydration, see page 48.)

One of the most significant differences you'll notice between flour made in a roller mill or stone ground mill and flour made at home is how pervasive, chunky, and sharp the bran is, even when sifted. The bran acts like tiny scissors in the dough, cutting at and weakening the gluten, and the bran is also very heavy. To ensure the dough reaches its optimal strength and volume, I like to sift out the bran from my flour made at home, soak it in warm water overnight, strain it, and add it into the dough when I mix in the salt and starter. Softening the bran improves gluten's chance at forming. I also adjust and increase the number of folds I perform, folding every 30 minutes for the first 2 hours and then on the hour. This initial burst of strength building and then resting will help make a structurally sound loaf.

Last, doughs made with home-ground flour can also gather strength through fermenting in the refrigerator. The cold air in the fridge tightens the gluten, and longer fermentation times add acidity to the dough, which (up to a point) increases strength, too. (For more on using the fridge to cold ferment, see page 52.)

WHAT'S IN A NUMBER?

In Europe, the number you'll see on a bag of flour is the ash content—the leftover mineral content of a sample of flour after it's burned—not the percentage of the bran removed as in the US (see above). Each number has a maximum amount of allowable ash. For example, Italian pizza flour has a designation of 00, meaning it's the whitest and finest flour possible, with an allowable ash content of 0.05%. In general, for both European and American flours, the lower the ash content, the whiter the flour (and the less fiber it has), and the higher the number, the more whole grain (and more fiber) it includes.

OPPOSITE FROM THE CENTER TO THE OUTER EDGE
Kamut, Einkorn, Oats, Turkey Red, Buckwheat, Emmer

COMMON
TYPES OF FLOUR

ALL-PURPOSE FLOUR (a blend of hard and soft wheats) is strong enough to trap gas for bread and tender enough for a cookie. It generally has a protein content of 12%. Many stone mills choose to use a white wheat for their all-purpose flour.

BREAD FLOUR, also called high-protein flour or high-gluten flour, is milled (generally) from hard red wheats with a protein content between 14% and 16%. This flour is excellent for baked goods that require a strong rise, like pizza, bagels, and bread. When baked, doughs made with bread flour have a chewy, tuggy quality.

HIGH EXTRACTION FLOUR is flour that is minimally sifted, having just the heaviest, largest portions of bran removed. It is lighter than a 100% whole wheat flour, but to the untrained eye and tongue, it will look and taste very similar. It is a great flour to use when you want a nice rise and depth of flavor.

PASTRY FLOUR is flour made from soft wheats that have a protein level of 12% or below. Pastry flour can come in a range of wholeness, from whole wheat to white, and it may be stone ground or roller milled. Pasty flour is wonderful for cookies, pies, cakes, and other baked goods where tenderness, flakiness, or featheriness is desired.

PIZZA FLOUR, or Italian 00 flour, is very fine flour with great extensibility. In Italy, the grading system goes 00, 0, 1, and 2 to delineate how fine the flour is, with 00 being the finest and 2 being coarsest. Pizza flour will be both extensible and elastic, making a crust that is easy to stretch and yet holds its shape. The protein content can range from 11% to 12%.

SIFTED FLOUR, or bolted flour, has had a considerable amount of the bran and large particles removed by being shaken over a series of sifters or brushed over fine-mesh screens. The remaining flour is fine and powdery. If it's been stone milled, it may still have small freckles of bran throughout.

WHITE WHEAT FLOUR is flour milled from white wheat varieties. It can be sold as 100% whole grain or sifted for a lighter flour. It is often used to make a whole-grain baked good without evoking the bitterness or heaviness red wheats are known for. It can come in hard and soft, with hard white wheats boasting a protein content anywhere between 10% and 14%.

WHOLE WHEAT FLOUR is 100% of the wheat berry, milled into flour. Remember that whole wheat flour can be made from different varieties of grain, and it may either be stone ground or roller milled. Stone ground whole wheat flour will contain the germ, and roller milled will not. Whole-grain flour is naturally high in fiber and enzymes and is quick to ferment.

STORING GRAINS, FLOURS, AND DRY GOODS

I STORE MY GRAINS (Turkey Red, einkorn, oats, etc.) in a cool place out of direct sunlight. Depending on how they come packaged, I may transfer them to a labeled, white, food-grade plastic tub with a lockable lid. I cut the label from the bag and tape it to the front of the tub. Although aesthetically this isn't the most romantic, I am confident they are always mold-, pest-, and critter-free, even in an old house during the summer in the South (and especially since I buy them in bulk, usually no less than ten pounds at a time).

I store flour the same as grain: I remove it from its packaging, transfer to an airtight container, and label with the type and date. I keep roller milled flour at room temperature since the perishable germ has been removed. Think of freshly milled flour as you would fresh produce: It can spoil—so I store stone ground and fresh flour in my freezer and let it come to room temperature before mixing my dough. When in doubt, touch, taste, and smell your flour for any off scents or pungent flavors. Yes, flour is a living ingredient and does not last forever!

I buy salt in bulk and keep a small deli container of it on my countertop and the backstock in a food-grade plastic tub. I am religious about using only Himalayan pink salt for the very mundane fact that I can visually distinguish it from all the other ingredients! (If I can't remember if I've added salt, all I need to do is look in the bowl.) It's the salt used for every bread in this book, so grab some for your future dough mixes.

SALT CHART

In general, whatever salt you have on hand will be okay for making bread. Because the salt amount in your dough is calculated by weight, you don't need to worry about swapping equivalents. However, if you use coarse salt, you'll need to either grind it to a finer texture in a coffee grinder or blender or dissolve it in a little hot water before adding it to the dough.

TYPE	TEXTURE	OKAY FOR BREAD?
Course sea salt	Large granules	Yes, but must be ground finer or dissolved
Fine sea salt	Fine	Yes
Flaky salt	Rough flakes	Just for topping
Himalayan pink salt	Fine	Yes, the only one I use!
Kosher salt (Diamond Crystal brand)	Large granules	Yes, but must be ground finer or dissolved
Kosher salt (Morton brand)	Various size granules	Yes, but must be ground finer or dissolved
Table salt	Fine	No, never use iodized salt

Fermenting Flour

HISTORIANS, BAKERS, AND BREWERS all like to debate the topic of which came first, beer or bread. Either way, one thing is clear: Humans have, for most of our history with cereal grains, fermented them in some way before enjoying them. It is the process of fermentation that is missing from most of the bread you find in the supermarket, and its revival is the key to good bread and happy bellies. Using sourdough to ferment your bread dough is a wonderful way to transform the flour into something tasty and nourishing.

Broadly speaking, sourdough refers to the various mixtures of flour and water that "catch" yeast and lactic acid bacteria and the bread that is made from them. The yeast and lactic acid bacteria digest the simple sugars in the flour and produce alcohol, acids, and gas. Around and around they go, eating and reproducing until there's no food left and they need to be fed. With consistent care, a sourdough mixture stabilizes, and the acidity keeps out any unwanted visitors. I also refer to my sourdough as my starter, since it's what kicks off the act of fermentation in the dough.

ABOVE

My three starters (*left to right*): sourdough, desem, and rye

THE YEAST AND BACTERIA in a sourdough starter come from environmental factors, such as the soil the grain was grown in, the flour itself, and the baker's body. The Korean phrase *son-mat*, literally "the taste of one's hand," helps explain how every baker's sourdough, even when tended with the same ingredients and methods, can be unique in its flavor and strength.

Ask around and you'll get a hundred different answers to the same question: What do you call your sourdough? A culture, a mother, a starter, or a leaven are all popular terms, as are geographic, pet, or family names. I'm too uptight to name any of my sourdoughs, but I sympathize with the desire to personalize the gluey mixture.

I keep three different kinds of sourdough: a ten-year-old white flour sourdough; an exclusively rye flour sourdough; and a whole-grain starter called desem (pronounced DAY-zum), which is hardly sour at all.

Each of my three starters began life differently, and they are fed different flours, hydrated with different amounts of water, fermented for different periods of time, kept at different temperatures, and used in different doughs. It's possible to keep only one starter, but I pair the starter with the end goal. If a dough calls for mostly white flour, I use my starter made with white flour; if it calls for rye, I use my rye starter; and if the dough is mostly whole wheat, I get out my desem.

WILD YEAST AND LACTOBACILLI

There are one hundred parts lactobacilli to one part yeast in a . . . sourdough starter.

YEAST, A NATURAL FUNGUS, is a single-celled organism with a distinct nucleus and a few tiny organs that generate energy, control growth, and direct reproduction. There are more than a thousand varieties of yeast in the world, and yet only a few, such as *Saccharomyces cerevisiae* (which means "sugar mold"), have the ability to live in a highly acidic environment and to digest the specific sugars in flour.

Yeast is primarily responsible for rising bread dough. When the yeasts consume simple sugars, they output gas that travels through the dough, joining large pockets of air already present through mixing (and in some cases, folding). These bubbles expand, filling the dough with air. Yeast also produces alcohol and acetic acid. When you leave your starter unfed for too long, you can actually see the alcohol as a thin, pungent layer of liquid on top of the starter. The alcohol in your loaf evaporates while baking, creating an intense aroma in the kitchen.

Lactobacilli are responsible for many of the health benefits associated with sourdough and its classic tangy "sourdough" flavor. There are one hundred parts lactobacilli to one part yeast in a typical sourdough starter (in a commercial bread made only with instant yeast, there would be none!), so you can see how impactful they are to culturing the dough. Lactobacilli predigest the simple sugars in flour, making sourdough less likely to cause blood sugar spikes, and they transform the dough into a prebiotic feast for the good bacteria in your stomach. A thriving colony of helpful bacteria can improve the overall vitality and function of your gut, easing digestion and inflammation. Yes! Good bread can prevent bloating!

LACTIC AND ACETIC ACIDS

Lactic acids impart a creamy yogurt-like flavor to the bread, while acetic acids make a tangy finish to your bite.

LACTOBACILLI ARE THE MAIN PLAYERS creating various acids in sourdough. A single sourdough starter, depending on its age and its care routine, can have up to three different kinds of lactobacilli. Homofermentative lactic acid bacteria (LAB) produce only lactic acids, heterofermentative LAB can produce both lactic and acetic acids, and the third variety of lactobacilli can switch between producing both. The flour you feed your starter, the amount of water you refresh it with, and the temperature at which you maintain it will all have direct effects on the diversity and population size of lactobacilli and hence the overall acidity and flavor profile of your starter.

Starters created and maintained with a high level of water and white flour (easy to stir with a spoon), kept on the countertop at room temperature (between 68° and 72°F), and used within a few hours of refreshment will produce an abundance of lactobacilli, making lots of lactic acids. Lactic acids impart a creamy, yogurt-like flavor to the baked bread. Fermented further, lactobacilli with respond with acetic acids, and the dough will develop a pronounced fruity apple cider flavor or even vinegar kick to the dough. If you'd like to make a sourdough with a mild flavor, then use your starter early on and bake your bread all in one day. If you'd like to pull out more of a punch, retard your dough in the fridge overnight or over the course of several days. (See cold bulk fermentation, page 52.)

Some bakers prefer to leave these complex tastes out of the bread, instead favoring to highlight the flavor of the grain itself by using starters that are stiffer (fed less water), fed more whole-grain flour (you might knead the starter rather than stir it), kept at cooler temperatures, and used after a prolonged period of fermentation. This combination of low hydration, sugars that take longer to access, and cooler temperatures curbs the production of lactobacilli and creates a starter with a robust yeast population, like the desem starter on page 136.

WATER

ABOVE
Happy lactobacilli rods and reproducing yeast

WATER SETS FERMENTATION INTO motion, homogenizes the dough, and binds the structure of bread. Water both hydrates and dissolves, allowing salt, sugar, and yeast to travel through the dough, eating and multiplying. It's essential for gluten development and the lasting power of a baked loaf. While you can use any water that is suitable to drink for tending to your starter or mixing your bread dough, whenever I get the chance to use pure spring water, my starters and doughs are wildly active—meaning they ferment in the blink of an eye, are covered in big bubbles, and rise to lofty, pillowy heights!

Water can be soft, meaning it's been either treated or distilled in such a way that there very little minerals left, or hard, meaning it contains an abundance of calcium and magnesium. Bread dough made with excessively soft water will be slow to ferment, slack, and sticky, while doughs made with excessively hard water will also have trouble fermenting and be stiff, tearing easily when folded or shaped. Water of a medium hardness is best for bread, but, again, if you would drink it, it's probably okay to use.

DEVELOPING YOUR (DOUGHY) INTUITION

Bake with your whole body.

INTUITION IS DATA ACCUMULATED by the body over time, so if you want to become a great baker, practice, practice, practice! Just like learning how to ride a bike, when we first make bread our bodies are awkward, stumbling, and unsure, but eventually we become confident and soon it's all muscle memory. Here are a few suggestions for finding your baker's intuition.

COMMIT TO MAKING BREAD ONCE A DAY FOR THIRTY DAYS. Forming a new habit (or getting rid of one) takes about thirty consecutive days. This news is great for the new sourdough baker, because sourdough is a daily rhythm. While it might sound nuts to try to bake every day, I guarantee this is THE quickest route to gaining intuition fast. It speeds up your physical skills and overall knowledge. It also takes the pressure off—if something goes wrong, eh, you've already got your other loaf going. The best bread to do this with is the Workweek Bread (page 74).

USE YOUR FIVE SENSES. There will come a point where you should stop listening to me and start listening to your fingertips, your eyes, and your nose. Fine-tuning your senses is imperative to developing a good internal timer. A recipe is really just a suggestion. Remember, you're working with living organisms—they don't really care about all this paperwork! They want your love, attention, and caress. You must bake with your whole body: Inhale deeply, lean in closely, and prod gently.

BE COOL WITH FAILING. The perfect bread really only happens once in a while, the rest is practice! Sometimes, even when you did everything right, your starter is going to be sluggish, or your bread isn't going to rise properly. As bakers we can attempt to control the outcome to our advantage, but part of the excitement is the relationship between you and your dough. Do yourself a favor and let go of expectations.

PICKING A RECIPE

Whether you're a beginner, intermediate, or advanced baker, it's all practice.

ALL THE RECIPES IN this book are sorted by difficulty, from beginner to advanced. In general, the recipes and starters in the book move from easy to difficult through each chapter.

BEGINNER: If you're making your first loaf of bread or are new to sourdough, focus on beginner recipes. You'll be getting used to the timeframes and overall techniques, and your confidence will grow as you bake.

INTERMEDIATE: As a proficient baker you may already have a weekly, or monthly, practice and can feed your starter and make bread with ease. If you're comfortable with the overall process of bread making, then start here.

ADVANCED: Advanced bakers are able to follow a lengthy and involved recipe, work with a variety of starters and grains, and may even write their own formulas, grow their own grain, and mill their own flour at home.

SETTING UP
YOUR WORK SPACE

ABOVE
Baking in a combo cooker is a great way to get perfect steam and color in a home oven.

MY BAKING SPACE IS BASIC. It's a simple metal table that's easy to clean, a digital scale, a 4-quart stand mixer, a dough tub (or sometimes I'll use a bowl with a plate for a lid), a dough scraper, and a hand towel. Underneath the table are two large bakery-style flour bins. I keep my recipes on a clipboard hanging on the wall with a pen attached. My worktable is by a window, so it gets natural light, and it's close to the sink, so I'm not trekking mess everywhere. I like to keep a wide-mouthed pitcher (like a restaurant-style water pitcher) of warm water on the table to wash my hands in or stick the dough scraper in when not in use. I clean up my space after every step, including doing the dishes, drying them, and putting them away. This keeps my work space tidy and allows me a minute to think about the next step for my dough.

ESSENTIAL TOOLS

BENCH KNIFE AND DOUGH SCRAPER

A bench knife is rigid and cuts through large portions of dough with a quick chop; it also makes cleaning up your work space a breeze. I use a metal one with a wooden handle to manipulate and cut my dough. Dough scrapers are flexible and generally made from some kind of plastic material; I use them for handling the dough in the bowl, scraping down the bowls, and shaping the dough.

COMBO COOKER

A combo cooker is a cast-iron pot and skillet, both with handles, that fit together nicely. For baking bread, the setup is inverted, so the skillet is on the bottom and the deeper pot acts as a lid. Bread dough can be turned out from the banetton directly into the shallow skillet, scored, then covered with the inverted pot as a lid, which allows ample space for the bread to rise. Because the loaf is turned out into a shallow pan, your hands and wrists are free to move around while you score, without the danger of touching a hot pan. It's my favorite thing to bake in.

DELI CONTAINERS

I store my starters and other ingredients like seeds or sprouts in deli/take-out containers (you can buy assorted sizes online from sites like Webstaurant Store; see Resources, page 294). They hold heat well, have clear sides so I can see starters rise, are very easy to clean, and don't take up much space, and I'm not worried about dropping one. I label them with the ingredient and date marked with a Sharpie on masking tape.

DIGITAL SCALE

Using a digital scale and gram measurements (grams are a more precise measurement than measuring cups) improves accuracy and is a very important part of making good bread. Using a scale ensures that you will get the ingredient amounts correct day-to-day and allows you to use one bowl to mix everything. This cuts down on the dishes and makes cleanup a breeze. I prefer a metal scale with a lifted platform, not a flat or glass one.

DIGITAL THERMOMETER

An accurate digital thermometer allows you to get the perfect temperature of water each time you mix bread dough, and it can be used to take the internal temperature of the bread toward the end of the bake. You can get a thermometer from the supermarket that costs ten bucks, or something long-lasting and professional, for around $100.

DOUGH BOWL AND COVER

An obvious necessity, this one is a personal choice. If you're new to baking, it can be helpful to ferment your dough in a clear container so you can see it rise. For large batches of dough, I like something with a thick wall and lid, like a 4-quart Cambro container (restaurant supply stores like Webstaurant Store have them; see Resources, page 294). Cold storage should also be considered—can your container fit in the fridge easily? For a single loaf of bread, I mix my dough in a ceramic bowl with a dinner plate for a lid (very high tech). You can also use a shower cap or sheet pan to cover the bowl. (Shower caps also work nicely to cover a shaped, proofing loaf of bread!)

DUTCH OVEN

A Dutch oven is a large, deep cast-iron pot (sometimes finished with an enamel inner coating) with a heavy lid. It sometimes has short handles on the sides or a thin bail handle on the top to hang it over a campfire. The pot's tall sides make it hard to easily flip a loaf out of its banneton and into the pot, and you can burn your wrists when scoring the loaf. So, instead of the loaf going directly into the pot, I turn it out of the banneton onto a precut round of parchment paper, score it, and then lower it into the pot by holding the sides of the parchment. The parchment stays under the bread while it bakes and is peeled off when the loaf cools.

LAME AND RAZOR

Lame (pronounced LAHM) is French for "blade," and it refers to a handheld tool designed to hold a double-edged razor blade at the end. A razor blade is important because the thinness of the metal gives the baker control and precision when making a cut. I use the kind with a wooden handle and a long metal end that slightly curves—I find these the most pleasing to hold.

MIXER

Most bread doughs in this book are intended to be mixed by hand. It's the best way to get in touch with the needs of the dough on any given day. However, there are a few enriched breads, cookies, and other treats that really do best in a standard tabletop mixer. I use a 4-quart KitchenAid that stores nicely under the counter.

PROOFING BASKETS/BANNETONS

Bannetons are baskets, often lined with linen cloth, used to proof shaped dough in. Loose doughs require the cloth liner, while firmer doughs can be proofed directly in the basket. The cloth needs a little "seasoning"—the crusty buildup of flour on the cloth after repeated use—for the dough to turn out easily. After use, I brush the bannetons out with a dustpan brush and let them dry, unstacked, while the bread is baking; I wash the cloth liners only in the summer when humidity encourages funky, colored mold to appear.

PULLMAN PAN

A Pullman pan is a straight-sided, perfectly rectangular pan with a flat removable lid. When loaded correctly, the top of the loaf hits the lid while baking, so no large air holes form, ensuring all sides come out soft, making the perfect texture and uniformity for a sandwich loaf. (You may bake bread with the lid off, too.) I use my 9-inch one constantly to make the Milk Bread on page 93.

SPRAY BOTTLE

I keep a spray bottle labeled "baking water" in my kitchen and use it to moisten my table while folding dough (see Folding, page 49), to gently spritz a loaf while it's proofing, and to moisten the top of my loaf in a Pullman pan or 9-inch loaf pan before baking (see The Importance of Steam, page 60).

TABLETOP MILL

The ability to mill your own flour is a game changer! I have a KoMo, a Mockmill, and Nutrimill to demonstrate in my workshops. I prefer the KoMo because of its appearance, but the Mockmill makes a comparable flour and has a lower price point. The Nutrimill is a great price point if you're not sure how much you'll use it (in my experience, it heated up the flour the fastest of all three brands and had the smallest stones for grinding, too). Don't bother using a coffee mill, Vitamix, or food processor to mill flour—their blades chop rather than crush the grain.

WELDING GLOVES

Regular oven mitts or pot holders aren't thick enough when handling hot cast iron, and they won't protect your wrists and forearms from the steam when the lid is removed. I use heavy-duty Hobart welding gloves instead (which I also use when working with my wood-fired oven and grill).

Methods for Bread Making

THIS CHAPTER WILL HELP you make magic, turning flour into bread. I will guide you through the basic steps to making delicious bread right in your home (you don't even need to get out of your pajamas!) and fill you in on some of the tips and tricks that I've taken from my often crusty but never boring journey with bread.

READING A RECIPE:
BAKER'S MATH AND PERCENTAGES

BEFORE YOU GRAB YOUR mixing bowl, it's important to familiarize yourself with the kind of math that bakers use to write their formulas. Baker's math allows all ingredients, be they solid or liquid, to be weighed with the same unit of measurement, and it's a common language by which bakers can easily and quickly assess the overall dough.

In a bread formula, flour is always 100% and all other ingredients are expressed in relation to the weight of the flour. As you can see in the example formula for Pizza Dough below, the total percentage goes over 100%, so think of each ingredient as "parts per" rather than a pie chart where all portions will add up to 100. There are other industry standards: Salt is generally 2% and starter ranges from 10% to 25%, depending on the season.

If this spooks you, don't worry, you can simply follow the recipes as written without having to pay attention to the percentages. However, as you become an advanced baker, you will come to love the creative aspect that baker's math offers you.

DETERMINING WEIGHTS FROM PERCENTAGES
PIZZA DOUGH
4 rounds of dough @ 250g each
Total amount of dough needed: 1,000g

PERCENTAGE	WEIGHT	INGREDIENT
100%	549g	Bread flour
70%	384g	Water
10%	55g	Starter
2%	12g	Salt
182%	1,000g	Totals

The weight of the flour is determined by dividing the total weight of the dough (1,000g) by the total percentage (182%) and then multiplying the result by 100 to switch from a decimal to a percentage (1,000 / 182 = 5.4945 × 100 = 549g). Once you have the flour weight, you can **calculate the remaining ingredient weights by multiplying the percentage, in decimal form, by the flour weight** (0.70 × 549 = 384g). Add all the weights together to check that the result matches the total amount of dough needed, and you're good to go!

When You Can't See the Bread for the Dough

Our grandmothers weren't pulling out digital scales and losing sleep over baker's math, yet they still made excellent bread. (They baked so frequently, their hands knew the weights and ratios.) If you become frustrated with the nitpicky details, I encourage you to take a step back and look at the whole process, lest you get meticulouosis: the (made-up) disease that causes you to overthink everything and steals the joy out of your baking (by about 80% to 81%, wink wink).

DETERMINING PERCENTAGES FROM WEIGHT

Understanding how to determine the percentage of an ingredient based on the weight will allow you greater flexibility and standardization in a formula.

PIZZA DOUGH
4 rounds of dough @ 250g each
Total amount of dough needed: 1,000g

PERCENTAGE	WEIGHT	INGREDIENT
100%	549g	Bread flour
70%	384g	Water
10%	55g	Starter
2%	12g	Salt
182%	1,000g	Totals

To get the percentage of an ingredient, divide the weight by the weight of the flour and multiply the result by 100 to switch from a decimal expression to a percentage. Here is an example using the weight of the water: 384 / 549 = 0.6999 × 100 = 69.9. In this case I would round up to 70 and arrive at water being 70% the weight of the flour. (I round down below 0.5 and up above 0.5.) Here is an example using the weight of starter: 55 / 549 = 0.1001 × 100 = 10.0 so the starter is 10% the weight of the flour.

THE OVERALL PROCESS OF MAKING BREAD

ALTHOUGH YOU CAN MIX and bake bread in a single day, there will always be a few steps that need to be taken care of ahead of time, like sprouting wheat berries and refreshing your starter. Once you are ready to begin, the key stages of making bread include: folding, shaping, proofing, and baking. (Working with rye flour requires different considerations; see the Rye chapter that begins on page 193 for specifics.) Each stage presents options, making bread a very real choose-your-own-adventure project. Keep in mind that time is an ingredient, and enjoy sinking into the rhythm.

A FEW DAYS AHEAD

SPROUTING

To prepare sprouts for bread: Pour the wheat berries into an 8-ounce wide-mouthed glass jar, cover with room temperature water, cover with a lid, slightly ajar, and rest on the counter for at least 8 hours, or overnight. Next, pour off any excess water and rinse the berries under cool water in a fine-mesh sieve. Transfer the berries back to the jar and, again, cover with a lid, slightly open. (You can buy jar lids with a mesh top specifically designed for sprouting so you don't have to transfer the berries from the jar to rinse.) Check your sprouts every 8 hours. In warm weather they will sprout in less than 24 hours, and in cool weather they will take up to 3 days. Once they have a little nub protruding from the germ, they are ready to use.

STARTER MAINTENANCE

If your starter is being kept in the fridge in between bakes, pull it out and give it a maintenance refreshment (see opposite page) 2 days ahead of when you will refresh it in the evening for mixing dough the following morning. This will balance out the flavor and make it easy to "wake up" later. For example: If I want to mix my bread dough Saturday morning, I will give my starter a maintenance refresh on Wednesday, return it to the fridge, and then refresh it again on Friday for a Saturday morning mix.

THE NIGHT BEFORE

PREPPING THE MIX

This is the baker's mise en place. It includes thoroughly reading the recipe all the way through, presoaking any ingredients, and scaling out the flours and other ingredients. For me, part of this process involves cleaning the space where the bread will be made and getting out any necessary tools or equipment that I'll need. (Save weighing out the water until you're ready to mix the dough, but do put out a wide-mouthed pitcher of water for easy access.)

TOASTING SEEDS AND NUTS

Toasting seeds and nuts brings out the oils and adds a wonderful flavor. Toast your seeds and/or nuts in a cast-iron skillet over medium heat, stirring constantly with a wooden spoon until they smell fragrant and are lightly browned. You can also toast them in the oven on a sheet pan at 225°F for 8 to 10 minutes. When done, carefully transfer the hot seeds and/or nuts to a bowl, or dinner plate, to cool. Once at room temperature, they can be stored in a deli container, with the lid on, for up to 3 days.

SOAKING SEEDS AND DEHYDRATED FRUIT

Dehydrated fruit and seeds will pull moisture out of bread dough, causing the dough to seize and stiffen. Soaking fruit and seeds overnight in warm water will turn the fruit juicy, plump up the seeds, and maintain the right level of hydration in the dough. Drain any excess water before adding the fruit or seeds to the dough.

REFRESHING YOUR STARTER

I refresh my sourdough starter the night before, mixing my bread dough about 6 to 10 hours later. Refreshing your starter simply means discarding a portion of what's in your jar and "feeding" the remaining starter flour and water. The refreshment process is key to developing a bread that rises properly (it provides ample food for the yeast) and tastes pleasing (it balances out any overpowering acidity). Step-by-step instructions for refreshing your sourdough can be found on page 67; step-by-step instructions for refreshing your desem can be found on page 136.

THE FOLLOWING MORNING

FIGURE OUT THE WATER TEMPERATURE

Just like making wine, beer, yogurt, or cheese, bread dough has a specific temperature range for optimal fermentation. Wheat-based doughs like to ferment, in bulk, between 75° and 78°F. The easiest way to control the overall temperature of the dough is through adjusting the water temperature. In a professional bakery, there is a large water meter on the wall that will control the temperature and amount of water that flows to the mixer. I encourage you to act like the pros and achieve the correct water temperature each time you mix your dough. Water temperature is calculated by following the Desired Dough Temperature formula on page 48. (If you skip this step, use room temperature water, between 68° and 72°F.)

HOW TO USE A DIGITAL SCALE

You must have a digital scale to make the bread in this book. If using a scale is new to you, take a minute to familiarize yourself with it before making a starter or dough. On most scales, there will be a power button, a button to switch between ounces and grams, a button to zero out (or tare, in baker speak) the scale, and a button to hold a weight. To mix bread dough, turn on the scale, set it to grams, and make sure it begins on zero. Set your empty bowl or dough container on the scale, then zero the scale. Add the flour, then zero it. Add the water, then zero it. Add the starter, then zero it. Add the salt, then zero it. You do not need to keep a notepad by the scale to add up each item, just return the scale to zero after every addition. If you splash a little too much water or accidentally add a glob more starter, if it's within 2 grams of the weight called for, don't worry too much. However, if you go above and beyond, use a spoon or ladle and remove the extra ingredient.

Desired Dough Temperature (DDT)

To calculate your water temperature, you need to know the temperature of the room, the temperature of the flour, the temperature of your starter, and the friction factor—which is the amount of heat added to the dough through mixing. When mixing by hand, the friction factor is 10°F. If you are using a stand mixer, like a KitchenAid, the friction factor goes up to 35°F.

Next, multiply the desired final dough temperature by the number of variables (in this case four: the room, the flour, the starter, and the friction factor) to get your total temperature. Finally, subtract the room temperature, the flour temperature, the starter temperature, and the friction factor from the final dough temperature. The remaining number is the water temperature!

Example: Let's say you want your bread dough to be 75°F when you're done mixing, and you're planning on mixing by hand so you can anticipate 10°F for the friction factor. Let's also say your kitchen is 70°F, the flour temperature is 68°F, and your starter is 72°F. So the equation would be: 75 (DDT) × 4 (the number of variables) = 300 (total temperature). And then, 300 − 70 − 68 − 72 − 10 = 80. So 80°F is the temperature you want your water to be.

In general, three degrees on either side of your desired dough temperature is acceptable. I use a digital thermometer and adjust my water from the faucet, filling up a pitcher of the correct temperature water for my bread dough. When adding the majority of the water, be sure it's at the correct temperature. Once you have practiced, you'll be able to gauge the temperature of the water just by passing your fingers under it. (My nerdy party trick!)

MIXING

FIRST MIX Now that you've prepped your ingredients, set up your work space, refreshed your starter, and considered your water temperature (see Desired Dough Temperature at left), you can get mixing. Bread dough can be mixed all at once, or in stages, with a first and second mix. In a dough with no second mix, all the flour, water, starter, salt, and any other additions are mixed together at the same time, like with Workweek Bread (page 74). You can see how many mixes each recipe needs by checking out the Snapshot description at the beginning of each recipe.

MIXING DOUGH BY HAND is the method I prefer. You can use a stand mixer to mix your dough, but your hands will provide you with invaluable information about the texture, temperature, and overall consistency of your dough. To mix dough by hand, squeeze it through your fingers, like you're extruding pasta! Once you can neither see nor feel any dry flour, scrape down the sides of the bowl with a dough scraper, mix again until the new bits are incorporated, and cover with an appropriate lid.

AUTOLYSE refers to mixing just the flour and water together, followed by an hour rest. By allowing all the water to go toward the formation of gluten (and not the salt or microorganisms), the dough becomes naturally strong and extensible.

DOUBLE HYDRATION Holding back a percentage of the overall water until after the autolyse is a technique called double hydration. This is helpful when you want to include a large portion of water in the dough (for an open crumb) or when working with fresh whole-grain flour (that can really soak up water). Adjustments can be made now for the right texture and feel.

FINAL MIX Sprinkle the salt and any remaining ingredients over the dough. Hold your hand like a pair of crab claws and, working from one side of the bowl to the other, pinch them in. You will feel the salt dissolve entirely, and any seeds, nuts, or fruits will be evenly distributed.

Have patience; the dough will fall apart and become stringy before it re-forms!

BULK FERMENTING

After mixing is complete, the dough is covered with a lid and set aside to ferment at room temperature (68° to 72°F) for 4 to 5 hours, or until it's risen about 30% in the bowl and, when gently pressed, it feels light and airy. While bulk fermenting, it's not a bad idea to take the temperature of the dough a few times. If the dough has cooled below the desired dough temperature, move it to a warmer location (not the oven), and if the dough has gotten too warm, move it to a cooler location (not the fridge). During bulk fermentation, the dough will undergo a series of folds to gather strength.

FOLDING

Folding strengthens gluten through a series of stretching motions. To fold dough, ready a pitcher of water and a dough scraper. Smear your work surface with a bit of water (dip your hand in a little water, too) and scoop the dough out of the bowl and onto the table. Imagine the dough in two portions, one top and one bottom. Pick up the entire dough from the table and gently slap the bottom half onto the table. It will stick. Pull the top half toward you (leaning back for a little extra tension), then quickly fold the top half over the bottom half. Repeat two or three times until the dough pulls itself together into a ball and has a smooth surface. If the surface of the dough is shredding or tearing, stop and allow the dough to rest on the table (covered with a kitchen towel) for a few minutes before trying again. Once folded, return the dough to the bowl, cover, and let it rest.

WINDOWPANE TEST

Taking a knob of dough and stretching it—called "pulling a window"—checks the strength of a dough. It can be done after the autolyse, if there is one, and at multiple points throughout the process, like before the first and second folds.

To pull a window: Dip your fingers in water and pull off a portion of dough the size of a golf ball. Gently stretch it, like you're making a mini pizza, and hold it up to a bright light. You'll be able to see the webs of gluten, and if there's any bran in the flour, you'll see speckles of that, too. The thinner you can stretch the dough without tearing it, the stronger it is and the better it will be at trapping gas.

▼ The dough during
bench rest

▲ "Crab claws" pinching in the salt

COLD BULK FERMENT

To further develop flavor or strength or to buy yourself some time (like if life gets in the way and you can't tend to your dough), after they undergo their folds many doughs can be covered with a lid, like a dinner plate or sheet pan, and transferred to the refrigerator overnight, or up to 24 hours. I love using my fridge with sourdough; it's a win-win for my schedule and the dough.

SHAPING

PRE-SHAPE Pre-shaping sets up the dough for its final form. Regardless of the ultimate shape of the bread, the pre-shape is always a round. Lightly dust your table with flour. Use a dough scraper to transfer and flip the dough onto the flour so that the top is now the bottom. Fold the edge of the dough closest to you up to meet the top, leaving a 1-inch lip at the top (brush off any excess flour). Take the sides of the dough, gently stretch them outward, then quickly cross them over each other so they are on top of each other, like swaddling a baby. Stretch the bottom of the dough up to meet the top and seal. Roll the dough so that the seam is now on the bottom and you're looking at a smooth top. Using the bench knife, gently drag the dough toward you so that the seam tucks underneath the round and the skin pulls together, smooth like the outside of a balloon.

BENCH REST Resting the dough after pre-shaping allows the gluten to relax (and the "bench" is just the baker term for your counter!). The dough is ready to be shaped again when it's visibly relaxed and slightly sloped on the sides, generally about 30 minutes after the pre-shape. When properly rested, it is easily extensible (meaning it will stretch in your hands without difficulty) and happily goes into a final shape without tearing.

FINAL SHAPING After the dough rests, it's ready for its final shaping—this is when you'll focus on getting good tension and uniformity to the shape and make any adjustments before it leaves your hands to rise in a banneton or pan. Lightly dust your table with flour. Use a dough scraper to flip over the pre-shape so the top is now the bottom. Be careful to not degas the dough or get flour onto the exposed top. Bring the bottom of the dough to meet the top, leaving a 1-inch lip. Dust off any

excess flour. Take the sides of the dough, gently stretch them outward a few inches, then quickly cross them over each other so they are on top of each other, like swaddling a baby. You're now looking at an envelope shape. Stretch the bottom of the dough up to meet the top of the envelope and press down to seal. The dough will now be a cylinder on its side with a seam running along the top.

For a **bâtard** or **loaf,** following the photos on pages 53–54 and 57, wind the dough onto itself until you've gotten proper tension (tight, but no tearing). Roll the seam underneath and seal the ends with a quick "chop" using the edge of your palm. If you're shaping a loaf for a Pullman pan, make it a little longer by overlapping slightly less on the swaddle. With the bench knife, flip the shaped loaf seam-side up and into a well-floured cloth-lined 9-inch oval banneton, or seam-side down into a lightly oiled 9-inch Pullman pan.

For a **round**, lightly dust a cloth-lined 9-inch round banneton with flour and set aside. Lightly dust your table with flour. Using a bench knife, flip over the relaxed round. Imagine the round into four quarters. Stretch the edge of each quarter to the center of the round, overlapping them slightly, about 1 inch, to make a pouch shape. Now turn the "pouch" on its side, cupping the portion that was flush with the table in one hand, and cinch the gathered portions together with the side of your palm, sealing the seam. Glide the dough down the table so that the seam is sealed between the edge of your hand and the table. With a bench knife, transfer the dough seam-side up to the floured banneton.

COATING

Rolling your shaped dough in seeds, oats, or nuts gives the crust a nice crunch. To coat the bread, moisten a kitchen towel (not terry cloth, as it can leave lint/fibers on the dough) and place it over one half of a sheet pan. (The towel does not need to be soaked, just slightly wet.) Cover the other half of the sheet pan with oats, seeds, grits, or whatever you wish to cover the bread in. Roll the dough over the towel and through the oats, grits, or seeds. Transfer seam-side up to a 9-inch round or oval cloth-lined banneton or seam-side down in a lightly oiled 9-inch Pullman pan.

SALT AND FOLDING

Add the salt after an autolyse.

Squeeze the dough through your fingers.

Pick up the entire dough from the table.

Fold it over itself.

Pick it up again.

Fold it again.

PRE-SHAPE

Fold the dough close to the top, leaving a one-inch lip.

Cross the sides of the dough.

Stretch the bottom on the dough to meet the top.

Roll it so the seam is now on the bottom.

Drag it on the table with the bench scraper.

Tuck the seam under.

PROOFING

During the proof, the bread will relax from any tension introduced through shaping and will fill up with gas, expanding about 35% in the basket or pan. This phase can take anywhere from 1 hour to 2 days, depending on the method you choose. You'll want to proof your bread in a warm spot, like on top of the dryer, on top of the fridge, near the woodstove, or on a high shelf. Take care to keep the loaf covered so it doesn't dry out, and keep it away from direct sunlight. (You don't want to bake it before it gets into the oven!)

During the proof, the loaf is periodically poked to check development. At the end of the proof, the dough is either put in the fridge (covered with a kitchen towel or shower cap) to be baked the following day, or the oven is readied and the loaf is baked.

Dough can be under proofed, correctly proofed, or over proofed. Under proofed dough, meaning it hasn't properly filled out with gas or relaxed from shaping, will bake up with a dense crumb, the scores will tear, and it will often blow out the side because so much gas is trying to escape. Correctly proofed bread will unfold nicely during the bake, hold a pleasing score, and have an open, irregular crumb. Over proofed bread will have risen and collapsed in the basket or pan—when baked, it will remain flat, the score will fail to open, and the crust will stay pale no matter how long you bake it.

I know it may sound horrifying, but pick a loaf and over proof it on purpose, then you will know just how far you can push it. Home bakers tend to chronically under proof their bread, so I encourage you to let the loaf *really* fill with air till it's almost on the verge of deflating—this is how you will get bakery-style bread in your own kitchen.

ABOVE
Left: Under proofed; *middle:* almost proofed; *right:* fully proofed

THE POKE TEST

To perform the poke test, use your index finger to firmly jab the dough. Watch how the dough rises back. If it springs back immediately, it's not relaxed enough and needs more time. If the poke leaves an indent that slowly rises back, then the bread is ready to be baked or transferred to the refrigerator. If you press your finger into the dough and you can hear gas escaping, then the dough has over proofed, and it should be baked immediately.

PROOFING SHAPED BREAD OVERNIGHT Once the bread has passed the poke test, it can be refrigerated overnight to deepen its flavor. This accentuates the tanginess of the dough, while the cold temperatures cause the loaf to contract, making it easy to remove from the basket and score.

BAKING

Hooray! You've made it through the bread making steps—now it's time to fill your kitchen with the smell of fresh bread. The first thing you'll need to do is preheat your oven. Thoroughly preheating your oven for about 1 hour at the temperature you're looking for—the recipes will specify—before baking ensures proper oven spring, an open crumb, a defined score, and excellent color. If baking in a combo cooker or Dutch oven, place it in the oven while it's preheating.

SCORE THE DOUGH Scoring involves slashing the top of your loaf with a razor blade. Scoring releases tension, directs steam, and controls the way the loaf blooms. It also creates a ridge, or ridges, of dough that lift away from the bread, called an ear or ears. Scores can also be meaningful and decorative, depicting a moon cycle or a family name. Get creative!

To score, hold the lame and razor (see page 40) with the blade at a 35-degree angle and slash the surface of the dough quickly from one end to the other (or however you would like; other common scores are two slashes running down the middle or an X on top). With proper steam, the 35-degree angle creates a flap of dough that will gracefully peel back and become a deeply colored ear. Score under proofed dough (see page 55) deeply, anticipating the bread will be releasing a fair amount of energy as it rises. Over proofed dough (see page 55) should be scored lightly or not at all.

TO BAKE IN A COMBO COOKER Once the oven and the combo cooker are at temperature (always preheat the cooker *while* preheating the oven), carefully remove the combo cooker. Lift off the inverted pot and flip the loaf from the banneton directly onto the hot skillet portion. Score. Cover with the inverted pot as a lid and load into the oven. Bake for 15 minutes. Remove the lid (careful of hot steam) and reduce the oven temperature

to 475°F. Bake for another 15 to 20 minutes, or until the loaf reaches an internal temperature of 190°F, is deeply browned, and sounds hollow when tapped on the bottom.

TO BAKE IN A DUTCH OVEN Have ready a round of parchment, a few inches wider all around than the bottom of your Dutch oven. Once the pot and the oven are at temperature (always preheat the Dutch oven *while* preheating the oven), carefully remove the Dutch oven and take off the lid. Flip the bread directly onto the parchment and score. Wearing welding gloves and holding the edge of the parchment, lower the bread into the pot. Cover with the lid and bake for 15 minutes. Remove the lid (be careful of hot steam) and reduce the oven temperature to 475°F. Bake for another 15 to 20 minutes. The loaf is done when its internal temperature reaches 190°F, or when it is deeply colored and sounds hollow when tapped on the bottom. (Peel off any bits of stuck parchment once the bread is cool.)

HOMEMADE PROOF BOX

In the winter my kitchen struggles to get above 65°F, so I make a proofer for my starter and a proofer for my dough to keep them warm and happy. For the starter, I line a large ceramic crock with a heating pad, nestle the starter in it, set the heating pad on low, and cover it with a cutting board. To proof my dough, I use a large cooler, like the kind you take to the beach, line it with the heating pad set on low, put my bowl of dough or shaped loaf inside, and close the lid.

FINAL TOUCHES AND PAN SHAPING

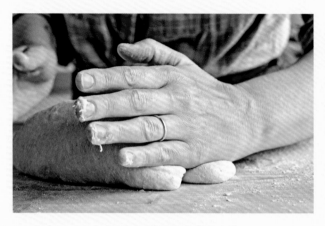

Seal the ends with a "chop."

Transfer seam-side up to a lightly floured banneton.

Leave less overlap for a sandwich-style loaf.

Roll the seam underneath the dough.

A nice long shape for the pan.

Transfer to the pan, seam-side down.

▲ Attach the razor
to the lame.

▼ Score on the skin of the dough at a 35-degree angle.

TO BAKE IN A PULLMAN PAN OR A 9-INCH LOAF PAN
For a perfectly rectangular loaf, if you have a Pullman pan, bake the loaf with the lid on for the first 15 minutes. Remove the lid, reduce the oven temperature to 475°F, and bake another 15 to 20 minutes, or until the loaf reaches an internal temperature of 190°F. If using a 9-inch loaf pan, preheat the oven, cover the pan with a sheet pan and something heavy, like a cast-iron pan or foil-wrapped brick, and bake the loaf with the lid on for the first 15 minutes. Remove the lid, reduce the oven temperature to 475°F, and bake another 15 to 20 minutes, or until the loaf is deeply browned and reaches an internal temperature of 190°F.

FOR A CLASSIC "SANDWICH BREAD" LOOK For bread with a domed top rather than flat one (like the Workweek Bread, page 74), gently spritz the top surface of the dough with water from a spray bottle before loading it into the oven. Bake for 15 minutes before reducing the oven temperature to 475°F. Bake another 15 to 20 minutes, or until the loaf has pulled away from the sides of the pan, is deeply browned, and reaches an internal temperature of 190°F.

MANAGING CRUST COLOR The most common complaint I get from my students is that the bottom of their beautiful bread is always burnt. Try removing your bread from the combo cooker or Dutch oven once it's firm enough and has started to brown, about 20 minutes into the bake, and finish baking it directly on the oven rack. This method will also work to even out any color difference between the top of your bread and the sides if you're baking in a Dutch oven with tall sides.

THE COOLDOWN
Your bread is still baking once it's removed from the oven, and the starches need time to set before you cut into it. To encourage a crisp crust on all sides, carefully remove the bread from the pan, Dutch oven, or combo cooker and let it sit on a wire rack for at least 1 hour. Listen closely: As the interior cools, it contracts and pulls on the crust, making tiny fractures so the bread sounds like it's singing.

STORING
Bread needs to breathe while it's being stored on your countertop, so avoid plastic bags and airtight containers. Instead, store fully cooled bread, cut-side down, in a paper bag inside of a cloth bag (like a market tote) for up to 5 days. The paper absorbs moisture, while the cloth bag allows air flow, preventing mold. (Never store bread in the fridge; it's the perfect place for it to become a Petri dish for whatever microbes are living there.)

THE IMPORTANCE OF STEAM

Commercial bakeries have large ovens with a special feature: steam injection. When bread is loaded onto the hearth, the baker pushes a button, and the hot chamber is filled with steam. Steam is crucial to a good loaf: It softens the exterior of the bread, allowing it to blossom and rise properly, and it adds moisture to the crust, setting off the Maillard reaction: a form of browning that occurs at high temperatures between amino acids and reducing sugars. In a home oven we are at a disadvantage, as trying to steam the whole inside of our ovens is difficult and even dangerous. (I've seen ice thrown directly onto a heating element before—yikes!) Baking your bread in a covered combo cooker or Dutch oven traps the steam released from the dough directly onto the surface of the bread (bread loses 15% of its weight in the form of steam as it bakes) and the result is a gorgeous (and tasty) loaf properly steamed every time!

FREEZING BREAD Sourdough bread freezes exceptionally well! If you're not going to eat the whole loaf right away, or you've been practicing daily and have a kitchen full of loaves, slice the bread and toss the slices in a 1-gallon zip-top plastic bag. Carefully press all the air out of the bag, double-bag it in another 1-gallon bag, and store in the freezer for up to 3 months. To revive all of it, simply take it out and thaw it on your countertop, letting the moisture from inside the bag rehydrate the loaf. To revive a piece at a time, take a slice out as you need it and toast (preferably in a hot cast-iron skillet with butter).

SLICING

Getting a great slice of bread at home can be a real challenge, so here's a trick: On a cutting board using a sharp bread knife, cut the loaf into two equal halves and stand one half on the cutting board so the exposed middle of the bread is flush with the cutting board and you're looking at the end, facing up. Now you can slice away, from left to right, at whatever slice thickness you prefer.

REHYDRATING STALE BREAD

I use this technique when the bread is about 5 to 6 days old. Preheat your oven to 225°F. When the oven is ready, run the whole loaf under lukewarm water, gently squeezing it. This will rehydrate the starches that have become dry as the loaf aged. You want the bread to be moist but NOT soggy, so just a few passes under running water will work. Next, wrap the bread in foil and reheat for 10 minutes at 225°F. Using pot holders or oven mitts, remove the loaf from the oven, take it out of the foil, and let it cool on a wire rack. Serve within a few hours.

> ## WHY DOES MY BREAD MAKE ME SO HAPPY?
>
> I'm not a psychologist, but I think that the whole process of bread making puts us back in touch with our basic humanity. When we make something from start to finish with our bare hands *and* it's delicious *and* it brings joy to friends and family, it becomes hard to do anything else *but* bake, am I right? Studies have shown that gardening is good for the body because it improves your microbiome, so perhaps the same can be said for plunging your fingers into vibrant flour or sourdough batters!

SEASONAL AND ENVIRONMENTAL CONSIDERATIONS

BE LIKE A FARMER when you bake! Study the weather for any changes and calibrate your starters and doughs accordingly. Every factor, including your environment, is either going to help your bread dough expand, or it's going to encourage it to contract. Here are some tips to help you get the best bread day in and day out.

COOL SEASONS

In the late fall, winter, and early spring, it's important to consider that your dough might need help rising in bulk fermentation and again during proofing. When your kitchen is between 65° and 68°F:

- Add an additional 5% of starter to the dough.
- Raise the desired dough temperature by 5°F.
- Don't mix your dough in a cold metal bowl. In cooler temperatures I use a thick-walled plastic 12-quart Cambro with a tight-fitting lid.
- Extend fermentation times. Build an extra hour or two into your bake schedule at both ends for the starter to become bubbly and active, and for the dough to fully proof.
- Find a warm spot to rise and proof in. I like the shelf above my woodstove. Some folks swear by the top of the dryer or near the water heater and some people even bring dough to bed with them (under the covers or not is your prerogative).
- Pop the dough in the oven with the pilot light on during bulk ferment and proofing. The light will gently warm up the chamber. (Oven off!!!)

WARM SEASONS

In the late spring, summer, and early fall, you can expect that your dough will move quickly, meaning that fermentation and proofing can happen at an accelerated rate. When your kitchen starts to creep above 77°F:

- Decrease the amount of starter in the dough by 5% to 10%.
- Lower the desired dough temperature by 5°F.

- Mix in the early morning hours, before the heat sets in.
- Mix and bulk ferment in a cool bowl, such as a metal, porcelain, or enamelware, with a towel placed over the top so the dough can breathe.
- Let the dough ferment in a cool location, out of direct sunlight. If you have easy access to a cellar or basement, this can be a good option.
- Use the fridge to start and stop the process—you can bulk ferment the dough in the fridge overnight, then shape and bake it the next day.

HUMIDITY

When humidity is high, make sure the flour that you're working with isn't moist or clumping. Store it in an airtight container and out of direct sunlight. Begin the mix, holding back a small portion of the water to see how the dough handles before adding the full amount called for. Humidity will speed things up and make a sticky dough. Stay on your toes.

DRY ENVIRONMENTS

In dry conditions, you want to keep the dough soft, supple, and moist so it doesn't develop a skin or dehydrate while fermenting. Use a spray bottle to moisten the surface while bulk fermenting and proofing. Proof it in a homemade steam chamber by boiling water in a pot and placing it in the bottom of the oven, set the pan or banneton on the middle rack and turn on the pilot light.

HIGH ALTITUDES

High elevation environments have low humidity, so you may also want to add 10% to 15% more water than a recipe calls for. Start by adding the amount specified, and if the dough is dry and lumpy, use the double hydration technique (see page 48) to work in more hydration. You'll also want to increase the oven temperature by 20° to 25°F and bake the bread for an extra 10 to 15 minutes.

CRUST AND CRUMB FLAVORS

VEGETAL
fresh grass
sprouts
tender greens
peas
potato

GRAIN
oats
rice
fresh
burnt toast
yeasty

SALTY
mineral
capers
saline

SWEET
corn
molasses
honey
vanilla

DAIRY
heavy cream
butter

FRUITY
grapefruit
lemon
green apple
banana

EARTHY
wet soil
moss
wood
tobacco

SOUR DAIRY
buttermilk
hard cheese
yogurt
sour cream

BOLD
black pepper
red wine
cinnamon
cocoa
charcoal

TOASTED
burnt
bacon
smoked
caramel

DRIED FRUIT
figs
raisins
currants
cherry

ABOVE

Just as you might attend a coffee or wine tasting, so, too, can you explore the complexity behind a bite of bread. Take a crouton-size bite of bread and slowly chew it 32 times. What do you taste? Here is some vocabulary (not to put words in your mouth) to get you going.

Sourdough

A CLASSIC SOURDOUGH STARTER, made with white flour and kept at a ratio of equal parts flour and water, is the easiest to create and the most versatile to bake with. The rough estimate for the time it takes this style of sourdough starter to come alive is 7 days. It will take another 7 days for the starter to stabilize, sorting out its microbiome and acidity levels. You should expect about 2 weeks' worth of daily attention to your starter before you can bake a loaf—and, honestly, it's not uncommon for it to take up to 3 weeks for a brand-new starter to be strong enough to make bread!

What I Mean When I Say "White" Flour

When I say "white flour," I mean commercially grown wheat, milled with an industrial roller mill, containing no bran or germ and found on the supermarket shelf. I buy white flour and use white flour, but I am picky about it. At the supermarket I prefer King Arthur organic bread flour. (For more information, see Resources, page 294.)

START THE FIRST DAY of a new starter's life with a blend of rye and white bread flour. I use rye in the first 24 hours because it has a high level of available sugars, is rich in enzymes, and is full of fiber, giving the white flour a boost of activity. If you don't have rye, you can substitute whole wheat flour. If you have neither rye nor whole wheat, then use all bread flour on Day One and anticipate a longer timeframe, about 2 more days, for the starter to come alive. Never use bleached, bromated, pastry, or cake flour to make a starter. If you have only rye flour or only whole wheat flour, and plenty of it, then skip this chapter and move on to a desem (see page 136) or 100% rye starter (see page 203), both of which involve no white flour at all.

Any water that you would drink is fine for creating and nurturing your starter. Chlorinated water *may* slow down the process. If you are worried about treated water, fill a pitcher the night before and let it stand, uncovered, on the counter for 6 to 8 hours, to dechlorinate.

MAKING A
SOURDOUGH STARTER

Refreshing your starter is key to growth and helps balance the acidity.

DAY ONE

To make a starter, choose a 1-quart wide-mouthed glass jar, or a ceramic or food-grade plastic container of a comparable size (your starter will double in size as it grows). Get the weight of your container in grams (just the container, not the lid) so you can reserve the correct amount of starter when you refresh it.

Combine 50g rye flour and 50g bread flour with 100g water. If your kitchen is warm, between 78° and 82°F, use cool water (about 70°F); if your kitchen is cool, between 60° and 72°F, use warm water (about 80°F). Stir vigorously with a spoon. Using a Sharpie, make a line directly on the container at the top of the starter. Label this mark: Day One. You will use this line to gauge if the starter has risen and, if so, by how much. Cover completely with a lid and let rest at room temperature (68° to 72°F) for 24 hours.

DAY TWO (REFRESHMENT)

Today the starter will begin a refreshment cycle. This involves saving a small portion of the original mixture, discarding the rest, and feeding the held-back portion flour and water. To refresh, zero your scale and then set your container with the starter in it on the scale. Discard until the number on the scale reflects 50g of the starter plus the weight

---

THE LID DILEMMA: TIGHT OR LOOSE?

One of the most frequent questions I get is whether you should tightly or loosely cover the container your sourdough starter lives in. The answer is: It depends on the container you keep it in. There will be gas produced by the yeast, and if you're using a glass container with the lid sealed tightly, there is a chance that the container could crack from internal pressure. This is why I choose food-grade plastic, like a deli container. It will either expand with the gas or "burp" itself by popping the lid when there's too much pressure. In short, if you use glass, leave the lid slightly ajar; if you use a flexible material, it's okay to cover tightly. Never leave the lid completely off; you don't want a crust to form or unwanted microbes to join the party.

OPPOSITE
City Queen Loaf (page 105)

of the container. To the remaining 50g, add 100g bread flour and 100g water. (You may also use a fresh container each time, adding 50g of the starter to it, along with 100g bread flour and 100g water—your call). If your kitchen is warm, between 78° and 82°F, use cool water (about 70°F); if your kitchen is cool, between 60° and 72°F, use warm water (about 80°F). Stir vigorously with a spoon. Mark the top of the starter and label it Day Two. Cover completely with a lid and let rest for 24 hours.

DAYS THREE THROUGH SIX

Follow the instructions for Day Two, with a fresh mark and date for each refreshment, and begin checking the starter every day 4 to 6 hours after refreshing. Note where the starter is now compared with the mark made earlier. Has it doubled? Risen at all? Once it begins to rise predictably at the 4- to 6-hour mark after refreshing, you have an active starter on your hands! Don't give up if your starter was highly active on Day Two and goes through a slump during this phase—it's totally normal.

DAY SEVEN

Refresh as you did on Day Two and use the excess that you'd usually discard to make the Workweek Bread (page 74) to gauge the leavening power of your starter. At this point the starter should be bubbly, rise predictably several hours after being fed, and smell like yogurt. If you slide a portion of the starter into a glass of water it should float (see The Float Test, at left). If it is not bubbly *at all*, doesn't rise *at all* after 7 days, start over (sorry!).

DAYS EIGHT THROUGH THIRTEEN

Continue refreshing your starter as directed on Day Two. Now you may use your discard to make any of the recipes in the Extra Credit chapter on page 251.

DAY FOURTEEN

Congratulations! Now you should have a healthy, active sourdough starter. Refresh as you did on Day Two and use the discard to make the Workweek Bread (page 74) again. Compared with the loaf you made on Day Seven, the bread should have more overall volume and an open, irregular interior. By Day Fourteen, the yeast and bacteria will be strong enough to undergo storage in cold temperatures.

PATIENCE
AS AN INGREDIENT

*Don't stress. . . .
Everything
necessary for
fermentation
is right there.*

IF AT ANY TIME you change a variable in the process of caring for your starter, such as forgetting to feed it, changing the flour, using cold water one day and hot water the next, or feeding it at different times, you will delay the time it takes to stabilize. Have patience and don't stress. This is an organic process and everything necessary for fermentation is right there; it just needs a little attention from you every few hours for the first few days (you are on the starter's timeline—it's not on yours!). Once the starter is bubbly, rises predictably after feeding, floats in water, and has the flavor and aroma of yogurt, you're ready for baking bread!

If you plan on baking daily or every other day: Leave the starter on the countertop and continue daily refreshments as instructed on Day Two.

If you plan on baking a loaf between once a week and once a month: Prepare your starter for cold storage in the fridge. See Preparing for Cold Storage (page 70).

If you plan on baking only a few times a year: Dehydrate the starter so you can have some at the ready whenever you'd like to revitalize the dried flakes. See Long-Term Storage (page 71).

TAKING CARE OF
YOUR SOURDOUGH STARTER

ABOVE

Left: Active sourdough. *Right:* The "hooch" created when left unattended.

IF YOU ARE ONLY planning to make bread once or twice a week, then you should keep your active starter in the fridge. To prepare your starter for a nap in the fridge, you'll want to stiffen it by reducing the amount of water. This slows down fermentation, which reduces activity and acid production (yeast and bacteria go dormant below 40°F).

PREPARING FOR COLD STORAGE

Weigh 50g of your starter into a clean container and add 100g of bread flour and 75g water. Stir vigorously. Cover with a lid and ferment at room temp (68° to 72°F) for 3 hours. The starter will have a few bubbles and have sightly risen, but not be filled with bubbles and doubled in size—that's okay! You want to put it away while there is still food left for the yeast and bacteria. Transfer it to the fridge.

You still need to feed your starter weekly (give it a maintenance refresh), even when it's dormant in the fridge. This keeps your starter alive and ready to bake on the other side of its hiatus.

To maintenance refresh, remove the starter from the fridge, discard all but 50g, and feed it 100g bread flour and 75g water. Cover with the lid and ferment at room temp (68° to 72°F) for 3 hours. The starter will have a few bubbles and have sightly risen, but not be filled with bubbles and doubled in size. Return it to the fridge.

While living in the fridge, your starter may separate or develop a layer of colored alcohol on the top, known as hooch. This does not mean that your starter is dead. The water and alcohol weigh less than the flour batter, so they float to the top (you'll pour this off before you revive it—see the next step). If you're not working with your starter often, then you might want to set a weekly calendar reminder so you don't forget to refresh it. If you do forget, miss a week, or go on vacation, don't stress: A starter can go dormant in the fridge for up to a month. When you're able, just take it out and maintenance refresh as described above.

REVIVING YOUR STARTER FROM COLD STORAGE
When you're getting ready to bake again, you'll need to pull your starter from the fridge and bring it up to speed.

To revive, pour off the hooch (any water/alcohol) at the surface and discard all but 50g of the starter. To the remaining 50g, mix in 100g bread flour and 100g water. Cover with the lid and ferment at room temp (68° to 72°F) for 24 hours. If your starter is looking great on the first refreshment—meaning it's doubled in size within 6 to 10 hours, smells like yogurt (not nail polish), and is bubbly—then skip ahead to making bread! If your starter is slow to rise and still smells pungent, refresh again before using.

LONG-TERM STORAGE
Dehydrating your starter into dry flakes is a great approach if you aren't planning on baking for a few months or you want to mail some starter to a friend or travel with your starter so you can make fresh sourdough while on a trip.

To dehydrate your starter, line a sheet pan with a silicone baking mat or parchment paper and have ready a flexible spatula or dough scraper. Mix warm water into the starter, a tablespoon at a time, to create a slurry that's the consistency of runny pancake batter. Then use the spatula or dough scraper to smear it across the mat or parchment.

Turn on your oven light. Place the sheet pan in the oven, close the door, and leave it to dehydrate for 24 hours. After 24 hours, the starter should be thin, dry, and crusty. Break it apart and transfer to small, resealable zip-top bags or other airtight containers, label, date, and transfer them to the freezer. Dehydrated starter can be stored in the freezer for up to 2 months.

To revive from dehydrated flakes, place 40g of the dehydrated starter flakes in a 1-quart wide-mouthed glass jar or a ceramic or food-grade plastic container of a comparable size, and add 100g bread flour and 100g warm water. Mix until incorporated, making sure there's no dry flour left. Cover with the lid and ferment at room temp (68° to 72°F) for 24 hours. Refresh (see page 67) every 6 to 10 hours, or until the starter doubles in size and has large, dish-soap-size bubbles on the surface and a pleasant sweet-and-sour smell. Now it's ready to use. Store the revived starter at room temperature, or in the fridge, and feed as instructed in Reviving Your Starter from Cold Storage (at left).

BEFORE YOU BAKE: USING YOUR SOURDOUGH STARTER

Warm (70° to 80°F) environments speed up starter activity, cooler conditions slow it down.

FOR ALL THE FORMULAS in this sourdough chapter, refresh your starter between 6 and 10 hours before you want to mix the dough. Keep in mind warm environments (70° to 80°F) will shorten the time it takes for the starter to become active, and cooler environments (60° to 68°F) will extend the time it takes for the starter to become active. You can use it as soon as it passes the float test (see page 68). I like to feed mine around 9:00 p.m., leave it somewhere cool, around 65°F, and mix the next morning around 6:00 a.m.

After you've pulled the amount of starter you need for the bread dough (look at the formula in the recipe to see how much you need), refresh the starter and cover with the lid. If you're planning on baking again the next day, leave it out at room temperature (you'll be refreshing it in the evening again). If you're not, stick it in the refrigerator.

OPPOSITE
Workweek Bread (page 74)

Refresh the sourdough starter 6 to 10 hours before mixing and folding the dough.
The dough is then chilled overnight before being shaped, proofed, and baked the following day.

1 LOAF AT 850G ——— **9-INCH PULLMAN PAN** ——— **DOUGH TEMP: 78°F** ——— **LEVEL: BEGINNER**

WORKWEEK BREAD

This half whole-grain, half white flour loaf is perfect to bake on a daily basis and
is a great starter loaf if you're new to sourdough—it's also the loaf I use to test
a new sourdough starter's strength and flavor at Day Seven (page 68) and Day
Fourteen (page 68). The dough is forgiving and spends time in the fridge before
going into a pan—making it easy to work around your schedule!

BAKER'S PERCENTAGES	WEIGHTS & INGREDIENTS
50%	203g bread flour
50%	203g whole wheat flour
80%	325g water
25%	102g sourdough starter
2%	8g salt

THE NIGHT BEFORE: SOURDOUGH STARTER REFRESH
Following the instructions on page 67, refresh your sourdough starter the
night before or up to 10 hours prior to mixing the dough.

DAY ONE: MIXING, FOLDING, AND CHILLING
Mix In a large bowl, thoroughly mix together the bread flour, whole wheat
flour, water, starter, and salt by hand until there are no patches of dry
flour. You can squeeze the dough through your hands, like extruding
pasta between your fingers! The dough will be sticky, gluey, and shaggy.

Pop a digital thermometer into the dough to take its temperature—it
should be between 75° and 81°F. (If the dough is above 81°F, stick
it in a cool spot—not the refrigerator—until it cools to between 75° and
78°F. If it is less than 75°F, place it in a warm location until it reaches
between 75° and 78°F.) Cover the bowl with a dinner plate or sheet pan
for a lid and let rest for 1 hour.

Fold Once the dough is relaxed, you will give it a series of three folds
spaced 1 hour apart. To fold, smear a little water onto your work surface.
Using a dough scraper, gather the dough together and, with a quick
motion, scoop the dough up with the dough scraper and flip it onto the
wet table. Using your hands, lift the dough off the table, then slap the
bottom half down, so that it sticks a little. Gently leaning back, stretch
the dough and then quickly lean forward, tossing the dough still in your
hands over the portion stuck to the table. Repeat three to four times. The
dough will become smooth and pull itself into a ball.

Using the dough scraper, return the dough to its container smooth-side
up and cover with the plate or sheet pan for 1 hour. Repeat the process
two more times, with 1 hour between folding sessions.

Chill After the final fold, transfer the dough back to the bowl, cover with the lid, and refrigerate for at least 8 hours, or up to 12.

DAY TWO: SHAPING, PROOFING, AND BAKING

Pre-shape Lightly dust your table with flour. Remove the dough from the fridge (there's no need to let it warm up before shaping). Using a dough scraper, gather the dough together in the bowl and, with a quick motion, scoop the dough up with the dough scraper and flip it onto the table. Pat into a rectangle with a short side facing you. Fold the edge of the dough closest to you over to the top (the edge farthest from you), leaving a 1-inch lip. Take the sides of the dough, gently stretch each outward a few inches, then quickly cross them over each other so they are on top of each other, like swaddling a baby. Next, stretch the edge of the dough closest to you up to the top, flush with the top edge. Gently press down to create a seam and seal.

Use your hands or a bench knife to gently drag the loaf on the table to create surface tension. You will see it tighten and become smooth as you drag. Make sure the top stays the top and the dough doesn't roll over as you go. The dough will curl into itself so the seam is now on the bottom and the top is smooth and roundish.

Bench rest Sprinkle the dough with flour, cover with a kitchen towel, and let rest 30 minutes.

Final shape Lightly oil a 9-inch Pullman pan. Dust your table with flour. Use a bench knife to flip over the pre-shape so the top is now the bottom. Bring the bottom of the dough to meet the top edge, leaving a 1-inch lip at the top. Gently stretch the sides outward a few inches, then quickly cross them over the middle of the dough, like swaddling a baby. You're now looking at an envelope shape. Stretch the bottom of the dough up to meet the top of the envelope and seal. The dough will now be a cylinder on its side with a seam facing away from you. Roll the seam underneath and seal the left and right ends using the edge of your palm. With the bench knife, flip it seam-side down, into the pan.

Proof Loosely cover the pan with a kitchen towel and proof the dough in a draft-free spot at room temperature for 3 hours. When fully proofed, the loaf will appear to have doubled in size, feel full of air, and pass the poke test (see page 55).

Preheat the oven to 500°F.

Bake When the oven is up to temperature, gently spritz the top surface of the dough with water from a spray bottle before loading it into the oven. (This loaf has no score.) Bake at 500°F for 15 minutes. After 15 minutes, reduce the oven temperature to 475°F and bake another 15 to 20 minutes, or until the loaf is deeply browned and reaches an internal temperature of 190°F. Carefully remove the bread from the pan and cool completely on a wire rack. Store for up to 5 days, cut-side down, in a paper bag tucked inside a cloth bag.

SNAPSHOT
Refresh the sourdough starter 6 to 10 hours before mixing
the dough. The dough is then folded, shaped, proofed, and baked.

1 BÂTARD AT 850G ——— 9-INCH OVAL BANNETON ——— DOUGH TEMP: 78°F ——— LEVEL: BEGINNER

LUNCH BOX LOAF

Picture the perfect bread for a decadent peanut butter and jelly or quick
BLT sandwich and that's what you have here. Fluffy, chewy, and slightly tangy,
these slices beg for mustard and mayonnaise. I'll plant a whole garden bed
of tomatoes in anticipation of perfect summer tomato and mayo sandwiches!

BAKER'S PERCENTAGES	WEIGHTS & INGREDIENTS
80%	354g bread flour
20%	89g whole wheat flour
70%	310g water
20%	89g sourdough starter
2%	9g salt

THE NIGHT BEFORE: SOURDOUGH STARTER REFRESH
Following the instructions on page 67, refresh your sourdough starter the
night before or up to 10 hours prior to mixing the dough.

DAY OF: MIXING THROUGH BAKING
Mix In a large bowl, thoroughly mix together the bread flour, whole wheat
flour, water, starter, and salt by hand until there are no patches of dry
flour. You can squeeze the dough through your hands, like extruding
pasta between your fingers! The dough will be sticky, gluey, and shaggy.

Pop a digital thermometer into the dough to take its temperature—it
should be between 75° and 81°F. (If the dough is above 81°F, stick
it in a cool spot—not the refrigerator—until it cools to between 75° and
78°F. If it is cooler than 75°F, place it in a warm location until it reaches
between 75° and 78°F.) Cover the bowl with a dinner plate or sheet pan
for a lid and let rest for 1 hour.

Fold Once the dough is relaxed, you will give it a series of three folds
spaced 1 hour apart. To fold, smear a little water onto your work surface.
Using a dough scraper, gather the dough together and, with a quick
motion, scoop the dough up with the dough scraper and flip it onto the
wet table. Using your hands, lift the dough off the table, then slap the
bottom half down, so that it sticks a little. Gently leaning back, stretch
the dough and then quickly lean forward, tossing the dough still in your
hands over the portion stuck to the table. Repeat three to four times.
The dough will become smooth and pull itself into a ball.

Using the dough scraper, return the dough to its container, smooth-side
up, cover with the plate or sheet pan, and let rest for 1 hour. Repeat the
process two more times, with 1 hour between folding sessions.

Recipe continues

Pre-shape Lightly dust your table with flour. Using a dough scraper, gather the dough together in the bowl and, with a quick motion, scoop the dough up with the dough scraper and flip it onto the table. Pat into a rectangle with a short side facing you. Bring the edge of the dough closest to you to the top (the edge farthest from you), leaving a 1-inch lip. Take the sides of the dough, gently stretch each outward a few inches, then quickly cross them over each other so they are on top of each other, like swaddling a baby. Next, stretch the edge of the dough closest to you up to the top, flush with the top edge. Gently press to create a seam.

Use your hands or a bench knife to gently drag the loaf on the table to create surface tension. You will see it tighten and become smooth as you drag. Make sure the top stays the top and the dough doesn't roll over as you go. The dough will curl into itself, so the seam is now on the bottom and the top is smooth and roundish.

Bench rest Sprinkle the dough with flour, cover with a kitchen towel, and let rest 30 minutes.

Final shape Lightly dust a cloth-lined 9-inch oval banneton with flour and set aside. Lightly dust the table with flour. Use a bench knife to flip over the pre-shape so the top is now the bottom. Bring the bottom of the dough to meet the top edge, leaving a 1-inch lip at the top. Gently stretch the sides outward a few inches, then quickly cross them over the middle of the dough, like swaddling a baby. You're now looking at an envelope shape. Stretch the bottom of the dough up to meet the top of the envelope and press down to seal. The dough will now be a cylinder on its side with a seam facing away from you. Roll the seam underneath and seal the left and right ends using the edge of your palm. With the bench knife, flip it seam-side up, into the banneton.

Proof Loosely cover the banneton with a kitchen towel and proof the dough in a draft-free spot and at room temperature for 2 to 3 hours. When fully proofed, the loaf will appear to have doubled in size, feel full of air, and pass the poke test (see page 55).

Preheat the oven. Set a combo cooker on a rack in the oven so the skillet is on the bottom and the pot is inverted as a lid. Preheat the oven (and the combo cooker) to 500°F.

Score Wearing welding gloves, remove the combo cooker from the oven (it's *hot!*) and quickly toss the dough seam-side down onto the hot skillet portion of the cooker. Use a lame and razor, with the blade at a 35-degree angle, to score in one long stroke, running lengthwise along the top of the bread.

Bake Immediately cover the bread with the inverted pot for a lid and load it back into the oven. Bake for 15 minutes. Remove the combo cooker from the oven and set on the stovetop. Remove the lid (be careful of hot steam) and reduce the oven temperature to 475°F. Return the bread, still on the skillet portion of the combo cooker, to the oven and bake another 15 to 20 minutes, or until the loaf is deeply browned, reaches an internal temperature of 190°F, and sounds hollow when tapped on the bottom. Carefully remove the bread from the skillet and cool completely on a wire rack. Store for up to 5 days, cut-side down, in a paper bag tucked inside a cloth bag.

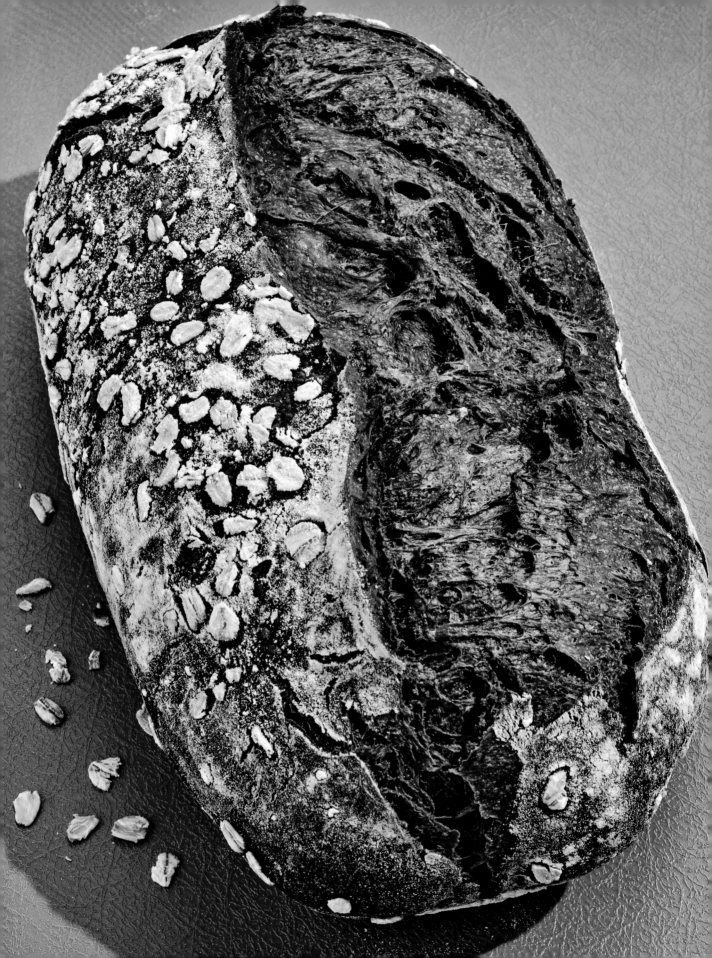

Refresh the sourdough starter 6 to 10 hours before mixing, folding, and shaping
the dough. Chill the shaped bâtard in the fridge overnight and bake it the following morning.

1 BÂTARD AT 850G ——— **9-INCH OVAL BANNETON** ——— **DOUGH TEMP: 78°F** ——— **LEVEL: BEGINNER**

CHOCOLATE BEER BREAD

Sturdy and stout, this loaf is a colorful favorite when you want something bitter
and malty to go with sharp cheese, pickles, and cured meats. Guinness and oatmeal
porters work exceptionally well here—stay away from funky sours and IPAs.

BAKER'S PERCENTAGES	WEIGHTS & INGREDIENTS
80%	320g bread flour
10%	40g whole wheat flour
10%	40g Dutch-process cocoa
75%	300g beer, at room temp
20%	80g sourdough starter
2%	8g salt

Rolled oats to roll the dough in

THE NIGHT BEFORE: SOURDOUGH STARTER REFRESH
Following the instructions on page 67, refresh your sourdough starter the
night before or up to 10 hours prior to mixing the dough.

DAY ONE: MIXING, FOLDING, SHAPING, PROOFING, AND CHILLING
Mix In a large bowl, thoroughly mix together the bread flour, whole wheat
flour, cocoa, beer, starter, and salt by hand until there are no patches of
dry flour. You can squeeze the dough through your hands, like extruding
pasta between your fingers! The dough will be sticky, gluey, and shaggy.

Pop a digital thermometer into the dough to take its temperature—it
should be between 75° and 81°F. (If the dough is above 81°F, stick
it in a cool spot—not the refrigerator—until it cools to between 75° and
78°F. If it is cooler than 75°F, place it in a warm location until it reaches
between 75° and 78°F.) Cover the bowl with a dinner plate or sheet pan
for a lid and let rest for 1 hour.

Fold Once the dough is relaxed, you will give it a series of three folds
spaced 1 hour apart. To fold, smear a little water onto your work surface.
Using a dough scraper, gather the dough together and, with a quick
motion, scoop the dough up with the dough scraper and flip it onto the
wet table. Using your hands, lift the dough off the table, then slap the
bottom half down, so that it sticks a little. Gently leaning back, stretch
the dough and then quickly lean forward, tossing the dough still in your
hands over the portion stuck to the table. Repeat three to four times. The
dough will become smooth and pull itself into a ball.

Using the dough scraper, return the dough to its container, smooth-side
up, cover with the plate or sheet pan, and let rest for 1 hour. Repeat the
process two more times, with 1 hour between folding sessions.

Recipe continues

Pre-shape Lightly dust your table with flour. Using a dough scraper, gather the dough together in the bowl and, with a quick motion, scoop the dough up with the dough scraper and flip it onto the table. Pat into a rectangle with a short side facing you. Bring the edge of the dough closest to you to the top (the edge farthest from you), leaving a 1-inch lip. Take the sides of the dough, gently stretch each outward a few inches, then quickly cross them over each other so they are on top of each other, like swaddling a baby. Next, stretch the edge of the dough closest to you up to the top, flush with the top edge. Gently press to create a seam.

Use your hands or a bench knife to gently drag the loaf on the table to create surface tension. You will see it tighten and become smooth as you drag. Make sure the top stays the top and the dough doesn't roll over as you go. The dough will curl into itself, so the seam is now on the bottom and the top is smooth and roundish.

Bench rest Sprinkle the dough with flour, cover with a kitchen towel, and let rest 30 minutes.

Ready the oats While the dough is resting, ready the oats that the dough will be rolled in by running a kitchen towel under water quickly (you want it damp, not soaking) and placing it over one half of a half-sheet pan. Toss a handful of rolled oats onto the pan opposite the kitchen towel. Set aside.

Final shape Lightly dust a cloth-lined 9-inch oval banneton with flour and set aside. Lightly dust your table with flour. Use a bench knife to flip over the pre-shape so the top is now the bottom. Bring the bottom of the dough to meet the top edge, leaving a 1-inch lip at the top. Gently stretch the sides outward a few inches, then quickly cross them over the middle of the dough, like swaddling a baby. You're now looking at an envelope shape. Stretch the bottom of the dough up to meet the top of the envelope and seal. The dough will now be a cylinder on its side with a seam facing away from you. Roll the seam underneath and seal the left and right ends using the edge of your palm. Roll the dough over the damp towel and through the whole oats. Transfer it seam-side up to the floured banneton.

Proof Loosely cover the banneton with a kitchen towel and proof the dough in a draft-free spot at room temperature for 2 to 3 hours. When fully proofed, the loaf will appear to have doubled in size, feel full of air, and pass the poke test (see page 55).

Chill When proofed, transfer the banneton, covered with a shower cap or kitchen towel, to the fridge for at least 6 hours and up to 24.

DAY TWO: BAKING
Preheat the oven Set a combo cooker on a rack in the oven so the skillet is the bottom and the pot is inverted as a lid. Preheat the oven (and the combo cooker) to 500°F.

Score Wearing welding gloves, remove the combo cooker from the oven (it's *hot!*) and quickly toss the cold dough seam-side down onto the hot skillet portion of the cooker. Use a lame and razor, with the blade at a 35-degree angle, to score in one long stroke, running lengthwise along the top of the bread.

Bake Immediately cover the bread with the inverted pot for a lid and load it back into the oven. Bake for 15 minutes. Remove the combo cooker from the oven and set on the stovetop. Remove the lid (be careful of hot steam) and reduce the oven temperature to 475°F. Return the bread, still on the skillet portion of the combo cooker, to the oven and bake another 15 to 20 minutes, or until the loaf is deeply browned, reaches an internal temperature of 190°F, and sounds hollow when tapped on the bottom. Carefully remove the bread from the skillet and cool completely on a wire rack. Store for up to 5 days, cut-side down, in a paper bag tucked inside a cloth bag.

Refresh the sourdough starter 6 to 10 hours before mixing the dough. The dough is then mixed and folded before being chilled overnight. The dough is shaped and baked the following morning.

1 ROUND AT 900G ——— **9-INCH ROUND BANNETON** ——— **DOUGH TEMP: 78°F** ——— **LEVEL: BEGINNER**

MICHE

A traditional miche can weigh anywhere from 1.5 to 5 kilos (3 to 11 pounds). This version is scaled down to a standard-size loaf for ease. The heavier weight reflects a time when it was common for bread to be baked in a communal, wood-fired oven once a week. Since whole-grain flour holds moisture so well, the large loaf would stay moist (and delicious) until the next village bake day.

BAKER'S PERCENTAGES	WEIGHTS & INGREDIENTS
70%	304g bread flour
20%	87g whole wheat flour
10%	43g whole-grain rye flour
80%	348g water
25%	108g sourdough starter
2%	9g salt

THE NIGHT BEFORE: SOURDOUGH STARTER REFRESH
Following the instructions on page 67, refresh your sourdough starter the night before or up to 10 hours prior to mixing the dough.

DAY ONE: MIXING, FOLDING, AND CHILLING
Mix In a large bowl, thoroughly mix together the bread flour, whole wheat flour, rye flour, water, sourdough starter, and salt by hand until there are no patches of dry flour. You can squeeze the dough through your hands, like extruding pasta between your fingers! The dough will be sticky, gluey, and shaggy.

Pop a digital thermometer into the dough to take its temperature—it should be between 75° and 81°F. (If the dough is above 81°F, stick it in a cool spot—not the refrigerator—until it cools to between 78° and 81°F. If it is less than 75°F, place it in a warm location until it reaches between 75° and 78°F.) Cover the bowl with a dinner plate or a sheet pan for a lid and set aside for 1 hour.

Fold Once the dough is relaxed, you will give it a series of three folds spaced 1 hour apart. To fold, smear a little water onto your work surface. Using a dough scraper, gather the dough together and, with a quick motion, scoop the dough up with the dough scraper and flip it onto the wet table. Using your hands, lift the dough off the table, then slap the bottom half down, so that it sticks a little. Gently leaning back, stretch the dough and then quickly lean forward, tossing the dough still in your hands over the portion stuck to the table. Repeat three to four times. The dough will become smooth and pull itself into a ball.

Recipe continues

Using the dough scraper, return the dough to its container, smooth-side up, and cover with the plate or sheet pan for 1 hour. Repeat the process two more times, with 1 hour between folding sessions.

Chill After the final fold, transfer the dough back to the bowl, cover with the lid, and refrigerate for at least 8 hours or up to 24.

DAY TWO: SHAPING, PROOFING, AND BAKING
Pre-shape Lightly dust your table with flour. Remove the dough from the fridge (there's no need to let it warm up before shaping). Using a dough scraper, gather the dough together in the bowl and, with a quick motion, scoop the dough up with the dough scraper and flip it onto the table. Pat into a rectangle with a short side facing you. Bring the edge of the dough closest to you to the top (the edge farthest from you), leaving a 1-inch lip. Take the sides of the dough, gently stretch each outward a few inches, then quickly cross them over each other so they are on top of each other, like swaddling a baby. Next, stretch the edge of the dough closest to you up to the top, flush with the top edge. Gently press to create a seam.

Use your hands or a bench knife to gently drag the loaf on the table to create surface tension. You will see it tighten and become smooth as you drag. Make sure the top stays the top and the dough doesn't roll over as you go. The dough will curl into itself so the seam is now on the bottom and the top is smooth and roundish.

Bench rest Sprinkle the dough with flour, cover with a kitchen towel, and let rest 30 minutes.

Final shape Lightly dust a cloth-lined 9-inch round banneton with flour and set aside. Lightly dust your table with flour. Using a bench knife, flip over the relaxed round. Imagine the round into four quarters. Stretch the edge of each quarter to the center of the round, overlapping them slightly, by about 1 inch, to make a pouch shape. Now turn the "pouch" on its side, cupping the portion that was flush with the table in one hand, and cinch the gathered portions together with the edge of your palm, sealing the seam. Glide the dough down the table so that the seam is sealed between the edge of your palm and the table. With a bench scraper, transfer the dough seam-side up into the floured banneton.

Proof Loosely cover the banneton with a kitchen towel and proof the dough in a draft-free spot at room temperature for 2 to 3 hours. When fully proofed, the loaf will appear to have doubled in size, feel full of air, and pass the poke test (see page 55).

Preheat the oven Set a combo cooker on a rack in the oven so the skillet is on the bottom and the pot is inverted as a lid. Preheat the oven (and the combo cooker) to 500°F.

Score Wearing welding gloves, remove the combo cooker from the oven (it's *hot!*) and quickly toss the dough seam-side down onto the hot skillet portion of the cooker. Use a lame and razor, with the blade at a 35-degree angle, to score a square, or X, on the top of the bread.

Bake Immediately cover the bread with the inverted pot for a lid and load it back into the oven. Bake for 15 minutes. Remove the combo cooker from the oven and set on the stovetop. Remove the lid (be careful of hot steam) and reduce the oven temperature to 475°F. Return the bread, still on the skillet portion of the combo cooker, to the oven and bake another 15 to 20 minutes, or until the loaf is deeply browned, reaches an internal temperature of 190°F, and sounds hollow when tapped on the bottom. Carefully remove the bread from the skillet and cool completely on a wire rack. Store for up to 5 days, cut-side down, in a paper bag tucked inside a cloth bag.

SNAPSHOT
Refresh the sourdough starter 6 to 10 hours before
mixing, folding, shaping, proofing, and baking the bread.

1 FREE-FORM LEAF SHAPE AT 500G ——— DOUGH TEMP: 78°F ——— LEVEL: BEGINNER

EVERYTHING BAGEL FOUGASSE

Fougasse is a French bread from Provence that is shaped like a leaf or an ear
of wheat. Typically, it is sprinkled with herbs and salt. I think it's the perfect
chewy, crispy vehicle for a boatload of salty, everything bagel topping. Try using
the everything bagel topping sprinkled on Cheddar and Black Pepper Biscuits
(page 258) or roll the City Queen Loaf (page 105) in it for a zesty bite.

TOPPING

WEIGHTS & INGREDIENTS

30g poppy seeds	30g sesame seeds
30g onion, dried minced	30g Maldon flaky salt
30g garlic, dried minced	

DOUGH

BAKER'S PERCENTAGES	WEIGHTS & INGREDIENTS
90%	228g bread flour
10%	25g whole wheat flour
70%	178g water
25%	64g sourdough starter
2%	10g salt

Light olive oil for brushing the dough

THE NIGHT BEFORE: SOURDOUGH STARTER REFRESH AND
PREP TOPPING
Following the instructions on page 67, refresh your sourdough starter the
night before or up to 10 hours prior to mixing the dough.

Prep everything bagel topping In a large bowl, mix together the poppy
seeds, onion, garlic, sesame seeds, and salt. Transfer to an airtight
container, like a 1-quart deli container, with the lid on, and shake! The mix
will keep for up to 1 month at room temperature.

DAY OF: MIXING THROUGH BAKING
Mix In a large bowl, thoroughly mix together the bread flour, whole wheat
flour, water, starter, and salt by hand until there are no dry patches
of flour. You can squeeze it through your hands, like extruding pasta
between your fingers! The dough will be sticky, gluey, and shaggy.

Pop a digital thermometer into the dough to take its temperature—it
should be between 75° and 81°F. (If the dough is above 81°F, stick
it in a cool spot—not the refrigerator—until it cools to between 75° and
78°F. If it is cooler than 75°F, place it in a warm location until it reaches
between 75° and 78°F.) Cover the bowl with a dinner plate or sheet pan
for a lid and let rest for 1 hour.

Fold Once the dough is relaxed, you will give it a series of three folds
spaced 1 hour apart. To fold, smear a little water onto your work surface.
Using a dough scraper, gather the dough together and, with a quick
motion, scoop the dough up with the dough scraper and flip it onto the
wet table. Using your hands, lift the dough off the table, then slap the
bottom half down, so that it sticks a little. Gently leaning back, stretch

Recipe continues

the dough and then quickly lean forward, tossing the dough still in your hands over the portion stuck to the table. Repeat three to four times. The dough will become smooth and pull itself into a ball.

Using the dough scraper, return the dough to its container, smooth-side up, cover with the plate or sheet pan, and let rest for 1 hour. Repeat the process two more times, with 1 hour between folding sessions.

Pre-shape Using a dough scraper, gather the dough together in the bowl and, with a quick motion, scoop the dough up with the dough scraper and flip it onto the table. Pat into a rectangle with a short side facing you. Fold the edge of the dough closest to you over to the top (the edge farthest from you), leaving a 1-inch lip. Take the sides of the dough, gently stretch each outward a few inches, then quickly cross them over each other so they are on top of each other, like swaddling a baby. Next, stretch the edge of the dough closest to you up to the top, flush with the top edge. Gently press down to create a seam and seal.

Use your hands or a bench knife to gently drag the loaf on the table to create surface tension. You will see it tighten and become smooth as you drag. Make sure the top stays the top and the dough doesn't roll over as you go. The dough will curl into itself so the seam is now on the bottom and the top is smooth and roundish.

Bench rest Sprinkle the dough with flour, cover with a kitchen towel, and let rest 30 minutes.

Final shape Line a sheet pan with parchment paper. Lightly dust each side of the dough with flour and gently pull into a triangle. This is your "leaf." Transfer to the lined pan and, leaving a portion of dough connecting at the top and at the bottom, cut a long line down the center of the triangle with a pizza wheel or sharp knife.

Score and top Cut small lines from the center line out, leaving a little dough between the center cut and the angle cut, like the pattern on a leaf. Gently pull apart the dough so the openings are visible. Brush the top with a minimal amount of olive oil, just enough to get the toppings to stick. Sprinkle generously with the everything bagel topping.

Proof Cover the sheet pan with a foil "tent" by placing a large sheet of foil over the tray, tall enough so it doesn't stick to the dough, and crimp the edges onto the rim of the sheet pan so that the foil is supported by the pan. Proof for 3 hours in a draft-free spot at room temperature. When fully proofed, the dough will feel full of air and will pass the poke test (see page 55).

Preheat the oven to 500°F.

Bake When the oven is up to temperature, slide the pan into the oven (with the foil tent) and bake for 10 minutes. Wearing welding gloves, remove the foil (it's hot!), reduce the oven temperature to 450°F, and bake another 15 minutes, or until the bread is deeply golden and crisp. If the toppings begin to burn, return the foil tent over the bread. Remove from the oven and serve warm or at room temperature—fougasse is best eaten within 24 hours of baking. If you have some left over, rip it up and soak in a hot soup to enjoy.

SNAPSHOT

Refresh the sourdough starter 6 to 10 hous before
mixing, folding, shaping, proofing, and baking the bread.

1 BUMPY LOAF AT 850G ——— 9-INCH PULLMAN PAN ——— DOUGH TEMP: 78°F ——— LEVEL: BEGINNER

MILK BREAD

This loaf came into motion while working through breastfeeding my daughter
at all hours of the day and night (up until now, I thought the time demands
of making bread were rigorous). I'd walk the halls with her at 3:00 a.m. and dream
(hallucinate?) of her eating sandwiches on tall, fluffy bread. This loaf is shaped like
a Japanese milk bread, with three soft mounds, like a curvy postpartum body.

EGG WASH

WEIGHTS & INGREDIENTS

28g whole milk

1 egg, large

DOUGH

BAKER'S PERCENTAGES	WEIGHTS & INGREDIENTS
75%	287g bread flour
25%	96g whole-grain spelt flour
85%	326g whole milk, at room temp
30%	115g sourdough starter
5%	20g butter, at room temp
2%	8g salt

THE NIGHT BEFORE: SOURDOUGH STARTER REFRESH AND MAKE THE EGG WASH

Following the instructions on page 67, refresh your sourdough starter the night before or up to 10 hours prior to mixing the dough.

Make the egg wash Whisk together the whole milk and egg in a pint-size deli container (or similar container), cover tightly with a lid, and refrigerate until needed.

DAY OF: MIXING THROUGH BAKING

Mix In a large bowl, thoroughly mix together the bread flour, spelt flour, milk, starter, butter, and salt by hand until there are no patches of dry flour or streaks of butter. You can squeeze the dough through your hands, like extruding pasta between your fingers! The dough will be sticky, gluey, and shaggy.

Pop a digital thermometer into the dough to take its temperature—it should be between 75° and 81°F. (If the dough is above 81°F, stick it in a cool spot—not the refrigerator—until it cools to between 75° and 78°F. If it is cooler than 75°F, place it in a warm location until it reaches between 75° and 78°F.) Cover the bowl with a dinner plate or sheet pan for a lid and let rest for 1 hour.

Fold Once the dough is relaxed, you will give it a series of three folds spaced 1 hour apart. To fold, smear a little water onto your work surface. Using a dough scraper, gather the dough together and, with a quick motion, scoop the dough up with the dough scraper and flip it onto the wet table. Using your hands, lift the dough off the table, then slap the bottom half down, so that it sticks a little. Gently leaning back, stretch

Recipe continues

the dough and then quickly lean forward, tossing the dough still in your hands over the portion stuck to the table. Repeat three to four times. The dough will become smooth and pull itself into a ball.

Using the dough scraper, return the dough to its container, smooth-side up, cover with the plate or sheet pan, and let rest for 1 hour. Repeat the process two more times, with 1 hour between folding sessions.

Shape Oil a 9-inch Pullman pan. Lightly dust your table with flour. Using the dough scraper, turn out the dough onto your floured work surface. Divide the dough into three 283g portions (or just eyeball it into three equal portions if that's easier for you). Shape each portion into a round by cupping your hand and, keeping the dough cuddled into your palm, make counterclockwise circles on the table, pressing down slightly so that as your hand makes the circular motions, the outer layers of dough are trapped under the bottom. The dough will pull itself into a ball, with a smooth top. The bottom will stay slightly stuck to the table. Repeat with the remaining two portions of dough. Place all three side by side in the Pullman pan.

Egg wash and proof Remove the egg wash from the refrigerator and, using a pastry brush, lightly brush the dough with the egg wash. Cover the pan with a kitchen towel and proof in a draft-free spot for 3 to 4 hours at room temperature. When proofed, the loaf will appear to have doubled in size, feel full of air, and pass the poke test (see page 55).

Preheat the oven to 500°F.

Egg wash and bake Brush the top of the loaf with more egg wash and load the bread into the oven. Bake for 15 minutes (uncovered). With welding gloves, carefully remove the pan, brush a final time with egg wash, and reduce the oven temperature to 475°F. Bake another 15 to 20 minutes, or until the loaf reaches an internal temperature of 190°F, and is a deep golden brown and has pulled away from the sides of the pan. Immediately remove the loaf from the pan and set it on a wire rack to cool completely. Store for up to 5 days, cut-side down, in a paper bag tucked inside a cloth bag.

Refresh the sourdough starter 6 to 10 hours before mixing, folding, and
shaping. The shaped loaf is chilled in the fridge overnight and baked the following day.

1 BÂTARD AT 850G —— **9-INCH OVAL BANNETON** —— **DOUGH TEMP: 78°F** —— **LEVEL: INTERMEDIATE**

TRAIL MIX BREAD

What's better than peanut butter on your bread? Peanut butter IN your bread!
This dough calls for silky smooth peanut butter, roasted peanuts, dark raisins, and
chopped chocolate: the essential components to any hike or outdoor adventure.
Make this bread before your next trip to the great outdoors.

BAKER'S PERCENTAGES	WEIGHTS & INGREDIENTS
SOAKER	
100%	35g raisins, red
100%	35g warm water
DOUGH	
90%	317g bread flour
10%	35g whole wheat flour
70%	247g water
25%	88g sourdough starter
12%	44g peanut butter, smooth
12%	44g semisweet chocolate
10%	35g roasted peanuts
10%	35g raisins, soaked
2%	7g salt

THE NIGHT BEFORE: SOURDOUGH STARTER REFRESH, SOAK RAISINS, PREP CHOCOLATE AND PEANUTS

Following the instructions on page 67, refresh your sourdough starter the night before or up to 10 hours prior to mixing the dough.

Soak the raisins In a pint-size deli container (or similar container), weigh out the raisins and add the warm water. Cover with a lid and soak overnight or until needed.

Prep the chocolate and peanuts Roughly chop the chocolate and roasted peanuts into pea-size pieces. Transfer them (they can be stored together) to a quart-size deli container (or similar container), cover with a lid, and set aside.

DAY ONE: MIXING, FOLDING, SHAPING, PROOFING, AND CHILLING
First mix In a large bowl, thoroughly mix together the bread flour, whole wheat flour, and water by hand until there are no patches of dry flour. You can squeeze the dough through your hands, like extruding pasta between your fingers! The dough will be sticky, gluey, and shaggy.

Pop a digital thermometer into the dough to take its temperature—it should be between 75° and 81°F. (If the dough is above 81°F, stick it in a cool spot—not the refrigerator—until it cools to between 75° and 78°F. If it is cooler than 75°F, place it in a warm location until it reaches between 75° and 78°F.)

Autolyse Cover the bowl with a dinner plate or sheet pan for a lid and let rest for 1 hour.

Final mix and additions Drain the raisins and pinch them into the dough along with the chopped chocolate, peanuts, peanut butter, starter, and

Recipe continues

salt. The dough will become stringy and fall apart; that's normal, just keep mixing until it re-forms into a cohesive mass. Cover and set aside to rest for 30 minutes.

Fold Once the dough is relaxed, you will give it a series of three folds spaced 1 hour apart. To fold, smear a little water onto your work surface. Using a dough scraper, gather the dough together and, with a quick motion, scoop the dough up with the dough scraper and flip it onto the wet table. Using your hands, lift the dough off the table, then slap the bottom half down, so that it sticks a little. Gently leaning back, stretch the dough and then quickly lean forward, tossing the dough still in your hands over the portion stuck to the table. Repeat three to four times. The dough will become smooth and pull itself into a ball.

Using the dough scraper, return the dough to its container, smooth-side up, cover with the plate or sheet pan, and let rest for 1 hour. Repeat the process two more times, with 1 hour between folding sessions.

Pre-shape Lightly dust your table with flour. Using a dough scraper, gather the dough together in the bowl and, with a quick motion, scoop the dough up with the dough scraper and flip it onto the table. Pat into a rectangle with a short side facing you. Fold the edge of the dough closest to you over to the top (the edge farthest from you), leaving a 1-inch lip. Take the sides of the dough, gently stretch each outward a few inches, then quickly cross them over each other so they are on top of each other, like swaddling a baby. Next, stretch the edge of the dough closest to you up to the top, flush with the top edge. Gently press down to create a seam and seal.

Use your hands or a bench knife to gently drag the loaf on the table to create surface tension. You will see it tighten and become smooth as you drag. Make sure the top stays the top and the dough doesn't roll over as you go. The dough will curl into itself so the seam is now on the bottom and the top is smooth and roundish.

Bench rest Sprinkle the dough with flour, cover with a kitchen towel, and let rest 30 minutes.

Final shape Lightly dust a cloth-lined 9-inch oval banneton with flour and set aside. Lightly dust your table with flour. Use a bench knife to flip over the pre-shape so the top is now the bottom. Bring the bottom of the dough to meet the top edge, leaving a 1-inch lip at the top. Gently stretch the sides outward a few inches, then quickly cross them over the middle of the dough, like swaddling a baby. Stretch the bottom of the dough up to meet the top of the envelope and seal. The dough will now be a cylinder on its side with a seam facing away from you. Roll the seam underneath and seal the left and right ends using the edge of your palm. Using a bench knife, transfer to the prepared banneton, seam-side up.

Proof Loosely cover the banneton with a kitchen towel and proof the dough in a draft-free spot at room temperature for 2 to 3 hours. When fully proofed, the loaf will appear to have doubled in size, feel full of air, and pass the poke test (see page 55).

Chill When proofed, transfer the banneton, covered with a shower cap or kitchen towel, to the fridge for at least 6 hours and up to 24.

DAY TWO: BAKING

Preheat the oven Set a combo cooker on a rack in the oven so the skillet is the bottom and the pot is inverted as a lid. Preheat the oven (and the combo cooker) to 500°F.

Score Wearing welding gloves, remove the combo cooker from the oven (it's hot!) and quickly toss the cold dough seam-side down onto the hot skillet portion of the cooker. Use a lame and razor, with the blade at a 35-degree angle, to score in one long stroke, running lengthwise along the top of the bread.

Bake Immediately cover the bread with the inverted pot for a lid and load it back into the oven. Bake for 15 minutes. Remove the combo cooker from the oven and set on the stovetop. Remove the lid (be careful of hot steam) and reduce the oven temperature to 475°F. Return the bread, still on the skillet portion of the combo cooker, to the oven and bake another 15 to 20 minutes, or until the loaf is deeply browned, reaches an internal temperature of 190°F, and sounds hollow when tapped on the bottom. Carefully remove the bread from the skillet and cool on a wire rack for 1 hour. Store for up to 5 days, cut-side down, in a paper bag tucked inside a cloth bag.

Refresh the sourdough starter 6 to 10 hours before mixing and folding the dough.
The dough is then chilled overnight and shaped, proofed, and baked the following day.

1 BÂTARD AT 900G —— **9-INCH OVAL BANNETON** —— **DOUGH TEMP: 78°F** —— **LEVEL: INTERMEDIATE**

PLOUGHMAN 2.0

The Ploughman was the only bread recipe in my first book, *A Baker's Year*. Back then I made one base dough for the farmers' market, sectioning off portions and adding in seeds or fruit for variation. This is a heartier version with a flavorful combination of flours. Use all freshly milled, stone ground flour for this dough (see Resources, page 294).

BAKER'S PERCENTAGES	WEIGHTS & INGREDIENTS
35%	160g whole-grain spelt flour
35%	160g whole wheat flour
30%	137g sifted bread flour
60%	275g water for the first mix
20%	91g sourdough starter
15%	68g water for the final mix
2%	9g salt

THE NIGHT BEFORE: SOURDOUGH STARTER REFRESH
Following the instructions on page 67, refresh your sourdough starter the night before or up to 10 hours prior to mixing the dough.

DAY ONE: MIXING, FOLDING, AND CHILLING
Mix In a large bowl, thoroughly mix together the whole-grain spelt flour, whole wheat flour, sifted bread flour, and water for the first mix by hand until there are no patches of dry flour. You can squeeze the dough through your hands, like extruding pasta between your fingers! The dough will be sticky, gluey, and shaggy.

Pop a digital thermometer into the dough to take its temperature—it should be between 75° and 81°F. (If the dough is above 81°F, stick it in a cool spot—not the refrigerator—until it cools to between 75° and 81°F. If it is cooler than 75°F, place it in a warm location until it reaches between 75° and 78°F.)

Autolyse Cover the bowl with a dinner plate or sheet pan for a lid and let rest for 1 hour.

Final mix Sprinkle the salt over the dough. Next, add the starter and the water for the final mix. Using your hands, start squeezing the salt, starter, and water into the dough. The dough will become stringy and fall apart; that's normal, just keep mixing until it re-forms into a cohesive mass. Cover and set aside to rest for 30 minutes.

Fold Once the dough is relaxed, you will give it a series of three folds spaced 1 hour apart. To fold, smear a little water onto your work surface. Using a dough scraper, gather the dough together and, with a quick motion, scoop the dough up with the dough scraper and flip it onto the

Recipe continues

wet table. Using your hands, lift the dough off the table, then slap the bottom half down, so that it sticks a little. Gently leaning back, stretch the dough and then quickly lean forward, tossing the dough still in your hands over the portion stuck to the table. Repeat three to four times, giving the dough a quarter-turn at each fold. The dough will become smooth and pull itself into a ball.

Using the dough scraper, return the dough to its container, smooth-side up, cover with the plate or sheet pan, and let rest for 1 hour. Repeat the process two more times, with 1 hour between folding sessions.

Chill After the final fold, transfer the dough back to the bowl, cover with the lid, and refrigerate for at least 8 hours or up to 24.

DAY TWO: SHAPING, PROOFING, AND BAKING
Pre-shape Lightly dust your table with flour. Remove the dough from the fridge (there's no need to let it warm up before shaping). Using a dough scraper, gather the dough together in the bowl and, with a quick motion, scoop the dough up with the dough scraper and flip it onto the table. Pat into a rectangle, with a short side facing you. Bring the edge of the dough closest to you to the top (the edge farthest from you), leaving a 1-inch lip. Take the sides of the dough, gently stretch each outward a few inches, then quickly cross them over each other so they are on top of each other, like swaddling a baby. Next, stretch the edge of the dough closest to you up to the top, flush with the top edge. Gently press to create a seam.

Use your hands or a bench knife to gently drag the loaf on the table to create surface tension. You will see it tighten and become smooth as you drag. Make sure the top stays the top and the dough doesn't roll over as you go. The dough will curl into itself, so the seam is now on the bottom and the top is smooth and roundish.

Bench rest Sprinkle the dough with flour, cover with a kitchen towel, and let rest 30 minutes.

Final shape Lightly dust a cloth-lined 9-inch oval banneton with flour and set aside. Lightly dust the table with flour. Use a bench knife to flip over the pre-shape so the top is now the bottom. Bring the bottom of the dough to meet the top edge, leaving a 1-inch lip at the top. Gently stretch the sides outward a few inches, then quickly cross them over the middle of the dough, like swaddling a baby. You're now looking at an envelope shape. Stretch the bottom of the dough up to meet the top of the envelope and press down to seal. The dough will now be a cylinder on its side with a seam facing away from you. Roll the seam underneath and seal the left and right ends using the edge of your palm. With the bench knife, flip it seam-side up, into the banneton.

Proof Loosely cover the banneton with a kitchen towel and proof in a draft-free spot at room temperature for 2 to 3 hours. When fully proofed, the loaf will appear to have doubled in size, feel full of air, and pass the poke test (see page 55).

Preheat the oven Set a combo cooker on a rack in the oven so the skillet is on the bottom and the pot is inverted as a lid. Preheat the oven (and the combo cooker) to 500°F.

Score Wearing welding gloves, remove the combo cooker from the oven (it's *hot!*) and quickly toss the dough seam-side down onto the hot skillet portion of the cooker. Use a lame and razor, with the blade at a 35-degree angle, to score two short strokes, running lengthwise along the top of the bread.

Bake Immediately cover the bread with the inverted pot for a lid and load it back into the oven. Bake for 15 minutes. Remove the combo cooker from the oven and set on the stovetop. Remove the lid (be careful of hot steam) and reduce the oven temperature to 475°F. Return the bread, still on the skillet portion of the combo cooker, to the oven and bake another 15 to 20 minutes, or until the loaf is deeply browned, reaches an internal temperature of 190°F, and sounds hollow when tapped on the bottom. Carefully remove the bread from the skillet and cool completely on a wire rack. Store for up to 5 days, cut-side down, in a paper bag tucked inside a cloth bag.

Refresh the sourdough starter 6 to 10 hours before mixing and folding the dough. The dough is chilled overnight and shaped, proofed, and baked the following day.

1 BÂTARD AT 850G —— **9-INCH OVAL BANNETON** —— **DOUGH TEMP: 78°F** —— **LEVEL: INTERMEDIATE**

CITY QUEEN LOAF

This bread is named for my friend Sara, who lives in Brooklyn. During the onset of COVID-19, we'd call each other every day at the same time. She'd have her elbows deep in this wet, white dough, and I'd be covered in whole wheat flour. Our daily check-ins, paired with our bread making, gave us (and so many others making sourdough for their first of a thousand times) a feeling of connectedness and comfort in strange and scary months.

BAKER'S PERCENTAGES	WEIGHTS & INGREDIENTS
100%	400g bread flour
80%	320g water for the first mix
20%	80g sourdough starter
10%	40g water for the final mix
2%	8g salt

THE NIGHT BEFORE: SOURDOUGH STARTER REFRESH
Following the instructions on page 67, refresh your sourdough starter the night before or up to 10 hours prior to mixing the dough.

DAY ONE: MIXING, FOLDING, AND CHILLING
First mix In a large bowl, thoroughly mix together the bread flour and water for the first mix by hand until there are no patches of dry flour. You can squeeze the dough through your hands, like you're extruding pasta between your fingers! The dough will be sticky, gluey, and shaggy.

Pop a digital thermometer into the dough to take its temperature—it should be between 75° and 81°F. (If the dough is above 81°F, stick it in a cool spot—not the refrigerator—until it cools to between 75° and 81°F. If it is cooler than 75°F, place it in a warm location until it reaches between 75° and 78°F.)

Autolyse Cover the bowl with a dinner plate or sheet pan for a lid and let rest for 1 hour.

Final mix Sprinkle the salt over the dough. Next, add the starter and the water for the final mix. Using your hands, start squeezing the salt, starter, and water into the dough. The dough will become stringy and fall apart; that's normal, just keep mixing until it re-forms into a cohesive mass. Cover and set aside to rest for 30 minutes.

Fold Once the dough is relaxed, you will give it a series of three folds spaced 1 hour apart. To fold, smear a little water onto your work surface. Using a dough scraper, gather the dough together and, with a quick motion, scoop the dough up with the dough scraper and flip it onto the

Recipe continues

wet table. Using your hands, lift the dough off the table, then slap the bottom half down, so that it sticks a little. Gently leaning back, stretch the dough and then quickly lean forward, tossing the dough still in your hands over the portion stuck to the table. Repeat three to four times. The dough will become smooth and pull itself into a ball.

Using the dough scraper, return the dough to its container, smooth-side up, cover with the plate or sheet pan, and let rest for 1 hour. Repeat the process two more times, with 1 hour between folding sessions.

Chill After the final fold, transfer the dough back to the bowl, cover with the lid, and refrigerate for at least 8 hours or up to 24.

DAY TWO: SHAPING, PROOFING, AND BAKING

Pre-shape Lightly dust your table with flour. Remove the dough from the fridge (there's no need to let it warm up before shaping). Using a dough scraper, gather the dough together in the bowl and, with a quick motion, scoop the dough up with the dough scraper and flip it onto the table. Pat into a rectangle with a short side facing you. Bring the edge of the dough closest to you to the top (the edge farthest from you), leaving a 1-inch lip. Take the sides of the dough, gently stretch each outward a few inches, then quickly cross them over each other so they are on top of each other, like swaddling a baby. Next, stretch the edge of the dough closest to you up to the top, flush with the top edge. Gently press to create a seam.

Use your hands or a bench knife to gently drag the loaf on the table to create surface tension. You will see it tighten and become smooth as you drag. Make sure the top stays the top and the dough doesn't roll over as you go. The dough will curl into itself, so the seam is now on the bottom and the top is smooth and roundish.

Bench rest Sprinkle the dough with flour, cover with a kitchen towel, and let rest 30 minutes.

Final shape Lightly dust a cloth-lined 9-inch oval banneton with flour and set aside. Lightly dust the table with flour. Use a bench knife to flip over the pre-shape so the top is now the bottom. Bring the bottom of the dough to meet the top edge, leaving a 1-inch lip at the top. Gently stretch the sides outward a few inches, then quickly cross them over the middle of the dough, like

swaddling a baby. You're now looking at an envelope shape. Stretch the bottom of the dough up to meet the top of the envelope and press down to seal. The dough will now be a cylinder on its side with a seam facing away from you. Roll the seam underneath and seal the left and right ends using the edge of your palm. With the bench knife, flip it seam-side up, into the banneton.

Proof Loosely cover the banneton with a kitchen towel and proof in a draft-free spot at room temperature for 2 to 3 hours. When fully proofed, the loaf will appear to have doubled in size, feel full of air, and pass the poke test (see page 55).

Preheat the oven Set a combo cooker on a rack in the oven so the skillet is on the bottom and the pot is inverted as a lid. Preheat the oven (and the combo cooker) to 500°F.

Score Wearing welding gloves, remove the combo cooker from the oven (it's hot!) and quickly toss the dough seam-side down onto the hot skillet portion of the cooker. Use a lame and razor, with the blade at a 35-degree angle, to score in one long stroke, running lengthwise along the top of the bread.

Bake Immediately cover the bread with the inverted pot for a lid and load it back into the oven. Bake for 15 minutes. Remove the combo cooker from the oven and set on the stovetop. Remove the lid (be careful of hot steam) and reduce the oven temperature to 475°F. Return the bread, still on the skillet portion of the combo cooker, to the oven and bake another 15 to 20 minutes, or until the loaf is deeply browned, reaches an internal temperature of 190°F, and sounds hollow when tapped on the bottom. Carefully remove the bread from the skillet and cool completely on a wire rack. Store for up to 5 days, cut-side down, in a paper bag tucked inside a cloth bag.

Refresh the sourdough starter 6 to 10 hours before mixing and folding two separate doughs. The doughs are layered together into one dough before shaping. The shaped dough is proofed overnight and baked the next day.

1 BÂTARD AT 1KG —— 9-INCH OVAL BANNETON —— DOUGH TEMP: 78°F —— LEVEL: INTERMEDIATE

MARBLED DELI RYE

This marbled bread made from a malted dough (with molasses) and a white dough (with 10% rye flour) is *the* rye used for Reubens!

BAKER'S PERCENTAGES	WEIGHTS & INGREDIENTS
MALTED DOUGH	
100%	236g bread flour
75%	177g water
15%	49g molasses, blackstrap
21%	47g sourdough starter
2%	5g salt
WHITE DOUGH	
90%	229g bread flour
10%	25g light rye flour
75%	190g water
20%	51g sourdough starter
2%	5g salt
ADDITION	
11%	28g caraway seeds

THE NIGHT BEFORE: SOURDOUGH STARTER REFRESH
Following the instructions on page 67, refresh your sourdough starter the night before or up to 10 hours prior to mixing the dough.

DAY ONE: MIXING, FOLDING, SHAPING, PROOFING, AND CHILLING
Mix the malted dough In a large bowl, thoroughly mix together the bread flour, water, molasses, starter, and salt by hand until there are no patches of dry flour. You can squeeze the dough through your hands, like extruding pasta between your fingers! The dough will be sticky, gluey, and shaggy.

Mix the white dough In a large bowl, thoroughly mix together the bread flour, light rye flour, water, starter, and salt by hand until there are no patches of dry flour. You can squeeze the dough through your hands, like extruding pasta between your fingers! The dough will be sticky, gluey, and shaggy.

Pop a digital thermometer into each dough—they should be between 75° and 81°F. (If the doughs are above 81°F, stick them in a cool spot—not the refrigerator—until they cool to between 75° and 78°F. If they are cooler than 75°F, place them in a warm location until they reach between 75° and 78°F.) Cover each bowl with a dinner plate or sheet pan for a lid and let rest for 1 hour.

Fold Once the doughs are relaxed, you will give them a series of three folds spaced 1 hour apart. To fold, smear a little water onto your work surface. Using a dough scraper, gather the malted dough together and, with a quick motion, scoop the dough up with the dough scraper and flip it onto the wet table. Using your hands, lift the dough off the table, then slap the bottom half down so that it sticks a little. Gently leaning back, stretch the dough and then quickly lean forward, tossing the dough still in your hands over the portion stuck to the table. Repeat three to four

Recipe continues

times. The dough will become smooth and pull itself into a ball.

Using the dough scraper, return the dough to its container, smooth-side up, cover with the plate or sheet pan, and let rest for 1 hour. Repeat the process with the white dough. Repeat the process on each dough two more times, with 1 hour between folding sessions.

Pre-shape Lightly dust your table with flour. Use a dough scraper to flip both doughs onto the table. Using a bench knife, cut each dough into 4 roughly equal pieces and sprinkle each with caraway seeds. (If you love caraway, you can be generous here.) Now stack the individual portions of dough, sprinkled with caraway, one on top of the other, alternating between malted and white.

Pat and press into a rectangle with a short side facing you. Bring the short side of the dough closest to you to the top (the edge farthest from you), leaving a 1-inch lip. Take the sides of the dough, gently stretch each outward a few inches, then quickly cross them over each other so they are on top of each other, like swaddling a baby. Next, stretch the edge of the dough closest to you up to the top, flush with the top edge. Gently press to create a seam.

Use your hands or a bench knife to gently drag the loaf on the table to create surface tension. You will see it tighten and become smooth as you drag. Make sure the top stays the top and the dough doesn't roll over as you go. The dough will curl into itself, so the seam is now on the bottom and the top is smooth and roundish.

Bench rest Sprinkle the dough with flour, cover with a kitchen towel, and let rest 30 minutes.

Final shape Lightly dust a cloth-lined 9-inch oval banneton with flour and set aside. Lightly dust the table with flour. Use a bench knife to flip over the pre-shape so the top is now the bottom. Bring the bottom of the dough to meet the top edge, leaving a 1-inch lip at the top. Gently stretch the sides outward a few inches, then quickly cross them over the middle of the dough, like swaddling a baby. You're now looking at an envelope shape. Stretch the bottom of the dough up to meet the top of the envelope and press down to seal. The dough will now be a cylinder on its side with

a seam facing away from you. Roll the seam underneath and seal the left and right ends using the edge of your palm. With the bench knife, flip it seam-side up, into the banneton.

Proof Loosely cover the banneton with a kitchen towel and proof in a draft-free spot at room temperature for 2 to 3 hours. When fully proofed, the loaf will appear to have doubled in size, feel full of air, and pass the poke test (see page 55).

Chill When proofed, transfer the banneton, covered with a shower cap or kitchen towel, to the fridge for at least 6 hours and up to 24.

DAY TWO: BAKING
Preheat the oven Set a combo cooker on a rack in the oven so the skillet is on the bottom and the pot is inverted as a lid. Preheat the oven (and the combo cooker) to 500°F.

Score Wearing welding gloves, remove the combo cooker from the oven (it's *hot!*) and quickly toss the cold dough seam-side down onto the hot skillet portion of the cooker. Use a lame and razor, with the blade at a 35-degree angle, to score in one long stroke, running lengthwise along the top of the bread.

Bake Immediately cover the bread with the inverted pot for a lid and load it back into the oven. Bake for 15 minutes. Remove the combo cooker from the oven and set on the stovetop. Remove the lid (be careful of hot steam) and reduce the oven temperature to 475°F. Return the bread, still on the skillet portion of the combo cooker, to the oven and bake another 15 to 20 minutes, or until the loaf is deeply browned, reaches an internal temperature of 190°F, and sounds hollow when tapped on the bottom. Carefully remove the bread from the skillet and cool completely. Store for up to 5 days, cut-side down, in a paper bag tucked inside a cloth bag.

Refresh the sourdough starter and prepare the grits 6 to 10 hours before
mixing the dough. The dough is mixed, folded, shaped, and proofed. The shaped
dough is chilled overnight and baked the following day.

1 ROUND AT 850G —— **9-INCH ROUND BANNETON** —— **DOUGH TEMP: 78°F** —— **LEVEL: INTERMEDIATE**

GRITS BREAD

This is one of my favorite breads of all time!
Try using Bloody Butcher grits for a gorgeous red-speckled dough.

BAKER'S PERCENTAGES	WEIGHTS & INGREDIENTS
GRITS	
293%	126g water
100%	43g grits, whole-grain
DOUGH	
90%	303g bread flour
10%	34g whole wheat flour
68%	230g water for the first mix
50%	169g cooked grits, cooled
25%	84g sourdough starter
7%	25g water for the final mix
2%	7g salt

Grits, uncooked, to roll the dough in

THE NIGHT BEFORE: SOURDOUGH STARTER REFRESH AND COOK GRITS
Following the instructions on page 67, refresh your sourdough starter the
night before or up to 10 hours prior to mixing the dough.

Cook the grits In a medium saucepan, combine the grits and water
and cook over medium heat, stirring constantly, until thick and creamy.
Remove from the heat, cool, and transfer to 1-quart deli container
or similar container and cool to room temperature. Cover with a lid and
set aside until you're ready to mix. (The grits will be fine to stay out
overnight, but if you prefer to transfer them to the fridge, bring them
up to room temperature prior to using.)

DAY ONE: MIXING, FOLDING, SHAPING, PROOFING, AND CHILLING
First mix In a large bowl, thoroughly mix together the bread flour, whole
wheat flour, and the water for the first mix by hand until there are
no patches of dry flour. You can squeeze the dough through your hands,
like you're extruding pasta between your fingers! The dough will be
sticky, gluey, and shaggy.

Pop a digital thermometer into the dough to take its temperature—it should
be between 75° and 81°F. (If the dough is above 81°F, stick it in a cool spot—
not the refrigerator—until it cools to between 75° and 81°F. If it is cooler
than 75°F, place it in a warm location until it reaches between 75° and 78°F.)

Autolyse Cover the bowl with a dinner plate or sheet pan for a lid and let
rest for 1 hour.

Final mix Sprinkle the salt over the dough. Next, add the starter, the water
for the final mix, and the cooked and cooled grits. Using your hands, start
squeezing the salt, starter, water, and grits into the dough. The dough
will become stringy and fall apart; that's normal, just keep mixing until
it re-forms into a cohesive mass. Cover and set aside to rest for 30 minutes.

Recipe continues

Fold Once the dough is relaxed, you will give it a series of three folds spaced 1 hour apart. To fold, smear a little water onto your work surface. Using a dough scraper, gather the dough together and, with a quick motion, scoop the dough up with the dough scraper and flip it onto the wet table. Using your hands, lift the dough off the table, then slap the bottom half down, so that it sticks a little. Gently leaning back, stretch the dough and then quickly lean forward, tossing the dough still in your hands over the portion stuck to the table. Repeat three to four times. The dough will become smooth and pull itself into a ball. Using the dough scraper, return the dough to its container, smooth-side up, cover with the plate or sheet pan, and let rest for 1 hour. Repeat the process two more times, with 1 hour between folding sessions.

Pre-shape Lightly dust your table with flour. Using a dough scraper, gather the dough together in the bowl and, with a quick motion, scoop the dough up with the dough scraper and flip it onto the table. Pat into a rectangle with a short side facing you. Bring the edge of the dough closest to you to the top (the edge farthest from you), leaving a 1-inch lip. Take the sides of the dough, gently stretch each outward a few inches, then quickly cross them over each other so they are on top of each other, like swaddling a baby. Next, stretch the edge of the dough closest to you up to the top, flush with the top edge. Gently press to create a seam.

Use your hands or a bench knife to gently drag the loaf on the table to create surface tension. You will see it tighten and become smooth as you drag. Make sure the top stays the top and the dough doesn't roll over as you go. The dough will curl into itself, so the seam is now on the bottom and the top is smooth and roundish.

Bench rest Sprinkle the dough with flour, cover with a kitchen towel, and let rest 30 minutes.

Ready the grits While the dough is resting, ready the grits that the dough will be rolled in: Run a kitchen towel under water quickly (you want it damp, not soaking) and place it over half of a sheet pan. Toss a handful of grits opposite the kitchen towel. Set aside.

Final shape Lightly dust a cloth-lined 9-inch round banneton with flour and set aside. Lightly dust your table with flour. Using a bench knife, flip over the relaxed round. Imagine the round into four quarters. Stretch the edge of each quarter to the center of the round, overlapping them slightly, about 1 inch, to make a pouch shape. Now turn the "pouch" on its side, cupping the portion that was flush with the table in one hand, and cinch the gathered portions together with the edge of your palm, sealing the seam. Glide the dough down the table so that the seam is sealed between the edge of your palm and the table. Roll the dough over the damp towel and through the grits and use the bench knife to transfer it to the round banneton, seam-side up.

Proof Loosely cover the banneton with a kitchen towel and proof in a draft-free spot at room temperature for 2 to 3 hours. When fully proofed, the loaf will appear to have doubled in size, feel full of air, and pass the poke test (see page 55).

Chill When proofed, transfer the banneton, covered with a shower cap or kitchen towel, to the fridge for at least 6 hours and up to 24.

DAY TWO: BAKING
Preheat the oven Set a combo cooker on a rack in the oven so the skillet is on the bottom and the pot is inverted as a lid. Preheat the oven (and the combo cooker) to 500°F.

Score Wearing welding gloves, remove the combo cooker from the oven (it's *hot!*) and quickly toss the cold dough seam-side down onto the hot skillet portion of the cooker. Use a lame and razor, with the blade at a 35-degree angle, to score a pattern of your choice on the top of the round.

Bake Immediately cover the bread with the inverted pot for a lid and load it back into the oven. Bake for 15 minutes. Remove the combo cooker from the oven and set on the stovetop. Remove the lid (be careful of hot steam) and reduce the oven temperature to 475°F. Return the bread, still on the skillet portion of the combo cooker, to the oven and bake another 15 to 20 minutes, or until the loaf is deeply browned, reaches an internal temperature of 190°F, and sounds hollow when tapped on the bottom. Carefully remove the bread from the skillet and cool completely. Store for up to 5 days, cut-side down, in a paper bag tucked inside a cloth bag.

Refresh the sourdough starter and prepare the potatoes 6 to 10 hours
before mixing, folding, shaping, and proofing the dough. The dough is then
chilled overnight before being baked the following day.

1 BÂTARD AT 850G —— **9-INCH OVAL BANNETON** —— **DOUGH TEMP: 78°F** —— **LEVEL: INTERMEDIATE**

POTATO BREAD

This tasty bread is dedicated to Randy and Eliza at Red Hen Baking Company,
where I took my first bite of potato bread and was forever hooked.

BAKER'S PERCENTAGES	WEIGHTS & INGREDIENTS
80%	280g bread flour
20%	70g whole wheat flour
70%	245g potato water
50%	176g Yukon Gold potato chunks, peeled (about 2 potatoes)
20%	70g sourdough starter
2%	7g salt

THE NIGHT BEFORE: SOURDOUGH STARTER REFRESH AND COOK POTATOES

Following the instructions on page 67, refresh your sourdough starter the night before or up to 10 hours prior to mixing the dough.

Cook the potatoes In a medium saucepan, combine the potatoes with water to cover. Bring to a boil over medium-high heat, reduce the heat to medium, and cook until tender and easily pierced with a fork, about 10 minutes (don't cook them so much they fall apart). Reserving the cooking liquid, drain the potatoes. Put the cooking liquid in a 1-quart deli container (or similar container), cover, and set aside. Pat the potato chunks dry and store in a separate container. Set aside.

DAY ONE: MIXING, FOLDING, SHAPING, PROOFING, AND CHILLING

First mix In a large bowl, thoroughly mix together the bread flour, whole wheat flour, and reserved potato water from cooking the potatoes (the measured amount in the chart) by hand until there are no patches of dry flour. You can squeeze the dough through your hands, like extruding pasta between your fingers! The dough will be sticky, gluey, and shaggy.

Pop a digital thermometer into the dough to take its temperature—it should be between 75° and 81°F. (If the dough is above 81°F, stick it in a cool spot—not the refrigerator—until it cools to between 75° and 78°F. If it is cooler than 75°F, place it in a warm location until it reaches between 75° and 78°F.)

Autolyse Cover the bowl with a dinner plate or sheet pan for a lid and let rest for 1 hour.

Final mix Sprinkle the salt over the dough. Add the starter and potatoes and mix the dough thoroughly by hand. The dough will become stringy and fall apart; that's normal, just keep mixing until it re-forms

Recipe continues

into a cohesive mass. Cover and set aside to rest for 30 minutes.

Fold Once the dough is relaxed, you will give it a series of three folds spaced 1 hour apart. To fold, smear a little water onto your work surface. Using a dough scraper, gather the dough together and, with a quick motion, scoop the dough up with the dough scraper and flip it onto the wet table. Using your hands, lift the dough off the table, then slap the bottom half down, so that it sticks a little. Gently leaning back, stretch the dough and then quickly lean forward, tossing the dough still in your hands over the portion stuck to the table. Repeat three to four times. The dough will become smooth and pull itself into a ball.

Using the dough scraper, return the dough to its container, smooth-side up, cover with the plate or sheet pan, and let rest for 1 hour. Repeat the process two more times, with 1 hour between folding sessions.

Pre-shape Lightly dust your table with flour. Using a dough scraper, gather the dough together in the bowl and, with a quick motion, scoop the dough up with the dough scraper and flip it onto the table. Pat into a rectangle with a short side facing you. Bring the edge of the dough closest to you to the top (the edge farthest from you), leaving a 1-inch lip. Take the sides of the dough, gently stretch each outward a few inches, then quickly cross them over each other so they are on top of each other, like swaddling a baby. Next, stretch the edge of the dough closest to you up to the top, flush with the top edge. Gently press to create a seam.

Use your hands or a bench knife to gently drag the loaf on the table to create surface tension. You will see it tighten and become smooth as you drag. Make sure the top stays the top and the dough doesn't roll over as you go. The dough will curl into itself, so the seam is now on the bottom and the top is smooth and roundish.

Bench rest Sprinkle the dough with flour, cover with a kitchen towel, and let rest 30 minutes.

Final shape Lightly dust a cloth-lined 9-inch oval banneton with flour and set aside. Lightly dust the table with flour. Use a bench knife to flip over the pre-shape so the top is now the bottom. Bring the bottom of the

dough to meet the top edge, leaving a 1-inch lip at the top. Gently stretch the sides outward a few inches, then quickly cross them over the middle of the dough, like swaddling a baby. You're now looking at an envelope shape. Stretch the bottom of the dough up to meet the top of the envelope and press down to seal. The dough will now be a cylinder on its side with a seam facing away from you. Roll the seam underneath and seal the left and right ends using the edge of your palm. With the bench knife, flip it seam-side up, into the banneton.

Proof Loosely cover the banneton with a kitchen towel and proof in a draft-free spot at room temperature for 2 to 3 hours. When fully proofed, the loaf will appear to have doubled in size, feel full of air, and pass the poke test (see page 55).

Chill When proofed, transfer the banneton, covered with a shower cap or kitchen towel, to the fridge for at least 6 hours and up to 24.

DAY TWO: BAKING
Preheat the oven Set a combo cooker on a rack in the oven so the skillet is the bottom and the pot is inverted as a lid. Preheat the oven (and the combo cooker) to 500°F.

Score Wearing welding gloves, remove the combo cooker from the oven (it's *hot!*) and quickly toss the cold dough seam-side down onto the hot skillet portion of the cooker. Use a lame and razor, with the blade at a 35-degree angle, to score one long stroke lengthwise on top of the bread.

Bake Immediately cover the bread with the inverted pot for a lid and load it back into the oven. Bake for 15 minutes. Remove the combo cooker from the oven and set on the stovetop. Remove the lid (be careful of hot steam) and reduce the oven temperature to 475°F. Return the bread, still on the skillet portion of the combo cooker, to the oven and bake another 15 to 20 minutes, or until the loaf is deeply browned, reaches an internal temperature of 190°F, and sounds hollow when tapped on the bottom. Carefully remove the bread from the skillet and cool completely on a wire rack. Store for up to 5 days, cut-side down, in a paper bag tucked inside a cloth bag.

Refresh the sourdough starter 6 to 10 hours before mixing, folding, shaping, and proofing the dough. The dough is then chilled overnight before being baked the following day.

1 BÂTARD AT 850G ———— 9-INCH OVAL BANNETON ———— DOUGH TEMP: 78°F ———— LEVEL: INTERMEDIATE

OLIVE BREAD

This loaf has bright and fruity green Castelvetrano olives and is the perfect blend of nutty and tangy. Serve toasted on a cheese plate with grapes and Marcona almonds, or offer it warmed and in a basket with cultured butter and flaky salt on the side. Be sure to buy already pitted olives (and always warn guests of potential remaining pits!).

BAKER'S PERCENTAGES	WEIGHTS & INGREDIENTS
75%	255g bread flour
25%	85g whole-grain spelt flour
75%	256g water
50%	170g pitted Castelvetrano olives (or another not-too-briny green or black olive)
20%	68g sourdough starter
2%	8g olive oil, light
2%	8g salt

THE NIGHT BEFORE: SOURDOUGH STARTER REFRESH

Following the instructions on page 67, refresh your sourdough starter the night before or up to 10 hours prior to mixing the dough.

DAY ONE: MIXING, FOLDING, SHAPING, PROOFING, AND CHILLING

First mix In a large bowl, thoroughly mix together the bread flour, spelt flour, and water by hand until there are no patches of dry flour. You can squeeze the dough through your hands, like extruding pasta between your fingers! The dough will be sticky, gluey, and shaggy.

Pop a digital thermometer into the dough to take its temperature—it should be between 75° and 81°F. (If the dough is above 81°F, stick it in a cool spot—not the refrigerator—until it cools to between 75° and 81°F. If it is cooler than 75°F, place it in a warm location until it reaches between 75° and 78°F.)

Autolyse Cover the bowl with a dinner plate or sheet pan for a lid and let rest for 1 hour.

Final mix Sprinkle the salt over the dough. Next, add the starter, olive oil, and olives. Using your hands, start squeezing the salt, starter, olive oil, and olives into the dough. The dough will become stringy and fall apart; that's normal, just keep mixing until it re-forms into a cohesive mass. Cover and set aside to rest for 30 minutes.

Fold Once the dough is relaxed, you will give it a series of three folds spaced 1 hour apart. To fold, smear a little water onto your work surface. Using a dough scraper, gather the dough together and, with a quick motion, scoop the dough up with the dough scraper and flip it onto the wet table. Using your hands, lift the dough off the table, then slap the

Recipe continues

bottom half down, so that it sticks a little. Gently leaning back, stretch the dough and then quickly lean forward, tossing the dough still in your hands over the portion stuck to the table. Repeat three to four times. The dough will become smooth and pull itself into a ball. If some olives pop out while you're folding, just smoosh them back in!

Using the dough scraper, return the dough to its container, smooth-side up, cover with the plate or sheet pan, and let rest for 1 hour. Repeat the process two more times, with 1 hour between folding sessions.

Pre-shape Lightly dust your table with flour. Using a dough scraper, gather the dough together in the bowl and, with a quick motion, scoop the dough up with the dough scraper and flip it onto the table. Pat into a rectangle with a short side facing you. Bring the edge of the dough closest to you to the top (the edge farthest from you), leaving a 1-inch lip. Take the sides of the dough, gently stretch each outward a few inches, then quickly cross them over each other so they are on top of each other, like swaddling a baby. Next, stretch the edge of the dough closest to you up to the top, flush with the top edge. Gently press to create a seam.

Use your hands or a bench knife to gently drag the loaf on the table to create surface tension. You will see it tighten and become smooth as you drag. Make sure the top stays the top and the dough doesn't roll over as you go. The dough will curl into itself, so the seam is now on the bottom and the top is smooth and roundish.

Bench rest Sprinkle the dough with flour, cover with a kitchen towel, and let rest 30 minutes.

Final shape Lightly dust a cloth-lined 9-inch oval banneton with flour and set aside. Lightly dust the table with flour. Use a bench knife to flip over the pre-shape so the top is now the bottom. Bring the bottom of the dough to meet the top edge, leaving a 1-inch lip at the top. Gently stretch the sides outward a few inches, then quickly cross them over the middle of the dough, like swaddling a baby. You're now looking at an envelope shape. Stretch the bottom of the dough up to meet the top of the envelope and press down to seal. The dough will now be a cylinder on its side with a seam facing away from you. Roll the seam underneath and seal the left and right ends using the edge of your palm. With the bench knife, flip it seam-side up, into the banneton.

Proof Loosely cover the banneton with a kitchen towel and proof in a draft-free spot at room temperature for 2 to 3 hours. When fully proofed, the loaf will appear to have doubled in size, feel full of air, and pass the poke test (see page 55).

Chill When proofed, transfer the banneton, covered with a shower cap or kitchen towel, to the fridge for at least 6 hours and up to 24.

DAY TWO: BAKING
Preheat the oven Set a combo cooker on a rack in the oven so the skillet is on the bottom and the pot is inverted as a lid. Preheat the oven (and the combo cooker) to 500°F.

Score Wearing welding gloves, remove the combo cooker from the oven (it's *hot!*) and quickly toss the cold dough seam-side down onto the hot skillet portion of the cooker. Use a lame and razor, with the blade at a 35-degree angle, to score in one long stroke, running lengthwise along the top of the bread.

Bake Immediately cover the bread with the inverted pot for a lid and load it back into the oven. Bake for 15 minutes. Remove the combo cooker from the oven and set on the stovetop. Remove the lid (be careful of hot steam) and reduce the oven temperature to 475°F. Return the bread, still on the skillet portion of the combo cooker, to the oven and bake another 15 to 20 minutes, or until the loaf is deeply browned, reaches an internal temperature of 190°F, and sounds hollow when tapped on the bottom. Carefully remove the bread from the skillet and cool on a wire rack. Store for up to 5 days, cut-side down, in a paper bag tucked inside a cloth bag.

Refresh the sourdough starter and prepare the yard butter 6 to 10 hours before mixing the dough. The dough is then mixed, folded, and chilled overnight. The following day it is shaped, proofed, and baked.

1 TWISTY LOAF AT 1KG ——— 9-INCH PULLMAN PAN ——— DOUGH TEMP: 78°F ——— LEVEL: ADVANCED

YARD BREAD

This bread is filled with aromatic herbs ideally from your kitchen garden, like rosemary and thyme, combined into butter. The butter is then slathered inside a babka-style twist for a savory delight.

YARD BUTTER

WEIGHTS & INGREDIENTS

113g (1 stick) butter, unsalted, at room temp

20g oregano, fresh, finely chopped

20g thyme, fresh, finely chopped

20g rosemary, fresh, finely chopped

20g sage, fresh, finely minced

20g lemon zest, grated

4 cloves garlic, minced

THE NIGHT BEFORE: SOURDOUGH STARTER REFRESH AND MAKE THE YARD BUTTER

Following the instructions on page 67, refresh your sourdough starter the night before or up to 10 hours prior to mixing the dough.

Make the yard butter In a stand mixer fitted with the whisk attachment, whip the butter on medium speed until creamy, about 2 minutes. Add the oregano, thyme, rosemary, sage, lemon zest, and garlic. Whip on medium speed until the herbs are evenly dispersed throughout the butter. Using a flexible spatula, transfer the butter to a 1-pint deli container (or similar container) and refrigerate until needed.

DAY ONE: MIXING, FOLDING, AND CHILLING

Mix In a stand mixer fitted with a dough hook, combine the bread flour, whole wheat flour, water, eggs, starter, vegetable oil, and salt and mix on low for 2 minutes. Stop the mixer and scrape down the bowl and hook with a dough scraper. Resume mixing on low speed for another 2 minutes, or until there are no patches of dry flour. Using a dough scraper, transfer the dough to a large bowl.

Pop a digital thermometer into the dough to take its temperature—it should be between 75° and 81°F. (If the dough is above 81°F, stick it in a cool spot—not the refrigerator—until it cools to between 75° and 78°F. If it is less than 75°F, place it in a warm location until it reaches between 75° and 78°F.) Cover the bowl with a dinner plate or sheet pan for a lid and let rest for 1 hour.

Fold Once the dough is relaxed, you will give it a series of three folds spaced 1 hour apart. To fold, smear a little water onto your work surface. Using a dough scraper, gather the dough together and, with a quick motion, scoop the dough up with the dough scraper and flip it onto the

Recipe and ingredients continue

wet table. Using your hands, lift the dough off the table, then slap the bottom half down, so that it sticks a little. Gently leaning back, stretch the dough and then quickly lean forward, tossing the dough still in your hands over the portion stuck to the table. Repeat three to four times. The dough will become smooth and pull itself into a ball.

Using the dough scraper, return the dough to its container, smooth-side up, cover with the plate or sheet pan, and let rest for 1 hour. Repeat the process two more times, with 1 hour between folding sessions.

Chill After the final fold, transfer the dough back to the bowl, cover with the lid, and refrigerate for at least 8 hours or up to 24.

DAY TWO: SHAPING, PROOFING, AND BAKING
Shape Remove the yard butter from the fridge and let it come to room temperature. Remove the dough from the fridge (no need to let it come to room temperature). Lightly flour your work surface and lightly oil a 9-inch Pullman pan. To shape, turn out the dough onto a well-floured surface. With a rolling pin, gently roll into a 10 × 12-inch rectangle. Using an offset spatula, evenly spread the yard butter over the rectangle, leaving a 1-inch border all around. With a long side facing you, roll the dough into itself, starting from the bottom, working toward the top, making a "jelly roll."

With a sharp knife, cut the roll down the center lengthwise. You now have two long halves. Place the halves side by side, with the cut sides facing up. Cross at the top to make an X. Twist the two ropes three to four times, always leaving the cut sides up. Use a bench knife to transfer the twist to the oiled Pullman pan with the cut sides facing up.

Proof Loosely cover the pan with a kitchen towel and proof the dough in a draft-free spot at room temperature for 2 to 3 hours. When fully proofed, the loaf will appear to have doubled in size, feel full of air, and pass the poke test (see page 55).

Preheat the oven to 500°F.

Bake When the oven is up to temperature, gently spritz the top surface of the dough with water from a spray bottle before loading it into the oven. (This bread has no score.) Bake at 500°F for 15 minutes. After 15 minutes, reduce the oven temperature to 475°F and bake another 15 to 20 minutes, or until the loaf is deeply browned and reaches an internal temperature of 190°F. Carefully remove the bread from the pan and cool completely on a wire rack. Store for up to 5 days, cut-side down, in a paper bag tucked inside a cloth bag.

DOUGH

BAKER'S PERCENTAGES	WEIGHTS & INGREDIENTS
80%	430g bread flour
20%	48g whole wheat flour
44%	213g yard butter
40%	215g water
20%	107g eggs, large, room temp
20%	107g sourdough starter
4%	22g vegetable oil
2%	11g salt

Smear the yard butter on the dough.

Roll it up like a "jelly roll."

Cut down the center.

Make an X to start the twist.

Twist the two ropes.

Transfer to a Pullman pan, cut-side up.

Refresh the sourdough starter 6 to 10 hours before mixing and folding the dough. The dough is then chilled overnight before being shaped, proofed, and baked the following day.

1 SWIRLY LOAF AT 850G ——— **9-INCH PULLMAN PAN** ——— **DOUGH TEMP: 78°F** ——— **LEVEL: ADVANCED**

CARDAMOM BUN BREAD

This bread is the perfect Scandinavian pull-apart treat!

FILLING

113g (1 stick) butter, unsalted, at room temp

100g sugar

10g cardamom, ground

DOUGH

BAKER'S PERCENTAGES	WEIGHTS & INGREDIENTS
75%	323g bread flour
25%	108g whole-grain spelt flour
75%	323g whole milk, at room temp
52%	223g filling
20%	86g sourdough starter
10%	43g butter, unsalted, at room temp
2%	9g salt
0.4%	2g cinnamon, ground
0.4%	2g nutmeg, freshly grated
0.4%	2g cardamom, ground

THE NIGHT BEFORE: SOURDOUGH STARTER REFRESH AND MAKE FILLING

Refresh your sourdough starter (page 67) the night before or up to 10 hours prior to mixing the dough.

Make the filling In a food processor, combine the butter, sugar, and cardamom until smooth and creamy. Transfer to an airtight container, cover, and refrigerate.

DAY ONE: MIXING, FOLDING, AND CHILLING

Warm the milk In a small saucepan, warm the milk and butter together over low heat, whisking until the butter is melted. Let cool to room temp before mixing it into the dough.

Mix In a large bowl, thoroughly mix together the bread flour, spelt flour, cooled milk/butter mixture, starter, salt, cinnamon, nutmeg, and cardamon until there are no patches of dry flour. You can squeeze the sticky dough through your hands, like extruding pasta between your fingers!

Pop a digital thermometer into the dough to take its temperature—it should be between 75° and 81°F. (If the dough is above 81°F, stick it in a cool spot—not the refrigerator—until it cools to between 75° and 78°F. If it is less than 75°F, place it in a warm location until it reaches between 75° and 78°F.) Cover the bowl and let rest for 1 hour.

Fold Once the dough is relaxed, you will give it a series of three folds every hour. To fold, smear a little water onto your work surface. Using a dough scraper, gather the dough together and, with a quick motion, scoop the dough up with the dough scraper and flip it onto the wet table. Using your hands, lift the dough off the table, then slap the bottom half down so that it sticks a little. Gently leaning back, stretch the dough and then quickly lean forward, tossing the dough still in your hands over the portion stuck to the table. Repeat three to four times. The dough will become smooth and pull itself into a ball.

Recipe continues

▲ Smear the filling over the dough.

▲ Fold the top half over the bottom half.

▲ Cut into four rectangular strips.

Using the dough scraper, return the dough to its container, smooth-side up, cover with a plate or sheet pan, and let rest for 1 hour. Repeat two more times, waiting 1 hour between folding sessions.

Chill After the final fold, transfer the dough back to the bowl, cover, and refrigerate for 8 to 24 hours.

DAY TWO: SHAPING, PROOFING, AND BAKING
Shape Remove the filling from the fridge and let it come to room temperature. Lightly flour your work surface. Lightly oil a 9-inch Pullman pan. Remove the dough from the fridge (no need to let it come to room temperature) and use a dough scraper to turn out the dough. Flip it over once or twice so both sides are nicely floured, and roll with a rolling pin to a 9 × 20-inch rectangle. (Use a soft touch so you don't press out all the gas.) Use an offset spatula to evenly smear the filling over the dough, all the way to the edges.

With a short side of the dough facing you, fold the top of the dough over to meet the bottom edge. You should now have a rectangle measuring 9 × 10 inches. Now make 4 pairs of "pants," each with a "waist" at the top and 2 "legs." Do this by using a bench knife or sharp kitchen knife to cut the rectangle of dough into 4 equal strips of dough roughly 2 inches wide and 10 inches long. Leave a 1-inch section uncut at the top of the strip (for the "waist") and make the "legs" by cutting down the center of the strip.

Now holding the "waist" between your pointer and middle fingers, wrap the pant legs around your fingers twice. On the third wrap, twist the legs, bring them over the side of the bun, and tuck them underneath, making the final bun. Repeat with the remaining dough. Squeeze the buns together, side by side, in the prepared Pullman pan.

Proof Cover the Pullman pan with the lid and proof in a draft-free spot at room temperature for 3 to 4 hours. When fully proofed, the loaf will appear to have doubled in size, feel full of air, and pass the poke test (see page 55).

Preheat the oven to 500°F.

Bake When the oven is up to temperature, load the bread into the oven with the Pullman pan lid still on and bake for 15 minutes. With welding gloves, carefully remove the lid and reduce the oven temperature to 475°F. Bake another 15 to 20 minutes, or until the loaf reaches an internal temperature of 190°F. Remove the pan from the oven and immediately remove the loaf from the pan. Transfer to a wire rack to cool completely. Store for up to 5 days, cut-side down, in a paper bag tucked inside a cloth bag.

Cut the center of each to make "pants."

Hold the top of the pants.

Wrap the "legs" around your fingers twice.

Twist the "legs."

Bring over the side of the bun and tuck underneath.

Squeeze the buns together in a lightly oiled Pullman pan.

▼ Alan's Bread (page 157)

Desem

THIS CHAPTER SHINES the spotlight on whole-grain flour and desem (pronounced DAY-zum), a Flemish style of leavening. Unlike sourdough starters and breads, known for their tangy bite, the desem starter, and breads made from it, have a wonderful fresh "wheaty" taste. Desem begins life as a stiff ball of dough made from whole wheat flour and water, buried in a container of whole wheat flour and stored for days at cool temperatures (50° to 65°F).

But shouldn't a bread made from wheat inherently taste "wheaty"? The answer is actually no! In a sourdough starter there are one hundred lactobacillus bacteria to every one yeast cell—the lactobacilli culture the bread, creating that famous sourdough sourness. This means that in sourdough bread you're often tasting the yogurt flavors produced by the lactobacilli rather than the flavor of the flour itself.

BECAUSE THE FLAVOR OF the wheat is so prominent in desem baking, this is a place where freshly milled whole-grain flour excels. If you have a tabletop mill, then *absolutely* mill your own flour from a hard, red winter wheat for the following starter and breads. If you have access to freshly milled whole-grain bread flour, choose that over roller milled flour. And if you just have access to whole wheat roller milled, then don't fret—that will work, too.

You *do* need to keep the desem between 50° and 65°F for the first two weeks while the microbial profile is developing. Desem doesn't have the same intense acidity to kill off unwanted microbes, so colder temperatures keep those unwanted microbes out as well as encourage yeast growth. Spring and fall, when it's warm (70°F) in the day and cool (40°F) at night, are excellent seasons for creating a desem starter.

Any water that you would drink is fine for creating and nurturing your desem starter. That being said, chlorinated water may slow down the process. If you are worried about treated water, fill a pitcher the night before and let it stand, uncovered, on the counter for 6 to 8 hours, to dechlorinate.

MY DESEM STORY

Coolish Water for Whole Grains

All the desem breads in this chapter have a desired dough temperature (DDT) of 75°F compared with a desired dough temp of 78°F in the Sourdough chapter that begins on page 65. (For more on DDT, see page 48.) This slightly lower temperature counteracts the high level of activity found in whole-grain flour, so that proper flavor development and bread strength come to completion in tandem.

I BEGAN MY FIRST of many desem starters during the final month I lived in Marshall, North Carolina, while I was running my small bakery, Smoke Signals. I had been hearing about it for years from my mentor, Jennifer Lapidus, who learned from her mentor, Alan Scott. Scott is a legendary figure in the bread world. He began building wood-fired ovens midway through his life, first helping author and cook Laurel Robertson with her backyard wood-fired oven. He created his own design, and it became the standard for homesteads, village bakeries, and anyone looking to have a wood-fired oven outside their back door. The oven was only one part of his overall worldview, which linked the oven with whole-grain bread and a human-scale economy (he was often seen walking around, passing out his bread from a canvas bag). Scott passed away in 2009, and his mill was sent to Jennifer Lapidus in Asheville, North Carolina, and became Carolina Ground, an artisanal flour mill in western North Carolina. When I closed Smoke Signals, I was sad to leave my baking family—as well as my oven built by Jennifer and Alan. Working on a desem starter was a way to bring my community (and its microbial profile) with me.

I used freshly milled Carolina Ground whole wheat flour to start the desem and buried it in a ceramic crock filled with five more pounds of fresh flour, using a wooden cutting board for the top. Once the desem was happy and active, I transferred it to a deli container, where it still lives with me in Virginia, all these years later. When I bake with it, I connect with my origins and something much larger than myself. Cared for and carried through time, a bread starter is a string that can tie a whole life together.

If you're wondering why you've never heard of desem until now, its lack of popularity goes hand in hand with a move away from whole grains to white bread. Its cousin, sourdough, has managed to survive only because it's made with readily available white flour. While desem may never become as common as sourdough, it is enjoying a resurgence thanks to farmers, millers, and bakers (like YOU) who are excited to work with flavorful and fun whole wheat flour.

OPPOSITE
Laurel's Loaf (page 153) is named after Laurel Robertson, who was a desem baker and friend of Alan Scott.

MAKING A DESEM STARTER

BEGINNING A DESEM IS not only straightforward but also relatively easier than a liquid-style sourdough. The desem will need to be fed every day for two weeks before it can be stored in the fridge. On Day Seven, and again on Day Fourteen, you'll make bread to test its progress and strength (just like you do for sourdough).

DAY ONE

Fill an opaque 1-quart food-grade container with whole wheat flour. (I use a tin pail with a wooden cutting board for a lid, but a plastic bucket with a lid or simply a brown paper bag that can be folded on top to enclose the flour and starter will work, too.)

In a medium bowl, knead together 110g of whole wheat flour and 70g of cool water until it makes a ball. Bury the ball in the flour in the container. Cover the container and place in a cool location between 50° and 65°F for 24 hours.

DAY TWO

Check the container periodically. Today you should see the surface of the flour start to "erupt," a sign that the yeast, naturally present in the flour, is coming alive and producing gas, causing the ball of dough to expand. You'll know the desem is working when it looks like a volcano has exploded in the center of the container!

DAY THREE

You'll now begin refreshing the desem. Remove the desem from the container, dusting any flour on the surface of the ball back into the container. Remove the outer layer of the starter (also referred to as the rind) and discard it, making sure to save 40g from the interior.

In a medium bowl, combine the 40g of reserved desem and 110g of the flour from the container with 70g of cool water. Knead this mixture into a ball and bury it back in the flour. (Replenish the flour in the container if the dough ball isn't fully covered.) Cover the container with a lid and rest between 50° and 65°F for 24 hours.

DAYS FOUR AND FIVE

Repeat the refreshment procedure outlined on Day Three. You should begin to see some webbing in the desem; it will be soft and maybe even a little wet in the middle. In general, it should smell like sprouted grain and have the texture of chewed bubble gum. If it smells sour or is weeping alcohol on the rind, don't worry—just make sure you're keeping it between 50° and 65°F and haven't missed a refreshment. If you need to replenish a little of the flour that surrounds the starter so that it's truly buried, then do so. If you don't see any webbing in the desem, no growth of the dough ball, no surface eruption, and no apple-cider-like aroma by Day Five, then start over. (Sorry!)

DAY SIX

Repeat the refreshment procedure outlined on Day Three, but afterward, instead of burying the desem back in flour, transfer it to the container it will now live in permanently—I use a 1-quart deli container, but any clean food-grade container with a lid will do. Continue to ferment in a cool location that's around 50°F (and cooler than 70°F), like the mudroom, garage, potting shed, or cellar. If there is any extra flour in the original container, you can save it for making bread.

DAY SEVEN (REFRESHMENT)

Discard all but 40g of the desem. In a medium bowl, combine the reserved desem with 110g of whole wheat flour and 70g of cool water. Use the desem discard to bake the Daily Desem (page 141). Although you'll likely have a dense, low-volume loaf, you'll learn about the strength of the desem and get a sneak peak of the flavor early on—which can be quite interesting.

DAYS EIGHT THROUGH THIRTEEN

Repeat the refreshment procedure outlined on Day Seven every day. During the second week, the desem will gain strength, ferment more quickly, and develop an intense flavor. (Use the discard to make Monica's Banana Bread, page 256, or Coffee Cake, page 265.)

Use the desem discard on Day Seven to learn about the strength and flavor of your new starter.

DAY FOURTEEN

Congratulations! Now you should have a healthy, active desem! By Day Fourteen, the desem should double in size between 6 and 8 hours after being refreshed, have a sweet fresh fruit (apple) smell, a domed top when fully risen, and a tender and webbed consistency. Repeat the refreshment procedure outlined on Day Seven and use the desem discard to bake the Daily Desem (page 141). The desem will now be strong enough to live on your countertop at room temperature or undergo storage in the fridge.

IF YOU PLAN ON BAKING DAILY OR EVERY OTHER DAY: Leave the desem on the countertop and continue daily refreshments as instructed on Day Seven.

IF YOU PLAN ON BAKING A LOAF BETWEEN ONCE A WEEK AND ONCE A MONTH: Prepare your desem for cold storage in the fridge. See Preparing for Cold Storage (page 138).

IF YOU PLAN ON BAKING ONLY A FEW TIMES A YEAR: Dehydrate the desem so you can have some at the ready whenever you'd like to revitalize the dried flakes. See Long-Term Storage (page 138).

TAKING CARE OF YOUR DESEM STARTER

IF YOU ARE PLANNING on baking once or twice a week, then you should keep your active desem in the fridge. To prepare your desem for a cold nap, you'll want to stiffen it by reducing the amount of water. This slows down fermentation, which reduces activity and acid production (yeast and bacteria go dormant under 40°F).

PREPARING FOR COLD STORAGE

Discard all but 40g of the desem. Refresh the reserved 40g with 110g of whole wheat flour and 60g of 65°F water. Knead into a stiff ball, place in a clean container, cover, and ferment for 3 hours at room temperature. Transfer to the refrigerator. Refresh the desem once a week to keep the flavor balanced and the yeast and bacteria well fed. You can do your weekly refresh right from cold storage—there's no need to let the starter come to room temp.

TO MAINTENANCE REFRESH Remove your desem from the fridge and discard all but 40g. Refresh the reserved 40g with 110g whole wheat flour and 60g water. Knead into a stiff ball and either return to the original container or transfer to a clean 1-quart container—your call. Cover and ferment for 3 hours at room temperature, then return to the refrigerator.

While living in the fridge, your desem may develop a layer of colored alcohol on the top, known as hooch, or become discolored on the surface. This does not mean that your desem is dead. Water and alcohol weigh less than the desem mixture, so they float to the top (you'll pour this off before you revive it—see the following step). If you forget, miss a week, or go on vacation, don't stress! Desem can go dormant in the fridge for up to 1 month. Take it out and refresh as described above.

REVIVING FROM COLD STORAGE

If you've been good to your desem, it should spring back to life with minimal worry. If you've neglected your weekly maintenance feedings, your desem may need to be refreshed more than once. If it's been months since you last touched the desem, you may want to simply begin a new one.

TO REVIVE YOUR DESEM FROM COLD STORAGE

Remove it from the refrigerator and discard all but 40g. Refresh the 40g with 70g water and 110g of whole wheat flour. The mixture will be stiff, but not as stiff as the initial ball. You can mix it up with a spoon or with your hands if you prefer. Cover the container and ferment at room temperature for 24 hours. If the desem smells fresh, cider-like, nutty, and feels full of air when gently pressed after a single refreshment, then go ahead and begin using it.

LONG-TERM STORAGE

Dehydrating your desem into dry flakes is a smart approach if you aren't planning on baking for a few months or want to mail some to a friend.

Line a sheet pan with a nonstick silicone baking mat or parchment paper and ready a flexible spatula or dough scraper. Mix room temp water into the desem, 1 tablespoon at a time, to create a slurry that's the consistency of runny pancake batter. Then use the spatula or dough scraper to smear it across the mat or parchment.

Turn on your oven light. Place the sheet pan in the oven and let it dehydrate there for 24 hours. After 24 hours, the starter should be thin, dry, and crusty. Break it apart and transfer to small air-tight bags or other airtight containers, label, date, and move to the freezer. It can be stored in the freezer for up to 2 months.

To revive from dehydrated desem flakes Combine 40g of the dehydrated flakes with 100g whole wheat flour and 90g warm water. Mix until incorporated, making sure there's no dry flour left. Cover with the lid and ferment at room temp for 24 hours. Repeat every 4 hours, or until the desem starter doubles in size and has a domed surface and a pleasant, hay-like smell. Now it's ready to use. Store the revived desem starter at room temperature or in the fridge and feed as instructed in Reviving from Cold Storage (above).

BEFORE YOU BAKE: USING YOUR DESEM STARTER

FOR ALL THE FORMULAS in this chapter, refresh your desem starter between 6 and 8 hours before you want to mix your dough. Keep in mind that warm environments (70° to 80°F) will shorten the time it takes for the desem to become active, and cooler environments (60° to 68°F) will extend the time it takes for the desem to become active. I like to feed mine around 9:00 p.m. and leave it somewhere cool, around 65°F, and mix the next morning around 6:00 a.m.

After you've pulled what you need for the bread dough (look at the formula in the recipe to see how much you need), refresh and cover with the lid. If you're planning on baking again the next day, leave it out at room temperature (you'll be refreshing it in the evening again). If you're not, stick it in the refrigerator.

Refresh the desem starter 6 to 8 hours before mixing and folding the dough.
The dough is then chilled overnight and shaped, proofed, and baked the following day.

1 ROUND AT 900G ——— **9-INCH ROUND BANNETON** ——— **DOUGH TEMP: 75°F** ——— **LEVEL: BEGINNER**

DAILY DESEM

*This loaf is the whole wheat bread I turn to on a daily basis for my family.
It's toothsome and tender, with a delightful chew and a dense crumb so my butter
and jam stay put. It's also the loaf to make on Day Seven and Day
Fourteen when testing the rising power and flavor of your new desem
starter. Happy whole wheat journey!*

BAKER'S PERCENTAGES	WEIGHTS & INGREDIENTS
SCALD	
200%	58g boiling water
100%	29g whole wheat flour
DOUGH	
100%	434g whole wheat flour
65%	282g water
20%	87g whole wheat scald
20%	87g desem starter
2%	9g salt

THE NIGHT BEFORE: DESEM STARTER REFRESH AND MAKE THE SCALD
Following the instructions on page 136, refresh your desem starter 6 to 8 hours before mixing the dough.

Prepare the scald Weigh out the whole wheat flour into a 1-pint deli container (or similar heat-safe container) and pour the boiling water over the flour. Stir vigorously until there are no patches of dry flour. Cover with the lid partially cracked and let rest for 6 to 8 hours, or until needed.

DAY ONE: MIXING, FOLDING, AND CHILLING
Mix In a large bowl, thoroughly mix together the whole wheat flour, water, scald, desem, and salt by hand until there are no patches of dry flour. You can squeeze the dough through your hands, like extruding pasta between your fingers! The dough will be sticky, gluey, and shaggy.

Pop a digital thermometer into the dough to take its temperature—it should be between 72° and 78°F. (If the dough is above 78°F, stick it in a cool spot—not the refrigerator—until it cools to between 75° and 78°F. If it is cooler than 72°F, place it in a warm location until it reaches between 72° and 75°F.) Cover the bowl with a dinner plate or sheet pan for a lid and let rest for 1 hour.

Fold Once the dough is relaxed, you will give it a series of three folds spaced 1 hour apart. To fold, smear a little water onto your work surface. Using a dough scraper, gather the dough together and, with a quick motion, scoop the dough up with the dough scraper and flip it onto the wet table. Using your hands, lift the dough off the table, then slap the bottom half down, so that it sticks a little. Gently leaning back, stretch the dough and then quickly lean forward, tossing the dough still in your

Recipe continues

hands over the portion stuck to the table. Repeat three to four times. The dough will become smooth and pull itself into a ball.

Using the dough scraper, return the dough to its container, smooth-side up, cover with the plate or sheet pan, and let rest for 1 hour. Repeat the process two more times, with 1 hour between folding sessions.

Chill After the final fold, transfer the dough back to the bowl, cover with the lid, and refrigerate for at least 8 hours or up to 24.

DAY TWO: SHAPING, PROOFING, AND BAKING
Pre-shape Lightly dust your table with flour. Remove the dough from the fridge (you don't need to let it warm up) and, using a dough scraper, scoop the dough up and flip it onto the table. Pat into a rectangle with a short side facing you. Bring the edge of the dough closest to you to the top (the edge farthest from you), leaving a 1-inch lip. Take the sides of the dough, gently stretch each outward a few inches, then quickly cross them over each other so they are on top of each other, like swaddling a baby. Next, stretch the edge of the dough closest to you up to the top, flush with the top edge. Gently press to create a seam.

Use your hands or a bench knife to gently drag the loaf on the table to create surface tension. You will see it tighten and become smooth as you drag. Make sure the top stays the top and the dough doesn't roll over as you go. The dough will curl into itself, so the seam is now on the bottom and the top is smooth and roundish.

Bench rest Sprinkle the dough with flour, cover with a kitchen towel, and let rest 30 minutes.

Final shape Lightly dust a cloth-lined 9-inch round banneton with flour and set aside. Lightly dust your table with flour. Using a bench knife, flip over the relaxed round. Imagine the round into four quarters. Stretch the edge of each quarter to the center of the round, overlapping them slightly, by about 1 inch, to make a pouch shape. Now turn the "pouch" on its side, cupping the portion that was flush with the table in one hand, and cinch the gathered portions together with the edge of your palm, sealing the seam. Glide the dough down the table so that the seam is sealed between the edge of your

hand and the table. Transfer seam-side up to the floured banneton.

Proof Loosely cover the banneton with a kitchen towel and proof in a draft-free spot at room temperature for 2 to 3 hours. When fully proofed, the loaf will appear to have doubled in size, feel full of air, and pass the poke test (see page 55).

Preheat the oven Set a combo cooker on a rack in the oven so the skillet is the bottom and the pot is inverted as a lid. Preheat the oven (and the combo cooker) to 500°F.

Score Wearing welding gloves, remove the combo cooker from the oven (it's *hot!*) and quickly toss the dough seam-side down onto the hot skillet portion of the cooker. Use a lame and razor, with the blade at a 35-degree angle, to score a square on the top of the round.

Bake Immediately cover the bread with the inverted pot for a lid and load it back into the oven. Bake for 15 minutes. Remove the combo cooker from the oven and set on the stovetop. Remove the lid (be careful of hot steam) and reduce the oven temperature to 475°F. Return the bread, still on the skillet portion of the combo cooker, to the oven and bake another 15 to 20 minutes, or until the loaf is deeply browned, reaches an internal temperature of 190°F, and sounds hollow when tapped on the bottom. Carefully remove the bread from the skillet and transfer to a wire rack to cool completely. Store for up to 5 days, cut-side down, in a paper bag tucked inside a cloth bag.

SNAPSHOT
Refresh the desem starter 6 to 8 hours before
mixing, folding, shaping, proofing, and baking the bread.

1 LOAF AT 1KG ——— 9-INCH PULLMAN PAN ——— DOUGH TEMP: 75°F ——— LEVEL: BEGINNER

CINNAMON-RAISIN DESEM

There are few fragrances as comforting as the smell of cinnamon-raisin bread
baking in the oven. I used Øland flour from Maine Grains as the whole
wheat flour base for this dough. A heritage grain from Denmark, the small, tender
berries are sweet and nutty with a toasted oat flavor that deepens
the experience of this classic bread.

BAKER'S PERCENTAGES	WEIGHTS & INGREDIENTS
SOAKER	
100%	167g raisins, dark or golden
100%	167g warm water
DOUGH	
70%	292g whole wheat flour
30%	125g bread flour
75%	313g water
40%	167g raisin soaker
20%	83g desem starter
2%	8g salt
1%	4g cinnamon, ground

THE NIGHT BEFORE: DESEM STARTER REFRESH AND SOAK RAISINS
Following the instructions on page 136, refresh your desem starter
6 to 8 hours before mixing the dough.

Soak the raisins Weigh the raisins out in a 1-pint deli container (or similar
container) and cover them with the warm water. Cover tightly with a lid
and soak overnight, or until needed.

DAY OF: MIXING THROUGH BAKING
Mix Drain any excess water from the raisin soaker. In a large bowl,
thoroughly mix together the whole wheat flour, bread flour, water, raisins,
desem, salt, and cinnamon by hand until there are no patches of dry
flour. You can squeeze the dough through your hands, like extruding
pasta between your fingers! The dough will be sticky, gluey, and shaggy.

Pop a digital thermometer into the dough to take its temperature—it
should be between 72° and 78°F. (If the dough is above 78°F, stick
it in a cool spot—not the refrigerator—until it cools to between 75° and
78°F. If it is cooler than 72°F, place it in a warm location until it reaches
between 72° and 75°F.) Cover the bowl with a dinner plate or sheet pan
for a lid and let rest for 1 hour.

Fold Once the dough is relaxed, you will give it a series of three folds
spaced 1 hour apart. To fold, smear a little water onto your work surface.
Using a dough scraper, gather the dough together and, with a quick
motion, scoop the dough up with the dough scraper and flip it onto the
wet table. Using your hands, lift the dough off the table, then slap the
bottom half down, so that it sticks a little. Gently leaning back, stretch
the dough and then quickly lean forward, tossing the dough still in your

Recipe continues

hands over the portion stuck to the table. Repeat three to four times. The dough will become smooth and pull itself into a ball.

Using the dough scraper, return the dough to its container, smooth-side up, cover with the plate or sheet pan, and let rest for 1 hour. Repeat the process two more times, with 1 hour between folding sessions.

Pre-shape Lightly dust your table with flour. Using a dough scraper, gather the dough together in the bowl and, with a quick motion, scoop the dough up with the dough scraper and flip it onto the table. Pat into a rectangle with a short side facing you. Fold the edge of the dough closest to you over to the top (the edge farthest from you), leaving a 1-inch lip. Take the sides of the dough, gently stretch each outward a few inches, then quickly cross them over each other so they are on top of each other, like swaddling a baby. Next, stretch the edge of the dough closest to you up to the top, flush with the top edge. Gently press down to create a seam.

Use your hands or a bench knife to gently drag the loaf on the table to create surface tension. You will see it tighten and become smooth as you drag. Make sure the top stays the top and the dough doesn't roll over as you go. The dough will curl into itself so the seam is now on the bottom and the top is smooth and roundish.

Bench rest Sprinkle the dough with flour, cover with a kitchen towel, and let rest 30 minutes.

Final shape Lightly oil a 9-inch Pullman pan. Lightly dust your table with flour. Use a bench knife to flip over the pre-shape so the top is now the bottom. Bring the bottom of the dough to meet the top edge, leaving a 1-inch lip at the top. Gently stretch the sides outward a few inches, then quickly cross them over the middle of the dough, like swaddling a baby. You're now looking at an envelope shape. Stretch the bottom of the dough up to meet the top of the envelope and seal. The dough will now be a cylinder on its side with a seam facing away from you. Roll the seam underneath and seal the left and right ends using the edge of your palm. With the bench knife, flip it seam-side down, into the pan.

Proof Cover the pan with the lid and proof in a draft-free spot at room temperature for 3 to 4 hours. When fully proofed, the loaf will appear to have doubled in size, feel full of air, and pass the poke test (see page 55).

Preheat the oven to 500°F.

Bake When the oven is up to temperature, load the bread into the oven with the Pullman pan lid still on and bake for 15 minutes. With welding gloves, carefully remove the lid and reduce the oven temperature to 475°F. Bake another 15 to 20 minutes, or until the loaf is deeply browned, pulls away from the sides of the pan, and reaches an internal temperature of 190°F. Remove the pan from the oven and immediately remove the loaf from the pan. Transfer to a wire rack to cool completely. Store for up to 5 days, cut-side down, in a paper bag tucked inside a cloth bag.

8 POCKET-STYLE ROUNDS AT 75G EACH ——————— **DOUGH TEMP: 75°F** ——————— **LEVEL: BEGINNER**

DESEM PITAS

I grew up on tunafish sandwiches stuffed into grocery store pitas instead
of on sandwich bread. I loved how floury, nutty, and yeasty the pita tasted against
the walnut-, grape-, and raisin-filled tuna salad my mom so expertly made.
As an adult, I grew to love making my pitas from scratch, and I hope that, one day,
my daughter likes her tuna sandwiches this way, too!

BAKER'S PERCENTAGES	WEIGHTS & INGREDIENTS
100%	320g whole wheat flour
65%	208g water
15%	48g desem starter
5%	17g vegetable oil
2%	7g salt

THE NIGHT BEFORE: DESEM STARTER REFRESH
Following the instructions on page 136, refresh your desem starter
6 to 8 hours before mixing the dough.

DAY OF: MIXING THROUGH BAKING
Mix In a large bowl, thoroughly mix together the whole wheat flour, water, desem, vegetable oil, and salt by hand until there are no patches of dry flour. You can squeeze the dough through your hands, like extruding pasta between your fingers! The dough will be sticky, gluey, and shaggy.

Pop a digital thermometer into the dough to take its temperature—it should be between 72° and 78°F. (If the dough is above 78°F, stick it in a cool spot—not the refrigerator—until it cools to between 75° and 78°F. If it is cooler than 72°F, place it in a warm location until it reaches between 72° and 75°F.) Cover the bowl with a dinner plate or sheet pan for a lid and let rest for 1 hour.

Divide the dough Lightly dust your work surface with flour and use a dough scraper to turn out the dough. Using a bench knife, divide the dough into eight 75g chunks. Place a chunk on the scale and take away from it or add to it (while it's still on the scale) to reach 75g. The fewer small bits of dough you have to add or pull off the better, so use the first chunk to eyeball the rest. Repeat with the remaining portions of dough. (You can also just eyeball it into 8 chunks, if that's easier for you.)

Pre-shape Shape the chunks into rounds by stretching the bottom edge of the small mound over the top so any extra bits are enclosed on the inside. Do this until the bits are completely enclosed by two or three dough flaps. Turn the mound over so that the seam is on the bottom and the smooth side is facing up. Hold your hand in a C shape

Recipe continues

and cuddle a portion of the dough against your palm. Moving your hand in counterclockwise circles, pinch/press a little dough between your palm and the table, to force it into a round. Repeat with the remaining pieces of dough.

Bench rest Sprinkle each round with a little flour, cover with a kitchen towel, and let rest 30 minutes.

Preheat the oven While the dough is resting, set a pizza stone or overturned 10-inch cast-iron skillet on a rack in the oven and preheat to 525°F.

Final shape Perform a final shape on the pita by rolling each out with a rolling pin into a roughly 7-inch round about ⅛ inch thick.

Bake Working with one at a time, slide a pita onto a well-floured peel (or floured and inverted sheet pan) and shake/shimmy the dough onto the hot pizza stone (or inverted skillet) and bake for 1 minute, or until it puffs up (this could take less than a minute, or slightly longer). Wearing welding gloves and using grill tongs, open the oven door and quickly flip over the pita, baking it on its second side for another minute. Remove from the oven and transfer to a basket (or plate) lined with a kitchen towel. Loosely cover the pita with another towel (or with the overhang of the towel being used to line the basket or plate) to steam while it cools. Bake the remaining pitas, adding them to the basket and covering with the kitchen towel as you go. The pitas will keep, wrapped in a kitchen towel in a canvas bag, for up to 24 hours, though they are best eaten just cooled from the oven.

SNAPSHOT

Refresh the desem starter 6 to 8 hours before mixing, folding, shaping, and
proofing the dough. The dough is then chilled overnight and baked the following day.

1 BÂTARD AT 1KG ———— 9-INCH OVAL BANNETON ———— DOUGH TEMP: 75°F ———— LEVEL: BEGINNER

LAUREL'S LOAF

I started reading Laurel Robertson's cookbooks about nutrition, pacifism,
and healthy cooking almost a decade ago, and I still cherish them to this day. Their
welcoming brown covers and woodcut illustrations provided a tangible relief from
the often-mechanized side of baking. When my hands are mixing this dough, I focus
my mind on those working to bring peace to the world, one loaf at a time.

BAKER'S PERCENTAGES	WEIGHTS & INGREDIENTS
100%	459g whole wheat flour
70%	321g water
20%	92g desem starter
20%	92g honey
6%	27g vegetable oil
2%	10g salt

Rolled oats to roll the dough in

THE NIGHT BEFORE: DESEM STARTER REFRESH
Following the instructions on page 136, refresh your desem starter
6 to 8 hours before mixing the dough.

DAY ONE: MIXING, FOLDING, SHAPING, PROOFING, AND CHILLING
Mix In a large bowl, thoroughly mix together the whole wheat flour, water,
desem, honey, vegetable oil, and salt by hand until there are no patches
of dry flour. You can squeeze the dough through your hands, like
extruding pasta between your fingers! The dough will be sticky, gluey,
and shaggy.

Pop a digital thermometer into the dough to take its temperature—it
should be between 72° and 78°F. (If the dough is above 78°F, stick
it in a cool spot—not the refrigerator—until it cools to between 75° and
78°F. If it is cooler than 72°F, place it in a warm location until it reaches
between 72° and 75°F.) Cover the bowl with a dinner plate or sheet pan
for a lid and let rest for 1 hour.

Fold Once the dough is relaxed, you will give it a series of three folds
spaced 1 hour apart. To fold, smear a little water onto your work surface.
Using a dough scraper, gather the dough together and, with a quick
motion, scoop the dough up with the dough scraper and flip it onto the
wet table. Using your hands, lift the dough off the table, then slap the
bottom half down, so that it sticks a little. Gently leaning back, stretch
the dough and then quickly lean forward, tossing the dough still in your
hands over the portion stuck to the table. Repeat three to four times. The
dough will become smooth and pull itself into a ball.

Using the dough scraper, return the dough to its container, smooth-side
up, cover with the plate or sheet pan, and let rest for 1 hour. Repeat

Recipe continues

the process two more times, with 1 hour between folding sessions.

Pre-shape Lightly dust your table with flour. Remove the dough from the fridge (there's no need to let it warm up before shaping). Using a dough scraper, gather the dough together in the bowl and, with a quick motion, scoop the dough up with the dough scraper and flip it onto the table. Pat into a rectangle with a short side facing you. Fold the edge of the dough closest to you over to the top (the edge farthest from you), leaving a 1-inch lip. Take the sides of the dough, gently stretch each outward a few inches, then quickly cross them over each other so they are on top of each other, like swaddling a baby. Next, stretch the edge of the dough closest to you up to the top, flush with the top edge. Gently press down to create a seam.

Use your hands or a bench knife to gently drag the loaf on the table to create surface tension. You will see it tighten and become smooth as you drag. Make sure the top stays the top and the dough doesn't roll over as you go. The dough will curl into itself so the seam is now on the bottom and the top is smooth and roundish.

Bench rest Sprinkle the dough with flour, cover with a kitchen towel, and let rest 30 minutes.

Ready the oats While the dough is resting, run a kitchen towel under water quickly (you want it damp, not soaking) and place it over half of a sheet pan. Toss a heaping handful of oats on the pan opposite the kitchen towel. Set aside.

Final shape Lightly dust a cloth-lined 9-inch oval banneton with flour and set aside. To shape the dough into a bâtard, lightly dust the table with flour. Use a bench knife to flip over the pre-shape so the top is now the bottom. Bring the bottom of the dough to meet the top edge, leaving a 1-inch lip at the top. Gently stretch the sides outward a few inches, then quickly cross them over the middle of the dough, like swaddling a baby. You're now looking at an envelope shape. Stretch the bottom of the dough up to meet the top of the envelope and press down to seal. The dough will now be a cylinder on its side with a seam facing away from you. Roll the seam underneath and seal the left and right ends using the edge of your palm. Roll the dough over the damp

towel and through the oats and use the bench knife to transfer it to the round banneton, seam-side up.

Proof Loosely cover the banneton with a kitchen towel and proof in a draft-free spot at room temperature, 2 to 3 hours. When fully proofed, the loaf will appear to have doubled in size, feel full of air, and pass the poke test (see page 55).

Chill When proofed, transfer the banneton, covered with a shower cap or kitchen towel, to the fridge for at least 6 hours and up to 24.

DAY TWO: BAKING
Preheat the oven Set a combo cooker on a rack in the oven so the skillet is the bottom and the pot is inverted as a lid. Preheat the oven (and the combo cooker) to 500°F.

Score Wearing welding gloves, remove the combo cooker from the oven (it's *hot!*) and quickly toss the dough seam-side down onto the hot skillet portion of the cooker. Use a lame and razor, with the blade at a 35-degree angle, to score in one long stroke, running lengthwise along the top of the bread.

Bake Immediately cover the bread with the inverted pot for a lid and load it back into the oven. Bake for 15 minutes. Remove the combo cooker from the oven and set on the stovetop. Remove the lid (be careful of hot steam) and reduce the oven temperature to 475°F. Return the bread, still on the skillet portion of the combo cooker, to the oven and bake another 15 to 20 minutes, or until the loaf is deeply browned, reaches an internal temperature of 190°F, and sounds hollow when tapped on the bottom. Carefully remove the bread from the skillet and cool completely on a wire rack. Store for up to 5 days, cut-side down, in a paper bag tucked inside a cloth bag.

SNAPSHOT
Refresh the desem starter 6 to 8 hours before
mixing, folding, shaping, proofing, and baking the bread.

1 ROUND AT 900G ——— **9-INCH ROUND BANNETON** ——— **DOUGH TEMP: 75°F** ——— **LEVEL: BEGINNER**

ALAN'S BREAD

Although I never met Alan Scott, for many years while I ran
my bakery, Smoke Signals, I was lucky to use a wood-fired oven that he built
with my mentor, Jennifer Lapidus. I thought of him often while I chopped
wood, lit fires, and mixed doughs. This loaf is perfect for using 100% home-milled
flour, as he would have. Bake a few loaves and pass them about your
neighborhood to keep the spirit of good bread alive and well.

BAKER'S PERCENTAGES	WEIGHTS & INGREDIENTS
60%	268g whole white wheat flour
40%	178g whole wheat flour
75%	335g water
25%	112g desem starter
2%	9g salt

THE NIGHT BEFORE: DESEM STARTER REFRESH
Following the instructions on page 136, refresh your desem starter
6 to 8 hours before mixing the dough.

DAY OF: MIXING THROUGH BAKING
Mix In a large bowl, thoroughly mix together the whole white wheat flour,
whole wheat flour, water, desem, and salt by hand until there are no patches
of dry flour. You can squeeze the dough through your hands, like extruding
pasta between your fingers! The dough will be sticky, gluey, and shaggy.

Pop a digital thermometer into the dough to take its temperature—it
should be between 72° and 78°F. (If the dough is above 78°F, stick
it in a cool spot—not the refrigerator—until it cools to between 75° and
78°F. If it is cooler than 72°F, place it in a warm location until it reaches
between 72° and 75°F.) Cover the bowl with a dinner plate or sheet pan
for a lid and let rest for 1 hour.

Fold Once the dough is relaxed, you will give it a series of three folds
spaced 1 hour apart. To fold, smear a little water onto your work surface.
Using a dough scraper, gather the dough together and, with a quick
motion, scoop the dough up with the dough scraper and flip it onto the
wet table. Using your hands, lift the dough off the table, then slap the
bottom half down, so that it sticks a little. Gently leaning back, stretch
the dough and then quickly lean forward, tossing the dough still in your
hands over the portion stuck to the table. Repeat three to four times. The
dough will become smooth and pull itself into a ball.

Using the dough scraper, return the dough to its container, smooth-side
up, cover with the plate or sheet pan, and let rest for 1 hour. Repeat the

Recipe continues

process two more times, with 1 hour between folding sessions. After the final fold, transfer the dough back to the bowl, cover with the lid, and let rest 30 minutes.

Pre-shape Lightly dust your table with flour. Remove the dough from the fridge (you don't need to let it warm up) and, using a dough scraper, scoop the dough up and flip it onto the table. Pat into a rectangle with a short side facing you. Bring the edge of the dough closest to you to the top (the edge farthest from you), leaving a 1-inch lip. Take the sides of the dough, gently stretch each outward a few inches, then quickly cross them over each other so they are on top of each other, like swaddling a baby. Next, stretch the edge of the dough closest to you up to the top, flush with the top edge. Gently press to create a seam.

Use your hands or a bench knife to gently drag the loaf on the table to create surface tension. You will see it tighten and become smooth as you drag. Make sure the top stays the top and the dough doesn't roll over as you go. The dough will curl into itself, so the seam is now on the bottom and the top is smooth and roundish.

Bench rest Sprinkle the dough with flour, cover with a kitchen towel, and let rest 30 minutes.

Final shape Lightly dust a cloth-lined 9-inch round banneton with flour and set aside. Lightly dust your table with flour. Using a bench knife, flip over the relaxed round. Imagine the round into four quarters. Stretch the edge of each quarter to the center of the round, overlapping them slightly, by about 1 inch, to make a pouch shape. Now turn the "pouch" on its side, cupping the portion that was flush with the table in one hand, and cinch the gathered portions together with the edge of your palm, sealing the seam. Glide the dough down the table so that the seam is sealed between the edge of your hand and the table.

Proof Loosely cover the dough with a kitchen towel and proof at room temperature in a draft-free spot for 2 to 3 hours. When fully proofed, the loaf will appear to have doubled in size, feel full of air, and pass the poke test (see page 55).

Preheat the oven Set a combo cooker on a rack in the oven so the skillet is on the bottom and the pot is inverted as a lid. Preheat the oven (and the combo cooker) to 500°F.

Score Wearing welding gloves, remove the combo cooker from the oven (it's *hot!*) and quickly toss the dough seam-side down onto the hot skillet portion of the cooker. Use a lame and razor, with the blade at a 35-degree angle, to score two large X's on the top of the round.

Bake Immediately cover the bread with the inverted pot for a lid and load it back into the oven. Bake for 15 minutes. Remove the combo cooker from the oven and set on the stovetop. Remove the lid (be careful of hot steam) and reduce the oven temperature to 475°F. Return the bread, still on the skillet portion of the combo cooker, to the oven and bake another 15 to 20 minutes, or until the loaf is deeply browned, reaches an internal temperature of 190°F, and sounds hollow when tapped on the bottom. Carefully remove the bread from the skillet and cool completely on a wire rack. Store for up to 5 days, cut-side down, in a paper bag tucked inside a cloth bag.

Refresh the desem starter 6 to 8 hours before mixing, shaping, and frying the paratha.

4 FLATBREADS AT 100G-ISH ———— DOUGH TEMP: NONE ———— LEVEL: BEGINNER

STUFFED ALOO PARATHA

I was introduced to paratha, an Indian flatbread, in a baking class
at Maine Grains, a stone ground mill and educational baking center in Maine.
Paratha is made up of many layers of cooked dough: The small dough
rounds are rolled out, brushed with ghee, folded into an envelope, and rolled
out again, creating a lamination (the layered effect). Here the paratha
is stuffed with potato and spices before being fried in a pan.

FILLING

WEIGHTS & INGREDIENTS

1 Yukon Gold potato, large

14g parsley or cilantro, chopped

5g cumin, ground

5g red pepper flakes

2g salt

DOUGH

BAKER'S PERCENTAGES	WEIGHTS & INGREDIENTS
100%	174g whole wheat flour
60%	104g water
20%	34g desem starter
2%	4g vegetable oil
2%	4g salt

Extra ghee for greasing the skillet

THE NIGHT BEFORE: DESEM STARTER REFRESH AND
POTATO ROASTING
Following the instructions on page 136, refresh your desem starter
6 to 8 hours before mixing the dough.

Roast the potato Preheat the oven to 400°F. Using the tines of a fork,
prick the potato several times and bake it directly on a rack for 45 minutes,
or until it's tender to the poke of a fork. Remove from the oven and wrap
in foil before setting aside to cool overnight.

DAY OF: MIXING THROUGH BAKING
Mix In a large bowl, thoroughly mix together the whole wheat flour, water,
desem, vegetable oil, and salt by hand until there are no patches of dry
flour. You can squeeze the dough through your hands, like extruding
pasta between your fingers! The dough will be sticky, gluey, and shaggy.

Pop a digital thermometer into the dough to take its temperature—it
should be between 72° and 78°F. (If the dough is above 78°F, stick
it in a cool spot—not the refrigerator—until it cools to between 75° and
78°F. If it is cooler than 72°F, place it in a warm location until it reaches
between 72° and 75°F.) Cover the bowl with a dinner plate or sheet pan
for a lid and let rest for 1 hour.

Prepare the filling In a food processor, pulse the cooked and cooled
potato (I like to leave the skin on) along with the parsley (or cilantro),
cumin, pepper flakes, and salt. Set aside.

Divide the dough Lightly dust your work surface with flour and use
a dough scraper to turn out the dough. Using a bench knife, divide the

Recipe continues

dough into four 80g chunks. Place a chunk on the scale and take away from it or add to it (while it's still on the scale) to reach 80g. (The fewer bits of dough you have to add or remove the better, so use the first chunk to visually gauge the rest.) Repeat with the remaining portions of dough. (It's also okay to just eyeball 4 pieces of dough.)

Pre-shape Shape the dough chunks into rounds by stretching the bottom edge of the small mound over the top so any extra bits are enclosed on the inside. Do this until the bits are completely enclosed by 2 or 3 dough flaps. Turn the mound over so that the seam is on the bottom and the smooth side is facing up. Hold your hand in a C shape and cuddle a portion of the dough against your palm. Move your hand in a counterclockwise motion, moving in circles and pinching/pressing a little dough between your palm and the table, to force it into a round. Repeat with the remaining pieces of dough.

Bench rest Sprinkle each with a little flour, cover with a kitchen towel, and let rest 30 minutes.

Fill and final shape Working with one paratha at a time, use a rolling pin to gently roll each portion of dough into a 4-inch round. Add a generous spoonful of the prepared potato filling to the center. Fold up 4 sides like a "purse," so they meet at the top, slightly overlapping over the potato filling, but not so much so that there is a large lump of dough. Gently press down on the paratha with the palm of your hand to seal the top. Sprinkle the top with flour and gently roll into an 8-inch round.

Heat the skillet Set a large cast-iron skillet over medium heat. Grease with a thin coating of ghee, leaving the remaining ghee out to add to the skillet as needed. Line a basket or plate with a kitchen towel and set aside.

Cook the stuffed paratha on the hot skillet until it is charred in spots and turns a deep golden brown, 1 to 2 minutes. Flip with a spatula and cook another 1 to 2 minutes. (While the first paratha is cooking, roll, fill, and reroll the next pieces of dough—and repeat this process for all the parathas.) Transfer the hot paratha to the cloth-lined basket or plate, folding the corners of the towel to keep it warm as you cook the remaining ones. Serve and eat immediately! If there are any left over, you can store them in an airtight container in the fridge for up to 3 days—I love to eat them cold, but you can also reheat them over medium heat on the stovetop in a skillet brushed with a light oil or ghee for a few minutes on each side.

1 LOAF AT 1KG ——— 9-INCH PULLMAN PAN ——— DOUGH TEMP: 75°F ——— LEVEL: INTERMEDIATE

WHOLE WHITE WHEAT BREAD

Whole white wheat is the best way to serve your friends or family
100% whole grain with a lighter color, mellower flavor, and less density than
breads made with 100% whole wheat flour milled from red wheat. This bread
has equal parts flour and water, which helps make a soft whole-grain loaf.

BAKER'S PERCENTAGES	WEIGHTS & INGREDIENTS
100%	450g whole white wheat flour
80%	360g water for the first mix
20%	90g desem starter
20%	90g water for the final mix
2%	9g salt

THE NIGHT BEFORE: DESEM STARTER REFRESH
Following the instructions on page 136, refresh your desem starter
6 to 8 hours before mixing the dough.

DAY OF: MIXING THROUGH BAKING
First mix In a large bowl, thoroughly mix together the whole white wheat
flour and the water for the first mix by hand until there are no patches
of dry flour. You can squeeze the dough through your hands, like extruding
pasta between your fingers! The dough will be sticky, gluey, and shaggy.

Pop a digital thermometer into the dough to take its temperature—it
should be between 72° and 78°F. (If the dough is above 78°F, stick
it in a cool spot—not the refrigerator—until it cools to between 75° and
78°F. If it is cooler than 72°F, place it in a warm location until it reaches
between 72° and 75°F.)

Autolyse Cover the bowl with a dinner plate or sheet pan for a lid and let
rest for 1 hour.

Final mix Sprinkle the salt over the dough. Next, add the desem and the
water for the final mix. Using your hands, start squeezing the salt, desem,
and water into the dough. The dough will become stringy and fall apart;
that's normal, just keep mixing until it re-forms into a cohesive mass. Cover
and set aside to rest for 30 minutes.

Fold Once the dough is relaxed, you will give it a series of three folds
spaced 1 hour apart. To fold, smear a little water onto your work surface.
Using a dough scraper, gather the dough together and, with a quick
motion, scoop the dough up with the dough scraper and flip it onto the
wet table. Using your hands, lift the dough off the table, then slap the
bottom half down, so that it sticks a little. Gently leaning back, stretch

Recipe continues

the dough and then quickly lean forward, tossing the dough still in your hands over the portion stuck to the table. Repeat three to four times. The dough will become smooth and pull itself into a ball.

Using the dough scraper, return the dough to its container, smooth-side up, and cover with the plate or sheet pan for 1 hour. Repeat the process two more times, with 1 hour between folding sessions.

Pre-shape Lightly dust your table with flour. Using a dough scraper, gather the dough together in the bowl and, with a quick motion, scoop the dough up with the dough scraper and flip it onto the table. Pat into a rectangle with a short side facing you. Fold the edge of the dough closest to you over to the top (the edge farthest from you), leaving a 1-inch lip. Take the sides of the dough, gently stretch each outward a few inches, then quickly cross them over each other so they are on top of each other, like swaddling a baby. Next, stretch the edge of the dough closest to you up to the top, flush with the top edge. Gently press down to create a seam.

Use your hands or a bench knife to gently drag the loaf on the table to create surface tension. You will see it tighten and become smooth as you drag. Make sure the top stays the top and the dough doesn't roll over as you go. The dough will curl into itself so the seam is now on the bottom and the top is smooth and roundish.

Bench rest Sprinkle the dough with flour, cover with a kitchen towel, and let rest 30 minutes.

Final shape Lightly oil a 9-inch Pullman pan. Lightly dust your table with flour. Use a bench knife to flip over the pre-shape so the top is now the bottom. Bring the bottom of the dough to meet the top edge, leaving a 1-inch lip at the top. Gently stretch the sides outward a few inches, then quickly cross them over the middle of the dough, like swaddling a baby. You're now looking at an envelope shape. Stretch the bottom of the dough up to meet the top of the envelope and seal. The dough will now be a cylinder on its side with a seam facing away from you. Roll the seam underneath and seal the left and right ends using the edge of your palm. With the bench knife, flip the dough seam-side down, into the pan.

Proof Cover the pan with a kitchen towel and proof in a draft-free spot at room temperature for 3 to 4 hours. When fully proofed, the loaf will appear to have doubled in size, feel full of air, and pass the poke test (see page 55).

Preheat the oven to 500°F.

Bake When the oven is up to temperature, gently spritz the top surface of the dough with water from a spray bottle before loading it into the oven. Bake at 500°F for 15 minutes. After 15 minutes, reduce the oven temperature to 475°F. Bake another 15 to 20 minutes, or until the loaf is deeply browned, pulls away from the sides of the pan, and reaches an internal temperature of 190°F. Remove the pan from the oven and immediately remove the loaf from the pan. Transfer to a wire rack to cool completely. Store for up to 5 days, cut-side down, in a paper bag tucked inside a cloth bag.

Refresh the desem starter 6 to 8 hours before
mixing, folding, shaping, proofing, and baking the bread.

1 LOAF AT 1KG ——— 9-INCH PULLMAN PAN ——— DOUGH TEMP: 75°F ——— LEVEL: INTERMEDIATE

SWEET POTATO AND BUCKWHEAT DESEM

My fondest memory of sweet potatoes comes from my farming days
in North Carolina. We'd get in a box of "slips" (sweet potato twigs with a leaf
on them), plant them, and then go back months later to unearth huge,
orange, flavorful potatoes! Paired with buckwheat flour to ground the natural
sweetness of the potato, this loaf is perfect for holiday tables.

BAKER'S PERCENTAGES	WEIGHTS & INGREDIENTS
70%	322g whole wheat flour
30%	138g bread flour
5%	23g buckwheat flour
70%	322g water
20%	92g desem starter
20%	92g sweet potato, about 1 medium
2%	9g salt

THE NIGHT BEFORE: DESEM STARTER REFRESH AND SWEET POTATO PREP
Following the instructions on page 136, refresh your desem starter
6 to 8 hours before mixing the dough.

Bake the sweet potato Preheat the oven to 400°F. Using the tines
of a fork, prick the potato several times and bake it directly on a rack for
45 minutes, or until it's tender to the poke of a fork. Remove from the oven
and cool slightly, then halve lengthwise and mash with a fork (I leave
the skin on for texture, but you can peel it off it you prefer). Transfer
to a 1-pint deli container (or similar container). Place the lid slightly ajar
and set aside until needed.

DAY OF: MIXING THROUGH BAKING
First mix In a large bowl, thoroughly mix together the whole wheat
flour, bread flour, buckwheat flour, and water by hand until there are
no patches of dry flour. You can squeeze the dough through your hands,
like extruding pasta between your fingers! The dough will be sticky,
gluey, and shaggy.

Pop a digital thermometer into the dough to take its temperature—it
should be between 72° and 78°F. (If the dough is above 78°F, stick
it in a cool spot—not the refrigerator—until it cools to between 75° and
78°F. If it is cooler than 72°F, place it in a warm location until it reaches
between 72° and 75°F.)

Autolyse Cover the bowl with a dinner plate or sheet pan for a lid and let
rest for 1 hour.

Recipe continues

Final mix Sprinkle the salt over the dough. Add the desem and the mashed sweet potato and mix the dough thoroughly by hand. The dough will become stringy and fall apart; that's normal, just keep mixing until it re-forms into a cohesive mass. Cover and set aside to rest for 30 minutes.

Fold Once the dough is relaxed, you will give it a series of three folds spaced 1 hour apart. To fold, smear a little water onto your work surface. Using a dough scraper, gather the dough together and, with a quick motion, scoop the dough up with the dough scraper and flip it onto the wet table. Using your hands, lift the dough off the table, then slap the bottom half down, so that it sticks a little. Gently leaning back, stretch the dough and then quickly lean forward, tossing the dough still in your hands over the portion stuck to the table. Repeat three to four times. The dough will become smooth and pull itself into a ball.

Using the dough scraper, return the dough to its container, smooth-side up, cover with the plate or sheet pan, and let rest for 1 hour. Repeat the process two more times, with 1 hour between folding sessions.

Pre-shape Lightly dust your table with flour. Using a dough scraper, gather the dough together in the bowl and, with a quick motion, scoop the dough up with the dough scraper and flip it onto the table. Pat into a rectangle with a short side facing you. Fold the edge of the dough closest to you over to the top (the edge farthest from you), leaving a 1-inch lip. Take the sides of the dough, gently stretch each outward a few inches, then quickly cross them over each other so they are on top of each other, like swaddling a baby. Next, stretch the edge of the dough closest to you up to the top, flush with the top edge. Gently press down to create a seam.

Use your hands or a bench knife to gently drag the loaf on the table to create surface tension. You will see it tighten and become smooth as you drag. Make sure the top stays the top and the dough doesn't roll over as you go. The dough will curl into itself so the seam is now on the bottom and the top is smooth and roundish.

Bench rest Sprinkle the dough with flour, cover with a kitchen towel, and let rest 30 minutes.

Final shape Lightly oil a 9-inch Pullman pan. Lightly dust your table with flour. Use a bench knife to flip over the pre-shape so the top is now the bottom. Bring the bottom of the dough to meet the top edge, leaving a 1-inch lip at the top. Gently stretch the sides outward a few inches, then quickly cross them over the middle of the dough, like swaddling a baby. You're now looking at an envelope shape. Stretch the bottom of the dough up to meet the top of the envelope and seal. The dough will now be a cylinder on its side with a seam facing away from you. Roll the seam underneath and seal the left and right ends using the edge of your palm. With the bench knife, flip the dough seam-side down, into the pan.

Proof Cover the pan with a kitchen towel and proof in a draft-free spot at room temperature for 3 to 4 hours. When fully proofed, the loaf will appear to have doubled in size, feel full of air, and pass the poke test (see page 55).

Preheat the oven to 500°F.

Bake When the oven is up to temperature, gently spritz the top surface of the dough with water from a spray bottle before loading it into the oven. Bake at 500°F for 15 minutes. After 15 minutes, reduce the oven temperature to 475°F and bake another 15 to 20 minutes, or until the loaf is deeply browned, pulls away from the sides of the pan, and reaches an internal temperature of 190°F. Carefully remove the bread from the pan and cool completely on a wire rack. Store for up to 5 days, cut-side down, in a paper bag tucked inside a cloth bag.

SNAPSHOT
Refresh the desem starter 6 to 8 hours before
mixing, folding, shaping, proofing, and baking the bread.

1 LOAF AT 1KG ——— 9-INCH PULLMAN PAN ——— DOUGH TEMP: 75°F ——— LEVEL: INTERMEDIATE

SPELT LOAF

Spelt is an ancient grain and the preferred grain of my favorite nun,
Hildegard von Bingen. In her 1855 work, *Physica*, she outlines food as powerful
medicine and cites spelt as the best grain for "strengthening the flesh
and purifying the blood." This loaf is dedicated to women around the world
who pull roots, talk to flowers, and defy tradition.

BAKER'S PERCENTAGES	WEIGHTS & INGREDIENTS
100%	508g whole-grain spelt flour
64%	325g water for the first mix
15%	81g water for the final mix
10%	51g desem starter
2%	10g salt

THE NIGHT BEFORE: DESEM STARTER REFRESH
Following the instructions on page 136, refresh your desem starter
6 to 8 hours before mixing the dough.

DAY OF: MIXING THROUGH BAKING
First mix In a large bowl, thoroughly mix together the spelt flour and the
water for the first mix by hand until there are no patches of dry flour. You
can squeeze the dough through your hands, like extruding pasta between
your fingers! The dough will be sticky, gluey, and shaggy.

Pop a digital thermometer into the dough to take its temperature—it should
be between 72° and 78°F. (If the dough is above 78°F, stick it in a cool spot—
not the refrigerator—until it cools to between 75° and 78°F. If it is cooler
than 72°F, place it in a warm location until it reaches between 72° and 75°F.)

Autolyse Cover the bowl with a dinner plate or sheet pan for a lid and let
rest for 1 hour.

Final mix Sprinkle the salt over the dough. Add the desem and the water
for the final mix. Using your hands, start squeezing the salt, desem, and
water into the dough. The dough will become stringy and fall apart; that's
normal, just keep mixing until it re-forms into a cohesive mass. Cover and
set aside to rest for 30 minutes.

Fold Once the dough is relaxed, you will give it a series of three folds
spaced 1 hour apart. To fold, smear a little water onto your work surface.
Using a dough scraper, gather the dough together and, with a quick
motion, scoop the dough up with the dough scraper and flip it onto the
wet table. Using your hands, lift the dough off the table, then slap the
bottom half down, so that it sticks a little. Gently leaning back, stretch

Recipe continues

the dough and then quickly lean forward, tossing the dough still in your hands over the portion stuck to the table. Repeat three to four times. The dough will become smooth and pull itself into a ball.

Using the dough scraper, return the dough to its container, smooth-side up, and cover with the plate or sheet pan for 1 hour. Repeat the process two more times, with 1 hour between folding sessions.

Pre-shape Lightly dust your table with flour. Using a dough scraper, gather the dough together in the bowl and, with a quick motion, scoop the dough up with the dough scraper and flip it onto the table. Pat into a rectangle with a short side facing you. Fold the edge of the dough closest to you over to the top (the edge farthest from you), leaving a 1-inch lip. Take the sides of the dough, gently stretch each outward a few inches, then quickly cross them over each other so they are on top of each other, like swaddling a baby. Next, stretch the edge of the dough closest to you up to the top, flush with the top edge. Gently press down to create a seam.

Use your hands or a bench knife to gently drag the loaf on the table to create surface tension. You will see it tighten and become smooth as you drag. Make sure the top stays the top and the dough doesn't roll over as you go. The dough will curl into itself so the seam is now on the bottom and the top is smooth and roundish.

Bench rest Sprinkle the dough with flour, cover with a kitchen towel, and rest 30 minutes.

Final shape Lightly oil a 9-inch Pullman pan. Dust your table with flour. Use a bench knife to flip over the pre-shape so the top is now the bottom. Bring the bottom of the dough to meet the top edge, leaving a 1-inch lip at the top. Gently stretch the sides outward a few inches, then quickly cross them over the middle of the dough, like swaddling a baby. You're now looking at an envelope shape. Stretch the bottom of the dough up to meet the top of the envelope and seal. The dough will now be a cylinder on its side with a seam facing away from you. Roll the seam underneath and seal the left and right ends using the edge of your palm. With the bench knife, flip the dough seam-side down, into the pan.

Proof Cover the pan with a kitchen towel and proof in a draft-free spot at room temperature for 2 to 3 hours. When fully proofed, the loaf will appear to have doubled in size, feel full of air, and pass the poke test (see page 55).

Preheat the oven to 500°F.

Bake When the oven is up to temperature, use a lame and razor to score a curvy stroke lengthwise across the top of the dough and gently spritz the top surface of the dough with water from a spray bottle before loading it into the oven. Bake at 500°F for 15 minutes. After 15 minutes, reduce the oven temperature to 475°F and bake another 15 to 20 minutes, or until the loaf is deeply browned, pulls away from the sides of the pan, and reaches an internal temperature of 190°F. Carefully remove the bread from the pan and cool completely on a wire rack. Store for up to 5 days, cut-side down, in a paper bag tucked inside a cloth bag.

SNAPSHOT
Refresh the desem starter 6 to 8 hours before
mixing, folding, shaping, proofing, and baking the bread.

1 LOAF AT 1KG ——— 9-INCH PULLMAN PAN ——— DOUGH TEMP: 75°F ——— LEVEL: INTERMEDIATE

100% EINKORN DESEM

Considered the original wheat from which all others are descended, *Einkorn*
in German means "single grain," referring to the one-seed-per-spikelet of this ancient
wheat. This dough is made with 100% einkorn flour, and it has a distinct fluidity and
taffy-like quality—yes, it's also incredibly sticky! Have patience during the folding
and watch for a slow proof; it's a gentle flour with not much gluten.

BAKER'S PERCENTAGES	WEIGHTS & INGREDIENTS
100%	508g whole-grain einkorn flour
75%	380g water for the first mix
10%	51g desem starter
10%	51g water for the final mix
2%	10g salt

THE NIGHT BEFORE: DESEM STARTER REFRESH
Following the instructions on page 136, refresh your desem starter
6 to 8 hours before mixing the dough.

DAY OF: MIXING THROUGH BAKING
First mix In a large bowl, thoroughly mix together the einkorn flour and
the water for the first mix by hand until there are no patches of dry flour.
You can squeeze the dough through your hands, like extruding pasta
between your fingers! The dough will be sticky, gluey, and shaggy.

Pop a digital thermometer into the dough to take its temperature—it should
be between 72° and 78°F. (If the dough is above 78°F, stick it in a cool spot—
not the refrigerator—until it cools to between 75° and 78°F. If it is cooler
than 72°F, place it in a warm location until it reaches between 72° and 75°F.)

Autolyse Cover the bowl with a dinner plate or sheet pan for a lid and let
rest for 1 hour.

Final mix Sprinkle the salt over the dough. Next, add the desem and the
water for the final mix. Using your hands, start squeezing the salt, desem,
and water into the dough. The dough will become stringy and fall apart;
that's normal, just keep mixing until it re-forms into a cohesive mass.
Cover and set aside to rest for 30 minutes.

Fold Once the dough is relaxed, you will give it a series of three folds
spaced 1 hour apart. To fold, smear a little water onto your work surface.
Using a dough scraper, gather the dough together and, with a quick
motion, scoop the dough up with the dough scraper and flip it onto the
wet table. Using your hands, lift the dough off the table, then slap the
bottom half down, so that it sticks a little. Gently leaning back, stretch

Recipe continues

the dough and then quickly lean forward, tossing the dough still in your hands over the portion stuck to the table. Repeat three to four times. The dough will become smooth and pull itself into a ball. (This dough is VERY sticky, so be patient and do your best.)

Using the dough scraper, return the dough to its container, smooth-side up, cover with the plate or sheet pan, and let rest for 1 hour. Repeat the process two more times, with 1 hour between folding sessions.

Pre-shape Lightly dust your table with flour. Using a dough scraper, gather the dough together in the bowl and, with a quick motion, scoop the dough up with the dough scraper and flip it onto the table. Pat into a rectangle with a short side facing you. Fold the edge of the dough closest to you over to the top (the edge farthest from you), leaving a 1-inch lip. Take the sides of the dough, gently stretch each outward a few inches, then quickly cross them over each other so they are on top of each other, like swaddling a baby. Next, stretch the edge of the dough closest to you up to the top, flush with the top edge. Gently press down to create a seam.

Use your hands or a bench knife to gently drag the loaf on the table to create surface tension. You will see it tighten and become smooth as you drag. Make sure the top stays the top and the dough doesn't roll over as you go. The dough will curl into itself so the seam is now on the bottom and the top is smooth and roundish.

Bench rest Sprinkle the dough with flour, cover with a kitchen towel, and let rest 30 minutes.

Final shape Lightly oil a 9-inch Pullman pan. Lightly dust your table with flour. Use a bench knife to flip over the pre-shape so the top is now the bottom. Bring the bottom of the dough to meet the top edge, leaving a 1-inch lip at the top. Gently stretch the sides outward a few inches, then quickly cross them over the middle of the dough, like swaddling a baby. You're now looking at an envelope shape. Stretch the bottom of the dough up to meet the top of the envelope and seal. The dough will now be a cylinder on its side with a seam facing away from you. Roll the seam underneath and seal the left and right ends using the edge of your palm. With the bench knife, flip the dough seam-side down, into the pan.

Proof Cover the pan with a kitchen towel and proof in a draft-free spot at room temperature for 2 to 3 hours. When fully proofed, the loaf will appear to have doubled in size, feel full of air, and pass the poke test (see page 55).

Preheat the oven to 500°F.

Bake When the oven is up to temperature, gently spritz the top surface of the dough with water from a spray bottle before loading it into the oven. (This bread has no score.) Bake at 500°F for 15 minutes. After 15 minutes, reduce the oven temperature to 475°F and bake another 15 to 20 minutes, or until the loaf is deeply browned, pulls away from the sides of the pan, and reaches an internal temperature of 190°F. Carefully remove the bread from the pan and cool completely on a wire rack. Store for up to 5 days, cut-side down, in a paper bag tucked inside a cloth bag.

Tip If the dough feels slack, increase the folds to every 30 minutes during bulk fermentation.

1 ROUND AT 1KG ——— 9-INCH ROUND BANNETON ——— DOUGH TEMP: 75°F ——— LEVEL: INTERMEDIATE

ANADAMA DESEM

Hailing from New England, anadama bread is said to originate from
an angry fisherman tossing his wife's inedible porridge into a bread and cursing
her: "Ana-damn-her." At any rate, it was my favorite loaf that we made
at the Morning Glory, a bakery I used to work at in Bar Harbor, Maine. In this
version I swap earthy sorghum in for the customary molasses.

BAKER'S PERCENTAGES	WEIGHTS & INGREDIENTS
SCALD	
200%	80g boiling water
100%	40g cornmeal
DOUGH	
70%	330g whole wheat flour
30%	142g bread flour
75%	354g water
25%	120g cornmeal scald
20%	95g desem starter
5%	24g sorghum syrup
2%	9g salt

Cornmeal for coating the loaf

THE NIGHT BEFORE: DESEM STARTER REFRESH AND SCALD
Following the instructions on page 136, refresh your desem starter the
night before or 6 to 8 hours before mixing the dough.

Make the scald Weigh out the cornmeal and transfer to a 1-pint deli
container (or similar heat-safe container) and pour the boiling water over
the top. Stir well with a spoon, cover (leaving the lid partially cracked),
and rest overnight or up to 8 hours.

DAY ONE: MIXING, FOLDING, AND CHILLING
Mix In a large bowl, thoroughly mix together the whole wheat flour,
bread flour, water, cornmeal scald, desem, sorghum syrup, and salt
by hand until there are no patches of dry flour. You can squeeze the
dough through your hands, like extruding pasta between your fingers!
The dough will be sticky, gluey, and shaggy.

Pop a digital thermometer into the dough to take its temperature—it
should be between 72° and 78°F. (If the dough is above 78°F, stick
it in a cool spot—not the refrigerator—until it cools to between 75° and
78°F. If it is cooler than 72°F, place it in a warm location until it reaches
between 72° and 75°F.) Cover the bowl with a dinner plate or sheet pan
for a lid and let rest for 1 hour.

Fold Once the dough is relaxed, you will give it a series of three folds
spaced 1 hour apart. To fold, smear a little water onto your work surface.
Using a dough scraper, gather the dough together and, with a quick
motion, scoop the dough up with the dough scraper and flip it onto the
wet table. Using your hands, lift the dough off the table, then slap the
bottom half down, so that it sticks a little. Gently leaning back, stretch

Recipe continues

the dough and then quickly lean forward, tossing the dough still in your hands over the portion stuck to the table. Repeat three to four times. The dough will become smooth and pull itself into a ball.

Using the dough scraper, return the dough to its container, smooth-side up, and cover with the plate or sheet pan for 1 hour. Repeat the process two more times, with 1 hour between folding sessions.

Chill After the final fold, transfer the dough back to the bowl, cover with the lid, and refrigerate for at least 8 hours or up to 24.

DAY TWO: SHAPING, PROOFING, AND BAKING
Pre-shape Lightly dust your table with flour. Remove the dough from the fridge (there's no need to let it warm up before shaping). Using a dough scraper, gather the dough together in the bowl and, with a quick motion, scoop the dough up with the dough scraper and flip it onto the table. Pat into a rectangle with a short side facing you. Fold the edge of the dough closest to you over to the top (the edge farthest from you), leaving a 1-inch lip. Take the sides of the dough, gently stretch each outward a few inches, then quickly cross them over each other so they are on top of each other, like swaddling a baby. Next, stretch the edge of the dough closest to you up to the top, flush with the top edge. Gently press down to create a seam.

Use your hands or a bench knife to gently drag the loaf on the table to create surface tension. You will see it tighten and become smooth as you drag. Make sure the top stays the top and the dough doesn't roll over as you go. The dough will curl into itself so the seam is now on the bottom and the top is smooth and roundish.

Bench rest Sprinkle the dough with flour, cover with a kitchen towel, and let rest 30 minutes.

Prepare the cornmeal While the dough is resting, ready the cornmeal that the dough will be rolled in by running a kitchen towel under water quickly (you want it damp, not soaking) and placing it over half of a sheet pan. Toss a heaping handful of cornmeal on the pan opposite the kitchen towel. Set aside.

Final shape Lightly dust your table with flour. Using a bench knife, flip over the relaxed round. Imagine the round into four quarters. Stretch the edge of each quarter to the center of the round, overlapping them slightly, by about 1 inch, to make a pouch shape. Now turn the "pouch" on its side, cupping the portion that was flush with the table in one hand, and cinch the gathered portions together with the edge of your palm, sealing the seam. Glide the dough down the table so that the seam is sealed between the edge of your hand and the table. Roll the dough over the damp towel and through the cornmeal and use a bench knife to transfer it to the round banneton, seam-side up.

Proof Loosely cover the banneton with a kitchen towel and proof in a draft-free spot at room temperature for 2 to 3 hours. When fully proofed, the loaf will appear to have doubled in size, feel full of air, and pass the poke test (see page 55).

Preheat the oven Set a combo cooker on a rack in the oven so the skillet is on the bottom and the pot is inverted as a lid. Preheat the oven (and the combo cooker) to 500°F.

Score Wearing welding gloves, remove the combo cooker from the oven (it's *hot!*) and quickly toss the dough seam-side down onto the hot skillet portion of the cooker. Use a lame and a razor, with the blade at a 35-degree angle, to score a pattern on top of the round.

Bake Immediately cover the bread with the inverted pot for a lid and load it back into the oven. Bake for 15 minutes. Remove the combo cooker from the oven and set on the stovetop. Remove the lid (be careful of hot steam) and reduce the oven temperature to 475°F. Return the bread, still on the skillet portion of the combo cooker, to the oven and bake another 15 to 20 minutes, or until the loaf is deeply browned, reaches an internal temperature of 190°F, and sounds hollow when tapped on the bottom. Carefully remove the bread from the skillet and cool completely on a wire rack. Store for up to 5 days, cut-side down, in a paper bag tucked inside a cloth bag.

Refresh the desem starter 6 to 8 hours before mixing and folding the dough.
The dough is then chilled overnight and shaped, proofed, and baked the following day.

1 ROUND AT 900G —— **9-INCH ROUND BANNETON** —— **DOUGH TEMP: 75°F** —— **LEVEL: INTERMEDIATE**

FENNEL, POPPY, AND YOGURT BREAD

The contrast between the golden-hued Kamut flour dough and the dark poppy
seeds make this a great loaf to score with a pattern or picture, like
the sun or the moon, since it will show up nicely after baking. The yogurt
adds a little tang and creaminess—YUM!

BAKER'S PERCENTAGES	WEIGHTS & INGREDIENTS
50%	215g bread flour
25%	108g whole wheat flour
25%	108g whole-grain Kamut flour
65%	279g water
20%	86g yogurt, plain, whole-milk
20%	86g desem starter
2%	9g fennel seeds
2%	9g salt

Poppy seeds for rolling the dough in

THE NIGHT BEFORE: DESEM STARTER REFRESH AND TOAST FENNEL SEEDS
Following the instructions on page 136, refresh your desem starter the
night before or 6 to 8 hours prior to mixing the dough.

Toast the fennel seeds In a small dry skillet, toast the fennel seeds until
fragrant, warmed, and golden, stirring constantly, 8 to 10 minutes. Once
toasted, transfer to a 1-pint deli container (or similar container), cool, and
cover with a lid. Set aside until needed.

DAY ONE: MIXING, FOLDING, AND CHILLING
First mix In a large bowl, thoroughly mix together the bread flour, whole
wheat flour, Kamut flour, and water by hand until there are no patches
of dry flour. You can squeeze the dough through your hands, like extruding
pasta between your fingers! The dough will be sticky, gluey, and shaggy.

Pop a digital thermometer into the dough to take its temperature—it should
be between 72° and 78°F. (If the dough is above 78°F, stick it in a cool
spot—not the refrigerator—until it cools to between 75° and 78°F.
If it is cooler than 72°F, place it in a warm location until it reaches between
72° and 75°F.)

Autolyse Cover the bowl with a dinner plate or sheet pan for a lid and let
rest for 1 hour.

Final mix Sprinkle the salt over the dough. Add the yogurt, desem starter,
and toasted fennel and mix the dough thoroughly by hand. The dough
will become stringy and fall apart; that's normal, just keep mixing until
it re-forms into a cohesive mass. Cover and set aside to rest for 30 minutes.

Recipe continues

Fold Once the dough is relaxed, you will give it a series of three folds spaced 1 hour apart. To fold, smear a little water onto your work surface. Using a dough scraper, gather the dough together and, with a quick motion, scoop the dough up with the dough scraper and flip it onto the wet table. Using your hands, lift the dough off the table, then slap the bottom half down, so that it sticks a little. Gently leaning back, stretch the dough and then quickly lean forward, tossing the dough still in your hands over the portion stuck to the table. Repeat three to four times. The dough will become smooth and pull itself into a ball.

Using the dough scraper, return the dough to its container, smooth-side up, cover with the plate or sheet pan, and let rest for 1 hour. Repeat the process two more times, with 1 hour between folding sessions.

Chill After the final fold, transfer the dough back to the bowl, cover with the lid, and refrigerate for at least 8 hours or up to 12.

DAY TWO: SHAPING, PROOFING, AND BAKING
Pre-shape Lightly dust your table with flour. Remove the dough from the fridge (there's no need to let it warm up before shaping). Using a dough scraper, gather the dough together in the bowl and, with a quick motion, scoop the dough up with the dough scraper and flip it onto the table. Pat into a rectangle with a short side facing you. Fold the edge of the dough closest to you over to the top (the edge farthest from you), leaving a 1-inch lip. Take the sides of the dough, gently stretch each outward a few inches, then quickly cross them over each other so they are on top of each other, like swaddling a baby. Next, stretch the edge of the dough closest to you up to the top, flush with the top edge. Gently press down to create a seam.

Use your hands or a bench knife to gently drag the loaf on the table to create surface tension. You will see it tighten and become smooth as you drag. Make sure the top stays the top and the dough doesn't roll over as you go. The dough will curl into itself so the seam is now on the bottom and the top is smooth and roundish.

Bench rest Sprinkle the dough with flour, cover with a kitchen towel, and let rest for 30 minutes.

Ready the poppy seeds While the dough is resting, run a kitchen towel under water quickly (you want it damp, not soaking) and place it over half of a sheet pan. Toss a heaping handful of poppy seeds on the pan opposite the kitchen towel. Set aside.

Final shape Lightly dust a cloth-lined 9-inch round banneton with flour and set aside. Using a bench knife, flip over the relaxed round. Bring the edges of the round to the middle, overlapping slightly by about 1 inch, to make a pouch shape. Now turn the "pouch" on its side, cupping the smooth side in your right hand, and pinch the gathered portions between the edge of your palm and the table, making a seam. Glide the dough down the table so that the seam is sealed between the edge of your hand and the table. Roll the dough over the damp towel and through the poppy seeds. Use a bench knife to transfer it seam-side up to the floured banneton.

Proof Loosely cover the banneton with a kitchen towel and proof in a draft-free spot at room temperature for 2 to 3 hours. When fully proofed, the loaf will appear to have doubled in size, feel full of air, and pass the poke test (see page 55).

Preheat the oven Set a combo cooker on a rack in the oven so the skillet is on the bottom and the pot is inverted as a lid. Preheat the oven (and the combo cooker) to 500°F.

Score Wearing welding gloves, remove the combo cooker from the oven (it's *hot!*) and quickly toss the dough seam-side down onto the hot skillet portion of the cooker. Use a lame and razor, with the blade at a 35-degree angle, to score a pattern on top of the bread.

Bake Immediately cover the bread with the inverted pot for a lid and load it back into the oven. Bake for 15 minutes. Remove the combo cooker from the oven and set on the stovetop. Remove the lid (be careful of hot steam) and reduce the oven temperature to 475°F. Return the bread to the oven and bake another 15 to 20 minutes, or until the loaf is deeply browned, reaches an internal temperature of 190°F, and sounds hollow when tapped on the bottom. Carefully remove the bread from the skillet and cool completely on a wire rack. Store for up to 5 days, cut-side down, in a paper bag tucked inside a cloth bag.

Refresh the desem starter 6 to 8 hours before mixing and folding the dough.
The dough is then chilled overnight and shaped, proofed, and baked the following day.

1 ROUND AT 900G —— **9-INCH ROUND BANNETON** —— **DOUGH TEMP: 75°F** —— **LEVEL: ADVANCED**

HAZELNUT AND HONEY DESEM

This bread incorporates roasted and chopped hazelnuts along with roasted hazelnut flour. A handsome loaf, file this one under sexy *and* sweet. Note that you'll need 100g of toasted hazelnuts: Half are used whole in the dough, and half are ground into flour. You may want to start with 120g to end up with the amount needed.

BAKER'S PERCENTAGES	WEIGHTS & INGREDIENTS
75%	297g sifted bread flour
25%	99g bread flour
75%	297g water
20%	79g desem
13%	50g hazelnuts, whole, skinless
13%	50g hazelnut flour
5%	20g honey
2%	8g salt

Sesame seeds for rolling the dough in

THE NIGHT BEFORE: DESEM REFRESH AND HAZELNUT PREP
Following the instructions on page 136, refresh your desem starter the night before or 6 to 8 hours before mixing the dough.

Toast the hazelnuts Preheat the oven to 400°F. Line a sheet pan with parchment, add all the hazelnuts, and bake until fragrant, lightly browned, and oily looking, 5 to 8 minutes. Remove from the oven and transfer to a plate to cool completely. Once cooled, weigh out 50g of the hazelnuts and transfer to a container, cover, and set aside.

Make the hazelnut flour Pulse the remaining hazelnuts in a coffee mill or Vitamix to make the hazelnut flour (don't overblend or you'll end up with hazelnut butter). Transfer to a container, cover, and set aside.

DAY ONE: MIXING, FOLDING, AND CHILLING
First mix In a large bowl, thoroughly mix together the sifted bread flour, bread flour, hazelnut flour, and water by hand until there are no dry patches. You can squeeze the sticky dough through your hands, like extruding pasta between your fingers!

Pop a digital thermometer into the dough to take its temperature—it should be between 72° and 78°F. (If the dough is above 78°F, stick it in a cool spot—not the refrigerator—until it cools to between 75° and 78°F. If it is cooler than 72°F, place it in a warm location until it reaches between 72° and 75°F.)

Autolyse Cover the bowl with a dinner plate or sheet pan and rest for 1 hour.

Final mix Sprinkle the salt over the dough. Add the desem, whole hazelnuts, and honey. Mix thoroughly by hand—the dough will become

Recipe continues

stringy and fall apart (that's normal)—just keep mixing until it re-forms into a cohesive mass. Cover and set aside for 30 minutes.

Fold Once the dough is relaxed, you will give it a series of three folds every hour. To fold, smear a little water onto your work surface. Using a dough scraper, gather the dough together and, with a quick motion, scoop the dough up with the dough scraper and flip it onto the wet table. Using your hands, lift the dough off the table, then slap the bottom half down so that it sticks a little. Gently leaning back, stretch the dough and then quickly lean forward, tossing the dough still in your hands over the portion stuck to the table. Repeat three to four times. The dough will become smooth and pull itself into a ball.

Using the dough scraper, return the dough to its container, smooth-side up, cover, and let rest for 1 hour. Repeat two more times, with 1 hour between folding sessions.

Chill After the final fold, transfer the dough back to the bowl, cover, and refrigerate for at least 8 hours or up to 12.

DAY TWO: SHAPING, PROOFING, AND BAKING
Pre-shape Lightly dust your table with flour. Remove the dough from the fridge (there's no need to let it warm up before shaping). Using a dough scraper, gather the dough together in the bowl and, with a quick motion, scoop the dough up with the dough scraper and flip it onto the table. Pat into a rectangle with a short side facing you. Fold the edge of the dough closest to you over to the top (the edge farthest from you), leaving a 1-inch lip. Take the sides of the dough, gently stretch each outward a few inches, then quickly cross them over each other so they are on top of each other, like swaddling a baby. Next, stretch the edge of the dough closest to you up to the top, flush with the top edge. Gently press down to create a seam and seal.

Use your hands or a bench knife to gently drag the loaf on the table to create surface tension. You will see it tighten and become smooth as you drag. Make sure the top stays the top and the dough doesn't roll over as you go. The dough will curl into itself, so the seam is now on the bottom and the top is smooth and roundish.

Bench rest Sprinkle the dough with flour, cover with a kitchen towel, and let rest for 30 minutes.

Ready the sesame seeds While the dough is resting, run a kitchen towel under water quickly (you want it damp, not soaking) and place it over half of a sheet pan. Toss a heaping handful of sesame seeds on the pan opposite the kitchen towel. Set aside.

Final shape Lightly dust a cloth-lined 9-inch round banneton with flour and set aside. Lightly dust your table with flour. Using a bench knife, flip over the relaxed round. Imagine the round divided into four quarters. Stretch the edge of each quarter to the center of the round, overlapping them slightly by about 1 inch, to make a pouch shape. Now turn the "pouch" on its side, cupping the portion that was flush with the table in one hand, and cinch the gathered portions together with the edge of your palm, sealing the seam. Glide the dough down the table so that the seam is sealed between the edge of your hand and the table. Transfer seam-side up to the floured banneton.

Proof Loosely cover the banneton with a kitchen towel and proof in a draft-free spot at room temperature for 2 to 3 hours. When fully proofed, the loaf will appear to have doubled in size, feel full of air, and pass the poke test (see page 55).

Preheat the oven Set a combo cooker on a rack in the oven so the skillet is on the bottom and the pot is inverted as a lid. Preheat the oven (and the combo cooker) to 500°F.

Score Wearing welding gloves, remove the combo cooker from the oven (it's hot!) and quickly toss the dough seam-side down onto the hot skillet. Use a lame and razor, with the blade at a 35-degree angle, to score a pattern, like an X or a square, on top of the bread.

Bake Immediately cover the bread with the inverted pot for a lid and load it back into the oven. Bake for 15 minutes. Remove the combo cooker from the oven and set on the stovetop. Remove the lid (be careful of hot steam) and reduce the oven temperature to 475°F. Return the bread, still on the skillet portion of the combo cooker, to the oven and bake for another 15 to 20 minutes, or until the loaf is deeply browned, reaches an internal temperature of 190°F, and sounds hollow when tapped on the bottom. Carefully remove the bread from the skillet and cool completely on a wire rack. Store for up to 5 days, cut-side down, in a paper bag tucked inside a cloth bag.

▲ Vollkornbrot (page 241)

Rye

I LOVE RYE for its earthy, mushroom-like, and malty flavor, but this wasn't always the case. Like a lot of people, growing up I knew rye only as a squishy, yeasted bread loaded with caraway and boasting a signature brown spiral in the middle. We brought it home from the supermarket on occasion, when my mom would make Reubens. For many years, the taste of caraway (with a hint of Thousand Island dressing) was synonymous in my mind with the taste of rye.

That is unfortunate, because rye has such a wide, lovely range of flavors—from sweet to spicy, and grassy to green—and its profile is much deeper and varied than wheat. Thinking about rye within such limited parameters (looking at you, marbled sandwich bread) is like comparing commercial white bread with an artisan loaf. Both are made with wheat, but they are so different from each other. Working with rye, more than any other grain, has helped me think outside the box and develop my (bready) intuition.

WHAT IS RYE?

RYE IS A CEREAL grain high in starch, commonly grown throughout northern and eastern Europe and across Scandinavia. In the United States, you'll find rye throughout the Northeast, Midwest, and Pacific Northwest. You'd be hard pressed to find it in the South (although it does exist!) and the Southwest, since it prefers a cooler climate and less sandy soil. Rye is used to create various flours, breads, beers, whiskeys, and specialty drinks like kvass, a lightly alcoholic drink made from fermenting stale rye bread. Like wheat berries, the rye berry itself can also be cooked and eaten whole or sprouted.

Rye has always lived in the shadow of its older sibling, wheat. Even its origin story defines it as a weed. When grain was domesticated throughout the Middle East, barley and einkorn dominated the cultivated fields, but the wild edges—and the rye that grew in them—crept in. Inevitably, a percentage of the following year's seed stock would contain this sneaky grass. This unintentional blend of grasses in a field, however, became a source of food security. When drought or cold weather struck and the wheat withered, the rye stood tall. Rye was eventually planted on purpose due to its adaptability and resiliency.

THE RYE BERRY— ANATOMY LESSON

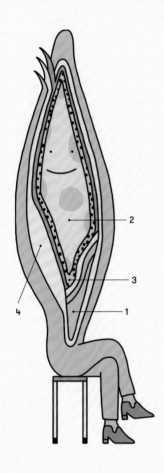

LIKE THE WHEAT BERRY, the rye berry is made up of three basic parts: the germ, the endosperm, and the bran.

GERM: The germ is by far the most nutritious part of the rye berry and makes up 2% of the overall weight. It's high in vitamin E and trace minerals, and with moisture and heat a taproot will burst from the germ and new life begins.

ENDOSPERM: The endosperm is the largest portion of the rye berry, approximately 85% (or more, depending on the variety) of the overall weight. The endosperm is a storehouse of starch and protein—and also where rye differs so greatly from wheat. Like wheat, rye has an aleurone layer (see below). In rye, this layer permeates the endosperm, going deeper into the core of the berry. The endosperm also lacks a balance of gliadin and glutenin, with only a high level of gliadin. These factors mean that flour made from the rye berry will be quite active (extra enzymes), quick to ferment (more sugar), and quite fragile (very little to no gluten).

ALEURONE LAYER: Transitioning between the bran and the endosperm is the aleurone layer, a sheath where enzymes and lactic acid bacteria live. The enzyme amylase works on unknitting simple sugars in the flour, while the lactic acid bacteria create the right levels of acidity for proper growth. Rye flour with bran included will show higher signs of activity in bread dough because it contains this extra dose of enzymes and microbes, ready to transform the flour.

BRAN: The bran is about 10% of the rye berry and is made of layers of cellulose and fiber. It protects the endosperm and absorbs water. Rye bran comes in a range of wonderful hues, from stormy purple to a fawn-colored brown, making rye flour often gray or even bluish.

ABOVE
(1) Germ, (2) endosperm, (3) aleurone layer, (4) bran

RYE FLOUR VARIETIES

THESE DISTINCTIONS IN THE rye berry translate to flour that performs and tastes quite different from flour made from wheat. Yet as with wheat, there are conventional varieties of rye grown for seed uniformity and high yields, and there are also bespoke varieties that artisan bakers love. The varieties I work with most frequently are Danko, Wrens Abruzzi, and Dylan. From a single variety, many kinds of flour can be made, depending on how the grain is milled. Here is what each milling style means.

LIGHT RYE FLOUR is flour made from the center of the endosperm. It is sifted so that the bulky bran is removed, helping the flour rise nicely when fermented. Light rye flour has a creamier, milder flavor than rye flour milled from the entire berry, and it creates a silky crumb when baked. Try the Finnish Rye Ring (page 220).

MEDIUM RYE FLOUR has a higher percentage of bran in the flour than light rye, but it is still a sifted flour, meaning the largest flecks have been removed. It's more flavorful and active than light rye, but it still rises easily when fermented properly. Try the Mountain Rye (page 214).

DARK RYE FLOUR is flour made from the outer layers of the endosperm with a portion of the bran included (what's left after making light rye flour). It contains the most pigment and tends to be coarse in texture, due to the bran. Dark rye flour has the most intense flavor and creates the densest crumb of all the rye flours. I love the dark rye flour in the Candied Ginger Rye (page 233).

100% WHOLE-GRAIN RYE FLOUR contains all the bran, endosperm, and germ of the rye berry and is packed with fiber and nutrients. Try the Buttermilk Orange Bread (page 228).

PUMPERNICKEL FLOUR is coarse and made from whole rye berries. Try the Pumpernickel (page 247).

RYE CHOPS (AKA CRACKED RYE) are chunky portions of the whole rye berry cut into rough pieces, like cracked wheat. Rye chops are often soaked to soften them or toasted to bring out a roasted sweetness. Try them in the Vollkornbrot (page 241).

OPPOSITE
Rye, Spelt, and Anise Loaf (page 218)

THE UNIQUENESS OF RYE DOUGH

ANYONE WHO'S EVER INNOCENTLY swapped rye flour for wheat flour in their favorite bread dough (raise your hand) knows that (wow) they are not the same! Due to the differences in the rye berry itself (more enzymes, more fiber, more sugar, little to no gluten), any bread dough made with more than 20% rye flour needs to ferment and bake in a different timeframe than dough for a wheat-based bread.

GLUTEN-POOR, PENTOSAN-RICH

In wheat breads, gliadin and glutenin knit together to form gluten. The gluten traps gas and, as these air pockets expand in the dough, it rises. When the dough is baked, it becomes light and chewy. Rye flour contains gliadin, but little glutenin, so it can't form gluten (making it great for those trying to avoid gluten!). In its place are pentosans, long chains of sugars that hold the dough together. Pentosans excel at attracting and holding water, but they take a long time to harden when baked and a long time to set, which is why many rye breads are baked for a long period before being "cured."

AMYLASE AND ACIDIFICATION OF RYE DOUGHS

Rye flour is naturally high in amylase, the enzyme responsible for breaking down starches into simple sugars. In wheat-based breads, the actions of amylase naturally sweeten the dough without damaging the structure. However, in rye breads, if there is too much amylase activity, the delicate chains of sugars holding the dough together crumble and the dough stays forever gummy, even after a long bake. This phenomenon is referred to as a starch attack. Starch attacks are most likely to occur when rye dough is held at a cool temperature for too long or when it is first loaded into the oven to bake (when the amylase is most active and before the starches have set).

The great news is that there is a natural way to counteract this in the dough: Use sourdough! Amylase is inactive in a low-pH environment, so if you acidify rye doughs by using sourdough and build the dough slowly in steps, you will increase the pH over time and make baking rye bread smooth sailing.

THE OVERALL PROCESS
OF MAKING RYE BREAD

ABOVE
I love rye bread thinly sliced and smeared with butter and sprinkled with salt.

ALTHOUGH MANY OF THE rye breads in this chapter can be mixed and baked within a single day, there will always be a few steps that need to be taken care of ahead of time, like sprouting rye berries, or refreshing your rye starter. The key stages of making rye bread are: mixing, fermenting, shaping, proofing, baking, and curing. Breads that have a combination of rye and wheat flours may need to be kneaded to develop the gluten in the wheat flour—if so, the recipe will specify. Consult the Methods for Bread Making chapter (starting on page 43) for refreshers on getting the correct water temperature for your dough, sprouting berries, and toasting seeds and nuts.

LEAVENS, SPONGES, AND MIXING FOR RYE BREADS

RYE DOUGH CAN BE mixed all at once or in several steps, or "builds" as bakers like to call them (you are building it out, increasing its size with each step). A leaven is made for any dough that requires a larger amount of leavening than the amount of starter you maintain. This is true for all breads—leavens make it possible to keep and maintain a small amount of starter and, from that, create a singular large bread (like the 1.4kg Rugbrod on page 243) or, in the case of a bakery, large batches of dough that will become many breads. The rye breads in this chapter may have a single leaven or two leaven builds with a final mix.

A sponge calls for the majority of the overall water in the recipe, and while it is also mixed before the final mix, it is larger and looser than a leaven. My favorite dough that requires a sponge is the one used to make the Rye, Spelt, and Anise Loaf on page 218. For doughs that have a leaven, several leavens, or a sponge, the mix is considered to begin when the first leaven or sponge is mixed. You can see how many mixes each recipe needs by checking out the Snapshot reference at the top of each recipe.

A FEW DAYS AHEAD OF MIXING RYE BREAD
STARTER MAINTENANCE
Regardless of whether the rye dough calls for a leaven or sponge, or simply just a portion of refreshed rye starter, if your rye starter is being kept in the fridge in between bakes, pull it out and give it a maintenance refreshment (see page 205) 2 days ahead of when you need to start mixing. The refreshment will balance out the acidity and make it easy to "wake up" later. For example: If I want to mix my rye bread dough Saturday morning, I will give my starter a maintenance refresh on Wednesday.

AFTERNOON PREPARATIONS FOR MIXING RYE BREAD
REFRESHING YOUR STARTER
If I am mixing a leaven, a leaven build one, or a sponge, I refresh my rye starter around lunchtime, or 6 to 8 hours before mixing the required pre-ferment. Check the Snapshot at the start of each recipe to see if you'll need to refresh your rye starter in the afternoon.

EVENING PREPARATIONS FOR MIXING RYE BREAD
REFRESHING YOUR STARTER
If my rye starter is going directly into the rye dough, I refresh the starter the night before, or 6 to 10 hours prior to mixing my bread dough. (After refreshing your starter, check to see if the recipe requires any fruit or seeds to be soaked, or any seeds or nuts to be toasted, and do so now.)

MIXING
MIXING A LEAVEN
The leaven is mixed by combining your healthy, active rye starter with a greater portion of flour and water. It's the leaven that goes into your bread, not the starter. The leaven will double in size, feel full of air when gently pressed, and smell like fresh apple cider when ready to use.

MIXING A LEAVEN BUILD ONE
The leaven build one is mixed the same way as a single leaven is, by combining your healthy active rye starter with a greater portion of water and flour, but it is followed the next day (or generally 6 to 8 hours later) by mixing a second leaven build. The leaven build one will double in size, feel full of air when gently pressed, and smell like fresh apple cider when ready to use.

MIXING A LEAVEN BUILD TWO
The leaven build two is made by mixing a greater portion of flour and water into the leaven build one, along with any other required ingredients. The leaven build two will double in size, feel full of air when gently pressed, and smell like fresh apple cider when ready to use.

MIXING A SPONGE

The sponge is made by mixing your healthy, active rye starter with a greater portion of flour and water. It's loose, like a batter, and it will double in size, have visible holes on the surface, and smell like fresh apple cider when it's ready to use.

FINAL MIX

This is when you add any remaining flour and water along with any other final ingredients. Add the required ingredients to the dough and thoroughly mix by hand until there are no dry patches of flour. In general, the dough is then shaped and proofed.

KNEADING

Doughs with both rye and wheat flours will benefit from some gentle strength building, but nothing like the intensive folding you perform on 100% wheat doughs. Kneading works best in this scenario. To knead a dough, lightly flour your work surface and turn out the dough onto the table using a dough scraper. Using the heel of your palm, gently push into the dough, stretching it away from you. It will be in a long swath now. Take the top portion, the part farthest away from you, and bring it back to the original starting point and, again, use the heel of your palm to push it away and then fold it back. Four or five good strokes and the dough should come together into a smoothish ball.

SHAPING

HOW TO PROPERLY PAN A RYE LOAF Use a dough scraper to scoop up the dough from the bowl or container and into a lightly oiled 9-inch Pullman pan. Next, dip your hand in water, shake off any excess, and use your palm to smooth and press down the top. Push the dough into each of the four corners evenly, using your fingers like a paddle (not individually). Make sure the dough has been pushed into each corner of the pan and that you have eliminated any air trapped on the sides between the pan and the dough. Avoid banging the pan, as you might degas the dough. Finally, dip a dough scraper in water and run it back and forth over the top of the loaf (like buttering bread) to create a smooth, level surface. Cover with the lid and proof as the recipe directs.

TO SHAPE A BÂTARD OR LOAF Gently pat the dough into a rectangle and roll it up like a jelly roll. Use a bench knife to transfer it seam-side up into a floured banneton, onto a 10-inch round of parchment, or into a 9-inch Pullman pan. In a pan, you may dust the top of your rye bread with a light flour, like a light rye or all-purpose flour, so the rise during proofing is highly visible—this also makes the final baked contrast between the dough and the flour striking. Don't use so much flour that you end up with a mouthful of burnt flour after it's baked!

TO SHAPE A ROUND. Lightly dust a cloth-lined 9-inch round banneton or cut a 10-inch round of parchment paper to proof the dough on—the recipe will specify which one to use. Lightly dust your table with flour. Turn out the rye dough with a bench scraper. Gently pat the dough into a loose round. Imagine the round into four quarters. Stretch the edge of each quarter to the center of the round, overlapping them slightly, by about 1 inch, to make a pouch shape. Now turn the "pouch" on its side, cupping the portion that was flush with the table in one hand, and cinch the gathered portions together with the edge of your palm, sealing the seam. It can also be quite easy to simply knead the dough into a round if that works for you. Use a bench knife to transfer it seam-side up into the floured banneton or seam-side down onto the parchment round.

PROOFING

PROOF Rye breads should be proofed in a warm environment whenever possible to get the best rise; they like slightly humid and warm conditions. Keeping the shaped breads at a steady 80°F while rising will make wonderful bread but can be a challenge. See my instructions for a Homemade Proof Box on page 56. When I had my bakery, I proofed my rye bread on a sheet pan at the top of a speed rack, covered with a plastic jacket, and with a space heater set on a sheet pan on the bottom rack. Shaped rye breads are proofed anywhere from as little as 30 minutes and up to 3 hours.

PINHOLES ON THE SURFACE Rye bread doesn't have an elastic skin to bounce back, so there's no poke test for proofing, but you should still touch the dough while proofing, pressing gently on the surface to feel for air building in the dough. Because rye flour is fragile, rather than showing visible surface bubbles, it may be covered in tiny dimples or holes once fully proofed.

CRACKING A cracked surface is another way to tell if rye dough is well proofed, and it's one of my favorite bread aesthetics. As the loaf swells with air, the weak surface develops fault lines and eventually splits in organic and fascinating ways. Don't assume the loaf is done proofing at the first sight of a crack. The cracking

will happen in stages: early cracking, mid-level cracking, and cracked so much it's oozing—the goal is the mid-level cracking stage. If you can see the structure of the dough between the cracks, you've gone too far. Don't stress if this happens—just go ahead and bake the loaf, then slice it very thinly for fun, extra-long crouton-like toasts!

SCORING (MAYBE)

Not all rye breads are scored; many are simply baked and allowed to crack (see above) into an interesting pattern. Some breads, like the Buttermilk Orange Bead on page 228, are scored—with a lame and razor— and hearty, large rye breads baked in pans, like the Pumpernickel on page 247, are scored with the end of a metal bench knife.

HOW TO SCORE RYE BREAD Dust the top of the loaf with a little flour. Start at one end of the pan and make indents (a scant ½ inch) with the long edge of the bench knife into the dough. You can make X's, diagonal lines, diamonds, or whatever else you can think of. While the scoring serves the same purpose as it does with the wheat loaf—directing the energy from the steam escaping—the dough won't develop the "ears" that a wheat loaf would.

BAKING

BAKING IN A COMBO COOKER FROM A DOUGH PROOFING IN A BANNETON Set a combo cooker on a rack in the oven so the skillet is on the bottom and the pot is inverted as a lid. Preheat both (the oven and the combo cooker) to 500°F. Wearing welding gloves, carefully remove the hot combo cooker from the oven and take off the lid. Turn out the dough from the banneton onto the hot skillet portion. Cover, using the inverted pot as a lid. Transfer to the oven and bake for 10 minutes at 500°F. Remove the combo cooker from the oven and set on the stovetop. Remove the lid (be careful of hot steam) and reduce the oven temperature to 450°F. Return the bread to the oven, just on the skillet, and bake for another 30 to 35 minutes, or until the loaf is deeply browned and reaches an internal temperature of 205°F.

BAKING IN A COMBO COOKER FROM A DOUGH PROOFING ON PARCHMENT Set a combo cooker on a rack in the oven so the skillet is on the bottom and the pot is inverted as a lid. Preheat both (the oven and the combo cooker) to 500°F. Wearing welding gloves, carefully remove the hot combo cooker from the oven and remove the lid. Still wearing the welding gloves, carefully pick up the parchment on either side of the bread round, lift it up, and gently lower it (still on the parchment) onto the skillet portion of the combo cooker. Cover, using the inverted pot as a lid. Transfer to the oven and bake for 10 minutes at 500°F. Remove the combo cooker from the oven and set on the stovetop. Remove the lid (be careful of hot steam) and reduce the oven temperature to 450°F. Return the bread to the oven, just on the skillet, and bake for another 30 to 35 minutes, or until the loaf is deeply browned and reaches an internal temperature of 205°F.

BAKING IN A PULLMAN PAN Preheat the oven to 500°F. Uncover the loaf and dust the top with flour, then gently press the metal edge of the bench knife into the top of the dough about a centimeter (a scant ½ inch) to score. Lightly spray the top of the lid with a light cooking oil and re-cover the dough with the lid. Transfer to the oven and bake for 10 minutes. Wearing welding gloves, carefully remove the Pullman pan lid and reduce the oven temperature to 450°F. Bake another 35 to 40 minutes, or until the loaf is deeply browned, pulls away from the sides of the pan, and reaches an internal temperature of 205°F.

CURING
The timeframe for a rye bread to properly cool and set can go well into the next day, thanks to the high volume of pentosans (see page 197). This period of cooling time is referred to as curing. To cure your rye breads, wrap them, completely covered, in plastic wrap, a recycled shopping bag, or tightly in a kitchen towel (not the terry cloth kind—linen and soft canvas work well here) and rest on a wire rack for the time indicated in the recipe (generally, anywhere from 5 to 25 hours). While a kitchen towel is nice, using plastic will trap the moisture being released by the loaf as it cools, softening the intense crust that can result from a lengthy bake. I use the same recycled bag over and over. You decide what works best for you.

SLICING
After the loaf is fully cooled (and cured, if it needs to be), rye bread should be sliced on the thin side (no Texas toast here) using a sharp bread knife. If you enjoy hearty rye breads baked in Pullman pans, like the Vollkornbrot (page 241), you can invest in a vintage rye cutter (I like the Danish Raadvad brand) that has a wooden cradle for the loaf to rest in, while a guillotine-like blade cuts paper-thin slices off the end (see page 249).

STORING
Store your rye bread in a paper bag, cut-side down, inside a cloth bag.

FREEZING RYE BREAD Rye bread freezes exceptionally well: If you're not going to eat the whole loaf right away, or you've made a hearty loaf like the Rugbrod (page 243) and you want to store half of it, slice the bread and toss the slices in a 1-gallon, zip-top plastic bag. Carefully press all the air out of the bag, double-bag it in another 1-gallon bag, and store in the freezer for up to 3 months. To revive all of it, simply take out and thaw on your countertop, letting the moisture from inside the bag rehydrate the loaf. To revive a piece at a time, take a slice out as you need it and toast (preferably in a hot cast-iron skillet with butter).

HOW TO START A 100% RYE STARTER

FOR A 100% RYE starter, use whole-grain rye flour. If you have a tabletop mill, mill your own flour for this starter. Yet like the desem starter (see page 136), if all that is available to you is supermarket rye flour, this will still work and be completely worth the effort!

DAY ONE

In a glass, ceramic, or food-grade plastic container that is large enough to hold your starter as it expands (it will double in size—I like to use a 1-quart deli container), combine 100g whole-grain rye flour with 90g of warm water. Mix until incorporated, making sure there are no patches of dry flour left. Cover tightly with the lid and rest at room temperature (68° to 72°F) for 24 hours.

DAY TWO (REFRESHMENT)

Today you will begin refreshing your starter, which involves removing most of the starter and "feeding" the remaining portion with rye flour and water. Discard all but 50g of the rye starter. To that 50g, add 100g rye flour and 90g water. Cover and let rest at room temp (68° to 72°F) for 24 hours.

DAYS THREE THROUGH SEVEN

Repeat the refreshment as directed on Day Two daily from Day Three to Day Seven. Is the starter rising predictably, within the same timeframe each day? Does it have a fragrant, peppery, grassy aroma? Do you see plenty of aeration when you check the sides of the container? When you press into the starter, do you feel air? These are all good things! If you said yes, then you have a healthy starter. If you said no, then remain diligent with your refreshments. If you see no rise and no domed surface and your starter hasn't doubled in size by the end of Day Seven, start over. (Sorry!)

DAY EIGHT

Congratulations! Now you should have a healthy, active rye starter! By Day Eight your rye starter should double in size between 6 and 8 hours after being refreshed, have a fresh fruit (apple) smell, and have a domed top when fully risen. Repeat the refreshment procedure outlined on Day Two and use the discard to bake Everyday Rye (page 208). The rye starter will now be strong enough to undergo storage in the fridge.

IF YOU PLAN ON BAKING DAILY OR EVERY OTHER DAY: Leave the rye starter on the countertop and continue daily refreshments as instructed on Day Two.

IF YOU PLAN ON BAKING A LOAF BETWEEN ONCE A WEEK AND ONCE A MONTH: Prepare your rye starter for cold storage in the fridge. See Preparing for Cold Storage (page 204).

IF YOU PLAN ON BAKING ONLY A FEW TIMES A YEAR: Dehydrate the rye starter so you can have some at the ready whenever you'd like to revitalize the dried flakes. See Long-Term Storage (page 205).

TAKING CARE OF YOUR RYE STARTER

ABOVE

Left: A healthy active rye starter

Right: The "hooch"

PREPARING FOR COLD STORAGE

If you're not baking rye bread every day, it's best to store your rye starter in the refrigerator where the yeast and bacteria can safely hibernate. To ready the starter, you'll stiffen it by reducing the amount of water. This slows down fermentation, curbing the production of alcohol and acid in the starter, keeping a balanced, fresh flavor.

To prepare your rye starter for a fridge rest, add 50g of your starter to a clean container (such as a 1-quart deli container) and mix in 100g whole-grain rye flour and 75g of warm water. Stir gently until there are no patches of dry flour. Cover tightly with a lid and leave out at room temp (68° to 72°F) for 3 hours, then transfer to the fridge.

While living in the fridge, your rye starter may separate or develop a layer of colored alcohol on the top, known as hooch. This does not mean that your rye starter is dead. The water and alcohol simply weigh less than the starter so they rise to the top (you'll pour this off before you revive it—see Waking Up Your Starter from Cold Storage, below). If you're not working with your starter daily, then you might want to set a weekly calendar reminder so you don't forget to feed your starter. If you forget, miss a week, or go on vacation, don't stress! A rye starter can go dormant in the fridge for up to 1 month; when you're ready, simply take it out and refresh as described on page 203.

MAINTAINING IN COLD STORAGE

To keep the yeast and bacteria happy under refrigeration, balance the flavors, and make the starter easy to revive, refresh your starter once a week, even if you're not planning on baking.

TO MAINTENANCE REFRESH Remove the rye starter from the fridge and discard all but 50g. To that 50g, add 100g whole-grain rye flour and 75g of warm water. Stir gently until there are no patches of dry flour, then cover and leave out at room temp (68° to 72°F) for 3 hours before transferring back to the fridge.

WAKING UP YOUR STARTER FROM COLD STORAGE

When you're getting ready to bake again, you'll need to pull your rye starter from the fridge and bring it back up to speed. If you have neglected maintenance feedings for a month, this process will take longer, and you may even consider just making another starter.

TO REVIVE YOUR RYE STARTER FROM COLD STORAGE Discard everything but 50g of the starter and feed it 100g whole-grain rye flour and 90g of 80°F water. Cover tightly with a lid and ferment at room temp (68° to 72°F) for 24 hours. If it's not rising, you can't see any aeration on the sides, and it smells like vinegar, repeat two more times, 12 hours apart for a total of three refreshments.

LONG-TERM STORAGE

If you aren't planning on baking for quite some time, you can easily dehydrate your starter. The dry flakes can be stored in the freezer for up to 2 months and are a great way to share with friends or family or for traveling.

Line a sheet pan with a silicone baking mat or parchment paper. You'll want a flexible spatula or dough scraper on hand. Mix warm water into the rye starter, 1 tablespoon at a time, to create a slurry. You don't want it too thick or too thin, but spreadable, like a thin pancake batter. Once it's ready, use the spatula or dough scraper to smear it across the mat or parchment.

Place the sheet pan in an oven with just the oven light on and let it dehydrate for 24 hours. If the starter gets above 100°F, the yeast and bacteria may die off, so check the temperature periodically with either a simple oven thermometer or a handheld infrared thermometer. After 24 hours the starter should be gray-chalky colored, thin, and brittle. Break it apart and transfer to the container(s) of your choice (like small resealable bags). Label and date the container(s) and store in the freezer. The starter can be frozen for up to 2 months.

TO REVIVE FROM DEHYDRATED RYE STARTER FLAKES Combine 40g of the dehydrated starter flakes with 100g whole-grain rye flour and 90g of 80°F water. Mix until incorporated, making sure there's no dry flour left. Cover tightly with a lid and ferment at room temp (68° to 72°F) for 24 hours.

Repeat up to three times, or until the starter doubles in size, you can see air pockets from the sides, the top has visible holes, and it smells fresh, fruity, and grassy.

BEFORE YOU BAKE: USING YOUR RYE STARTER

Refresh your rye starter 6 to 8 hours before making a leaven or sponge.

FOR ALL THE FORMULAS in this chapter, refresh your rye starter between 6 and 8 hours before you want to mix the dough or make the leaven or sponge. Keep in mind that warm environments (70° to 80°F) will shorten the time it takes for the starter to become active, and cooler environments (60° to 68°F) will extend the time it takes for the rye starter to become active.

After you've pulled what you need for the leaven, sponge, or bread dough (look at the formula for each recipe to see how much you need), refresh and cover the starter with a lid. If you're planning on baking again the next day, leave it out at room temperature (you'll be refreshing it in the evening again). If you're not, stick it in the refrigerator.

OPPOSITE
Everyday Rye (page 208)

Refresh the rye starter 6 to 8 hours before mixing the leaven. The leaven is then fermented overnight.
The following morning the dough is mixed, shaped, proofed, and baked before being cured for 5 hours.

1 ROUND AT 1.2KG ——— **A ROUND OF PARCHMENT** ——— **DOUGH TEMP: 82°F** ——— **LEVEL: BEGINNER**

EVERYDAY RYE

Rye flour doesn't possess the elasticity that wheat flour does, so when
gas builds up in the dough, rather than trapping a bubble under the surface,
the dough cracks—this is totally okay! Don't bake the loaf at the very
first sign of a fracture; instead, let it crack over the entire surface, but not
so much so that the interior of the bread is revealed.

BAKER'S PERCENTAGES	WEIGHTS & INGREDIENTS
LEAVEN	
100%	131g whole-grain rye flour
75%	98g water
10%	13g rye starter
FINAL DOUGH	
100%	540g light rye flour
75%	406g water
45%	243g leaven
2%	11g salt

THE AFTERNOON BEFORE: RYE STARTER REFRESH
Following the instructions on page 203, refresh your rye starter in the
afternoon, or 6 to 8 hours before mixing your leaven.

THE NIGHT BEFORE: MIX THE LEAVEN
In a 1-quart deli container (or similar container), mix together the rye
starter, whole-grain rye flour, and room temperature water. Cover with
a lid and let rest overnight or up to 10 hours.

DAY OF: MIXING THROUGH BAKING
Mix In a large bowl, thoroughly mix together the light rye flour, water,
leaven, and salt by hand until there are no patches of dry flour. You can
squeeze the dough through your hands, like extruding pasta between
your fingers! The dough will feel like wet cement and be viscous and
sticky—this is normal.

Pop a digital thermometer into the dough to take its temperature—it
should be between 79° and 85°F. (If the dough is above 85°F, stick
it in a cool spot to proof—not the refrigerator—until it cools to between
82° and 85°F. If it is less than 79°F, place it in a warm location to proof
until it reaches 79° to 82°F.)

Shape Cut out a 10-inch round of parchment paper. Set aside. Lightly
flour your work surface and use a dough scraper to turn the dough out
onto the table. Gently knead the dough into a uniform mass and then
knead it into a round with a smooth top and a seam on the bottom, about
10 inches in diameter. Use a bench knife to transfer the round, smooth-
side up, onto the parchment.

Proof Loosely cover the dough with a kitchen towel and proof in a draft-
free spot for 1 to 2 hours, or until it almost doubles in size, feels full of air,
and cracks on the surface.

Preheat the oven Set a combo cooker on a rack in the oven so the skillet is on the bottom and the pot is inverted as a lid. Preheat the oven (and the combo cooker) to 500°F.

Bake Wearing welding gloves, carefully remove the hot combo cooker from the oven and remove the lid. Still wearing the welding gloves, carefully pick up the parchment on either side of the round, lift it up, and gently lower it (still on the parchment) into the skillet portion of the combo cooker. Re-cover with the inverted pot as a lid. Transfer to the oven and bake for 10 minutes at 500°F. Remove the combo cooker from the oven and set on the stovetop. Remove the lid (be careful of hot steam) and reduce the oven temperature to 450°F. Return the bread, still on the skillet portion of the combo cooker, to the oven and bake for another 30 to 40 minutes, or until the loaf is deeply browned and reaches an internal temperature of 205°F.

Cure Remove the loaf from the pan and immediately wrap in a kitchen towel. Let it rest for 5 hours before cutting. Store for up to 5 days, cut-side down, in a paper bag tucked inside a cloth bag.

Refresh the rye starter 6 to 8 hours before mixing the dough. The dough
is then mixed, divided, and packed into 1-pint cardboard cartons, then baked for 8 hours.

2 (406G) LOAVES ——— 1-PINT CARTONS ——— DOUGH TEMP: NONE ——— LEVEL: BEGINNER

MILK CARTON RYE

My dear friend Melissa Martin takes a break from her New Orleans restaurant
Mosquito Supper Club when the weather is too hot to cook. Last year she went to
Iceland and made rye bread in a milk carton, generously sharing the recipe with me.

BAKER'S PERCENTAGES	WEIGHTS & INGREDIENTS
86%	370g dark rye flour
14%	50g whole wheat flour
48%	200g whole milk, at room temp
24%	100g cane syrup
20%	84g rye starter
2%	8g salt
0.9%	4g baking soda

THE NIGHT BEFORE: RYE STARTER REFRESH
Following the instructions on page 203, refresh your rye starter the night before, or 6 to 8 hours before mixing the dough.

DAY OF: MIXING THROUGH BAKING
Preheat the oven to 210°F.

Mix In a large bowl, thoroughly mix together the dark rye flour, whole wheat flour, milk, cane syrup, rye starter, salt, and baking soda by hand until there are no patches of dry flour. You can squeeze the dough through your hands, like extruding pasta between your fingers! The dough will feel like wet cement and be viscous and sticky—this is okay.

Divide and "pan" Using a flexible spatula or dough scraper, divide the dough into 2 equal portions (you can eyeball it). Transfer each portion into its own clean 1-pint milk carton, with the top portion cut off so you're left with a rectangular box that is open at the top. Dip your fingers in water and gently push the dough into the corners of the carton. Cover the open end with a foil tent. Transfer both cartons to the oven and set directly on the middle rack.

Bake at 210°F for 8 hours. Wearing welding gloves, remove the cartons from the oven and set them on a wire rack.

Cure Let the loaves sit, still in the cartons, for 8 to 10 hours, then remove the foil and peel off the carton. (Since the loaves are small, and you'll likely go through them quickly, you can open just one and keep the other in the carton until you're ready for it.) Slice thin and enjoy with a large smear of cultured butter and a glass of milk. Store unwrapped bread for up to 5 days, cut-side down, in a paper bag tucked inside a cloth bag.

SNAPSHOT
Refresh the rye starter 6 to 8 hours before mixing the
dough. The dough is then mixed, shaped, rolled out, and baked.

4 ROUND CRISPS AT 80G EACH ———————— **DOUGH TEMP: 82°F** ———————— **LEVEL: BEGINNER**

KNACKEBROD

Every Scandinavian country has its own version of this crisp (a thin,
crunchy, cracker-like "bread"); this one is from Sweden. Traditionally these crisps
would be made in large batches twice a year, shaped into rings and hung on a pole
over the hearth. They are my go-to cracker for picnics and dinner parties!

BAKER'S PERCENTAGES	WEIGHTS & INGREDIENTS
100%	162g dark rye flour
48%	78g water
20%	39g rye starter
15%	24g butter, unsalted, at room temp
10%	16g honey
2%	3g caraway seeds, ground
2%	3g salt

THE NIGHT BEFORE: RYE STARTER REFRESH
Following the instructions on page 203, refresh your rye starter the night
before, or 6 to 8 hours before mixing your dough.

DAY OF: MIXING THROUGH BAKING
Mix In a large bowl, thoroughly mix together the dark rye flour, water, rye
starter, butter, honey, caraway, and salt by hand until there are
no patches of dry flour. You can literally squeeze the dough through your
hands, like extruding pasta between your fingers! The dough will feel like
wet cement and be viscous and sticky—this is okay.

Preheat the oven Insert a pizza stone (square or round is fine, at least
10 inches wide) and preheat the oven to 450°F. While you're waiting for
the oven to preheat, divide and roll out the dough.

Divide Using a bench knife, divide the dough into 80g chunks. Place
a portion on the scale and take away from it or add to it (while it's still
on the scale) to reach 80g. The fewer bits of dough you have to add
or remove, the better, so use the first portion of dough to gauge the rest.
Repeat with the remaining portions of dough. (You can also just eyeball
4 pieces of dough, if that's easier for you.)

Pre-shape With your hand in a C shape, cuddle a portion of dough
in your palm, allow a little to stick to the table, and swirl your hand
in a counterclockwise motion, coaxing the dough into a small, smooth
round. Repeat with the remaining 3 portions of dough. Transfer the
rounds, using the dough scraper, to a clean portion of your work space,
dust away any excess flour with a pastry brush, and cover them with
a damp (not wet) kitchen towel.

ABOVE
Knackebrod

Final shape Lightly dust your work surface with flour and, using a rolling pin, roll out a portion of dough into a 7-inch round about ⅛ inch thick. Roll over each round with a decorative rolling pin or prick with a fork in an interesting pattern. Punch a 1-inch hole in the middle with a cookie cutter or shot glass if you wish to do so. Repeat with the remaining 3 portions of dough.

Bake Slide a well-floured peel or floured inverted sheet pan beneath a round and transfer to the hot stone, using a quick jerk to slide the dough from the peel or pan to the stone. Bake 3 to 4 minutes, or until it has tiny bubbles all over the surface and turns deep brown around the edges. Wearing welding gloves and using grill tongs, flip over the crisp and bake another 1 to 2 minutes, until deeply browned. Wearing welding gloves, use the grill tongs to remove the crisp from the stone and transfer to a wire rack to cool. Bake the remaining crisps, letting the pizza stone reheat for a minute or two between crisps. These are best eaten within 24 hours. Do not store in a plastic bag; they will soften too much. Instead, wrap leftovers in a tea towel or parchment paper.

Refresh the rye starter 6 to 8 hours before mixing the leaven. The leaven
is mixed up to 10 hours before mixing the dough. The following morning, the dough
is mixed, kneaded, shaped, proofed, baked, and cured for 5 hours.

1 ROUND AT 1.2KG ——— 9-INCH ROUND BANNETON ——— DOUGH TEMP: 82°F ——— LEVEL: INTERMEDIATE

MOUNTAIN RYE

Abruzzi rye has a citrusy, spicy, subtly sweet profile.

BAKER'S PERCENTAGES	WEIGHTS & INGREDIENTS
LEAVEN	
100%	72g whole rye flour
100%	72g water
10%	8g rye starter
SCALD	
200%	102g boiling water
100%	50g dark rye flour
FINAL DOUGH	
40%	202g Wrens Abruzzi rye flour
30%	152g whole wheat flour
30%	151g bread flour
75%	380g water
30%	152g leaven
30%	152g scald
2%	10g salt

THE AFTERNOON BEFORE: RYE STARTER REFRESH
Following the instructions on page 203, refresh your rye starter in the afternoon, or 6 to 8 hours before mixing the leaven.

THE NIGHT BEFORE: MIX THE LEAVEN AND PREPARE THE SCALD
Mix the leaven In a 1-quart deli container (or similar container), mix the rye starter with the whole rye flour and room temperature water. Cover with a lid and let rest overnight, or 8 to 10 hours.

Make the scald In a 1-pint deli container (or similar container), combine the dark rye flour and boiling water and mix thoroughly until there is no dry flour. Cover with a lid, slightly ajar, and let rest overnight or up to 10 hours.

DAY OF: MIXING THROUGH BAKING
Final mix In a large bowl, thoroughly mix together the rye flour, whole wheat flour, bread flour, water, leaven, scald, and salt by hand until there are no patches of dry flour. You can squeeze the dough through your hands, like extruding pasta between your fingers! The dough will feel like wet cement and be viscous and sticky—this is okay.

Pop a digital thermometer into the dough to take its temperature—it should be between 79° and 85°F. (If the dough is above 85°F, stick it in a cool spot—not the refrigerator—until it cools to between 82° and 85°F. If it is less than 79°F, place it in a warm location until it reaches 79° to 82°F.) Cover the bowl with a dinner plate or sheet pan for a lid and set aside for 1 hour.

Knead Lightly flour your work surface and use a dough scraper to turn out the dough onto the table. Gently knead for a minute or two to develop a little of the gluten from the whole wheat and bread flours—the dough will become smooth and form into a ball as you go. Use the dough scraper to lift and return the dough to the bowl, smooth side up. Cover and let rest for 1 hour.

Recipe continues

Shape Lightly flour a cloth-lined 9-inch round banneton and set aside. Dust your work surface with flour. Use the dough scraper to turn the dough out onto the table, touching the tacky dough as little as possible. Knead the dough into a uniform mass and then knead it into a round with a smooth top and a seam on the bottom. Use a dough scraper or bench knife to help lift the shaped round and transfer it seam-side up to the floured banneton.

Proof Loosely cover the banneton with a kitchen towel and proof in a draft-free spot at room temperature for 1 to 3 hours. When fully proofed, the loaf will appear to have doubled in size and feel full of air.

Preheat the oven Set a combo cooker on a rack in the oven so the skillet is on the bottom and the pot is inverted as a lid. Preheat the oven (and the combo cooker) to 500°F.

Bake Wearing welding gloves, carefully remove the hot combo cooker from the oven and remove the lid. Turn out the dough onto the hot skillet (this bread has no score) and cover with the inverted pot. Transfer to the oven and bake for 10 minutes at 500°F. Remove the combo cooker from the oven and set on the stovetop. Remove the lid (be careful of hot steam) and reduce the oven temperature to 450°F. Return the bread, still on the skillet portion of the combo cooker, to the oven and bake for another 30 minutes, or until the loaf is deeply browned and reaches an internal temperature of 205°F.

Cure Remove the loaf from the skillet and immediately wrap in a kitchen towel. Cure for 5 hours before cutting. Store for up to 5 days, cut-side down, in a paper bag tucked inside a cloth bag.

1 ROUND AT 1.2KG ——— **9-INCH ROUND BANNETON** ——— **DOUGH TEMP: 82°F** ——— **LEVEL: INTERMEDIATE**

RYE, SPELT, AND ANISE LOAF

The loaf opens beautifully in the oven with a delicate spiral and has a slightly sweet and entirely unique flavor thanks to the licorice-like aniseed.

BAKER'S PERCENTAGES	WEIGHTS & INGREDIENTS
SPONGE	
50%	149g whole rye flour
50%	149g whole wheat flour
100%	298g water
10%	30g rye starter
FINAL DOUGH	
200%	626g sponge
50%	156g medium rye flour
50%	156g spelt flour
50%	156g whole milk, at room temp
20%	62g honey
10%	31g butter, unsalted, at room temp
4%	12g salt
1%	3g aniseed

THE AFTERNOON BEFORE: RYE STARTER REFRESH

Following the instructions on page 203, refresh your rye starter in the afternoon, or 6 to 8 hours before mixing the sponge.

THE NIGHT BEFORE: MIX THE SPONGE

Mix the sponge In a large bowl, thoroughly mix together the rye starter, whole rye flour, whole wheat flour, and water by hand until there are no patches of dry flour. You can squeeze it through your hands, like extruding pasta between your fingers! The sponge will be viscous and sticky—this is okay. Cover the bowl with a dinner plate or sheet pan for a lid and ferment overnight, or 8 to 10 hours, until it doubles in size, is slightly domed, and smells fresh and apple-cider-like.

DAY OF: MIXING THROUGH BAKING

Final mix To the bowl with the overnight sponge, add the medium rye flour, spelt flour, milk, honey, butter, salt, and aniseed and thoroughly mix by hand until there are no patches of dry flour and the butter is fully incorporated. The dough will be sticky—this is okay.

Pop a digital thermometer into the dough to take its temperature—it should be between 79° and 85°F. (If the dough is above 85°F, stick it in a cool spot—not the refrigerator—until it cools to between 82° and 85°F. If it is less than 79°F, place it in a warm location until it reaches 79° to 82°F.)

Shape Lightly flour a 9-inch round banneton and flour your work surface. Use a dough scraper to turn the sticky dough out onto the table. Lightly dust the dough with flour. Work the dough into a log that's about 12 inches long. Curl the log into a spiral and use a bench knife to flip it over (so the bottom becomes the top) into the banneton.

Proof Loosely cover the banneton with a kitchen towel and proof in a draft-free spot at room temperature for 2 to 3 hours. When fully proofed, the loaf will appear to have doubled in size and feel full of air.

Preheat the oven Set a combo cooker on a rack in the oven so the skillet is on the bottom and the pot is inverted as a lid. Preheat the oven (and the combo cooker) to 500°F.

Bake Wearing welding gloves, remove the combo cooker from the oven (it's *hot!*) and quickly toss the dough seam-side down onto the hot skillet portion of the cooker. Immediately cover the bread with the inverted pot for a lid (this bread has no score) and load it back into the oven. Bake for 10 minutes. Remove the combo cooker from the oven and set on the stovetop. Remove the lid (be careful of hot steam) and reduce the oven temperature to 450°F. Return the bread, still on the skillet portion of the combo cooker, to the oven and bake another 20 to 30 minutes, or until the loaf is deeply browned and reaches an internal temperature of 205°F.

Cure Remove the loaf from the skillet and wrap immediately in a kitchen towel. Cure for 5 hours before cutting. Store for up to 5 days, cut-side down, in a paper bag tucked inside a cloth bag.

Refresh the rye 6 to 8 hours before mixing the sponge. The sponge is then
mixed 8 to 10 hours before mixing the final dough. The following morning, the
dough is mixed, shaped, proofed, baked, and cured for 2 to 3 hours.

2 (400G) RINGS —— **10-INCH ROUNDS OF PARCHMENT** —— **DOUGH TEMP: 82°F** —— **LEVEL: INTERMEDIATE**

FINNISH RYE RING

I was searching for a delicate rye when I came across a video of Finnish
women mixing this dough in buckets, with no scales in sight, gossiping while
tending to a wood-fired oven. It was like I dropped into heaven.

BAKER'S PERCENTAGES	WEIGHTS & INGREDIENTS
SPONGE	
150%	304g water
100%	203g dark rye flour
10%	20g rye starter
FINAL DOUGH	
200%	528g sponge
100%	264g light rye flour
3%	8g salt

THE AFTERNOON BEFORE: RYE STARTER REFRESH
Following the instructions on page 203, refresh your rye starter in the
afternoon, or 6 to 8 hours before mixing the sponge.

THE NIGHT BEFORE: MIX THE SPONGE
In a large bowl, thoroughly mix together the water, dark rye flour, and
rye starter by hand until there are no patches of dry flour. You can
squeeze it through your hands, like extruding pasta between your fingers!
The sponge will be viscous and sticky—this is okay. Cover the bowl with
a dinner plate or sheet pan for a lid and ferment overnight, or 8 to
10 hours, or until it doubles in size, is slightly domed, and smells fresh
and apple-cider-like.

DAY OF: MIXING THROUGH BAKING
Final mix To the bowl with the sponge, add the light rye flour and salt
and thoroughly mix by hand until there are no patches of dry flour. You
can squeeze the dough through your hands, like extruding pasta between
your fingers! The dough will feel like wet cement and be viscous and
sticky—this is okay.

Pop a digital thermometer into the dough to take its temperature—it
should be between 79° and 85°F. (If the dough is above 85°F, stick
it in a cool spot—not the refrigerator—until it cools to between 82° and
85°F. If it is less than 79°F, place it in a warm location until it reaches
79° to 82°F.)

Divide Lightly flour your work surface and use the dough scraper to turn
out the dough onto the table. Eyeball the dough into 2 equal portions.

Recipe continues

Shape Cut two pieces of parchment paper into 10-inch rounds (the rings will get baked on the parchment). Sprinkle the parchment with flour and, using a dough scraper, transfer each portion of dough onto a parchment round. Lightly flour the dough and hand-pat each into an 8-inch ring that's about 1½ inches thick with a 2-inch hole in the center. Decorate each one as you wish: You can use a bench knife to make long lines, indenting the surface of the dough like the pattern of a stone from a stone mill, or gently press a cookie cutter (like a heart shape) on the surface of the dough, or use the end of a chopstick to poke indentations all over the surface (they do not need to go all the way through). Or just leave it plain!

Proof Loosely cover each ring with a kitchen towel and proof in a draft-free spot for 1 to 2 hours, or until the rings appear to have almost doubled in size and when pressed, feel full of air and have slightly cracked.

Preheat the oven Set a combo cooker on a rack in the oven so the skillet is on the bottom and the pot is inverted as a lid. Preheat the oven (and the combo cooker) to 500°F.

Bake Wearing welding gloves, carefully remove the hot combo cooker from the oven and remove the lid. Still wearing the welding gloves, carefully pick up the parchment on either side of one of the rings rounds, lift it up, and gently lower it (still on the parchment) into the skillet portion of the combo cooker. Re-cover with the inverted pot as a lid and transfer back to the oven. Bake for 10 minutes at 500°F. Wearing welding gloves, carefully remove the combo cooker from the oven and set it on the stovetop. Remove the lid (be careful of hot steam!) and reduce the oven temperature to 450°F. Return the ring, still on the skillet portion of the combo cooker, to the oven and bake another 20 minutes, or until it's deeply browned and reaches an internal temperature of 205°F. Return the combo cooker to the oven and let it come back up to 500°F before baking the second ring.

Cure Wrap the rings in a kitchen towel and let rest for 2 to 3 hours. The towel will hold in some steam, helping to soften the outside. You can store them on a pole or string for up to a month or two. After 2 to 3 days, the bread will be quite hard and stale; once it reaches this point, you can break it apart and dunk it into soup or stew.

Refresh the rye starter 6 to 8 hours before mixing the first leaven build. Mix the first leaven build 8 to 10 hours before mixing the second leaven build. The second leaven build is fermented for 4 hours. The final dough is then mixed, shaped, proofed, baked, and then cured for 5 hours.

1 ROUND AT 1.2KG —— **9-INCH SPRINGFORM PAN** —— **DOUGH TEMP: 82°F** —— **LEVEL: INTERMEDIATE**

APPLE-OAT RYE

Two stages of leavening give the dough time to reach a perfect, flavorful balance of sweet and tangy. I recommend using a crunchy/firm apple like a Jonagold, Gold Rush, Arkansas Black, or Pink Lady for the mix-in.

BAKER'S PERCENTAGES	WEIGHTS & INGREDIENTS
LEAVEN BUILD ONE	
100%	89g light rye flour
100%	89g water
10%	9g rye starter
LEAVEN BUILD TWO	
100%	187g leaven build one
100%	187g light rye flour
100%	187g water

THE AFTERNOON BEFORE: RYE STARTER REFRESH

Following the instructions on page 203, refresh your rye starter in the afternoon, or 6 to 8 hours before mixing the leaven build one.

THE NIGHT BEFORE: MIX THE LEAVEN BUILD ONE AND PREP THE APPLES

Mix the leaven build one In a 1-quart deli container (or similar container) mix the rye starter, light rye flour, and room temperature water. Cover with a lid and let rest overnight, or 8 to 10 hours.

Preheat the oven to 400°F.

Prep the apples Core and cut the apples into ½-inch chunks. In a lightly oiled large skillet or lightly oiled sheet pan, spread out and bake the apple chunks for 45 to 50 minutes, roasting them until they are fragrant, fork-tender, and caramelized on the edges. Remove from the oven and set aside to cool. Transfer to an airtight container and cover. Set aside until needed.

DAY OF: LEAVEN BUILD TWO THROUGH BAKING

Mix the leaven build two In a large bowl, thoroughly mix together the leaven build one, light rye flour, and water by hand until there are no patches of dry flour. You can squeeze the dough through your hands, like extruding pasta from your fingers! The dough will feel like wet cement and be viscous and sticky—this is okay. Cover with a dinner plate or sheet pan for a lid and ferment for 4 hours, or until doubled in size with small holes on the surface and an apple-cider-like smell.

Final mix To the bowl with the leaven build two, add the dark rye flour, spelt flour, oat flour, water, roasted apples, and salt and thoroughly mix by hand until there are no patches of dry flour.

Recipe and ingredients continue

FINAL DOUGH

200%	561g leaven build two
50%	141g dark rye flour
30%	85g spelt flour
20%	56g oat flour
75%	210g water
50%	140g apples (about 3)
2%	6g salt

Pop a digital thermometer into the dough to take its temperature—it should be between 79° and 85°F. (If the dough is above 85°F, stick it in a cool spot to proof—not the refrigerator—until it cools to between 82° and 85°F. If it is less than 79°F, place it in a warm location to proof until it reaches 79° to 82°F.)

Shape Spray a 9-inch springform pan with a light cooking oil and use a dough scraper to transfer the dough to the pan. Wet your hand and use it to gently pat the dough into the pan, filling it out evenly.

Proof Spray a square of aluminum foil with a light cooking oil and cover the pan with it, oil-side down, loosely tenting it, and crimp it around the sides of the pan. Proof for 2 to 3 hours at room temperature, or until it is slightly risen (about 30% in the pan) and feels full of air when you press on it gently.

Preheat the oven to 500°F.

Bake When the oven is up to temperature, load the bread (still covered in foil) into the oven and bake for 10 minutes. Remove the foil and reduce the oven temperature to 450°F. Bake another 20 minutes, or until the bread has pulled away from the sides, is deeply browned, and reaches an internal temp of 205°F. Remove from the oven and let cool for a few minutes. Run a sharp knife between the edge of the pan and the bread. Pop open the springform side and remove the ring, then remove the loaf from the bottom disk of the pan.

Cure Wrap the bread in a kitchen towel while still warm and cure for 5 hours before cutting. Store for 3 to 4 days, cut-side down, in a paper bag tucked inside a cloth bag.

Refresh the rye starter 6 to 8 hours before mixing the first leaven build. The first
leaven build is fermented 8 to 10 hours. The second leaven build is fermented for 4 hours.
The final dough is then mixed, shaped, proofed, baked, and then cured for 5 hours.

1 BÂTARD AT 1.2KG —— 9-INCH OVAL BANNETON —— DOUGH TEMP: 82°F —— LEVEL: INTERMEDIATE

BUTTERMILK ORANGE BREAD

This is a wonderful bread to make when oranges are
in season, as its fresh citrus flavor brightens any wintry day.

BAKER'S PERCENTAGES	WEIGHTS & INGREDIENTS
LEAVEN BUILD ONE	
100%	171g whole-grain rye flour
100%	171g water
10%	17g rye starter
SCALD	
200%	36g boiling water
100%	18g whole-grain rye flour

THE AFTERNOON BEFORE: RYE STARTER REFRESH
Following the instructions on page 203, refresh your rye starter in the afternoon, or 6 to 8 hours before mixing the leaven build one.

THE NIGHT BEFORE: MIX THE LEAVEN BUILD ONE AND MIX THE SCALD
Mix the leaven build one In a 1-quart deli container (or similar container), mix the rye starter, whole-grain rye flour, and room temperature (68° to 72°F) water. Cover with a lid and let rest overnight, or 8 to 10 hours.

Mix the scald In a 1-pint deli container (or similar heat-safe container), combine the whole-grain rye flour and boiling water and mix together thoroughly with a spoon until there are no patches of dry flour. Cover loosely with a lid and let rest overnight or 8 to 10 hours.

DAY OF: LEAVEN BUILD TWO THROUGH BAKING
Mix the leaven build two In a large bowl, thoroughly mix together the light rye flour, spelt flour, buttermilk, leaven build one, and scald by hand until there are no patches of dry flour. You can squeeze the dough through your hands, like extruding pasta from your fingers! The dough will feel like wet cement and be viscous and sticky—this is okay. Cover with a dinner plate or sheet pan for a lid and ferment for 4 hours.

Final mix To the bowl with the leaven build two, add the rye flour, spelt flour, water, salt, and orange zest and thoroughly mix by hand until there are no patches of dry flour.

Pop a digital thermometer into the dough to take its temperature—it should be between 79° and 85°F. (If the dough is above 85°F, stick it in a cool spot to proof—not the refrigerator—until it cools to between 82° and 85°F. If it is less than 79°F, place it in a warm location to proof until it reaches 79° to 82°F.)

Recipe and ingredients continue

LEAVEN BUILD TWO

200%	360g leaven build one
70%	126g light rye flour
30%	54g whole-grain spelt flour
80%	144g buttermilk, whole, at room temp
30%	54g scald

FINAL DOUGH

300%	738g leaven build two
50%	123g whole-grain rye flour
50%	123g whole-grain spelt flour
80%	197g water
5%	12g salt
5%	12g grated orange zest

Shape Lightly flour a 9-inch oval banneton. Lightly flour your work surface and use a dough scraper to turn the sticky dough out onto the table. Sprinkle the dough with a little flour. Knead the dough into a uniform mass and then use your hands to pat it into a rectangle with a short side facing you. Roll up the dough into a cylinder with a seam on the bottom and a smooth top. Pinch the ends shut. Use a bench knife to flip the dough, seam-side up, into the floured banneton.

Proof Loosely cover the banneton with a kitchen towel and proof in a draft-free spot at room temperature for 2 to 3 hours. When fully proofed, it will have almost doubled in size and will feel full of air when gently pressed.

Preheat the oven Set a combo cooker on a rack in the oven so the skillet is on the bottom and the pot is inverted as a lid. Preheat the oven (and the combo cooker) to 500°F.

Score Wearing welding gloves, remove the combo cooker from the oven (it's hot!) and quickly toss the dough seam-side down onto the hot skillet portion of the cooker. Use a lame and razor, with the blade at a 35-degree angle, to score the top of the loaf in a crosshatch or pattern of your choice.

Bake Cover with the inverted pot for a lid and transfer back to the oven. Bake for 10 minutes. Remove the combo cooker from the oven and set on the stovetop. Remove the lid (be careful of hot steam) and reduce the oven temperature to 450°F. Return the bread, still on the skillet portion of the combo cooker, to the oven and bake for another 30 minutes, or until the loaf is deeply browned and reaches an internal temperature of 205°F.

Cure Wrap the bread in a kitchen towel while still warm and cure for 5 hours before cutting. Store for 3 to 4 days, cut-side down, in a paper bag tucked inside a cloth bag.

SNAPSHOT
Refresh the rye starter 6 to 8 hours before mixing the sponge.
The sponge is mixed 8 to 10 hours before mixing the final dough. The final
dough is mixed, shaped, proofed, baked, and cured for 5 hours.

1 ROUND AT 1KG ——— 9-INCH SPRINGFORM PAN ——— DOUGH TEMP: 82°F ——— LEVEL: INTERMEDIATE

CANDIED GINGER RYE

The combination of candied ginger, ground ginger,
cinnamon, and cloves in this bread is like a hug from the inside out.

BAKER'S PERCENTAGES	WEIGHTS & INGREDIENTS
SPONGE	
75%	188g whole-grain spelt flour
25%	63g whole-grain rye flour
100%	251g water
10%	25g rye starter
CANDIED GINGER SOAKER	
100%	100g candied ginger
100%	100g boiling water

THE AFTERNOON BEFORE: RYE STARTER REFRESH

Following the instructions on page 203, refresh your rye starter in the afternoon, or 6 to 8 hours before mixing the sponge.

THE NIGHT BEFORE: MIX THE SPONGE AND MAKE THE CANDIED GINGER SOAKER

Mix the sponge In a large bowl, thoroughly mix together the spelt flour, rye flour, water, and rye starter by hand until there are no patches of dry flour. You can squeeze it through your hands, like extruding pasta between your fingers! The sponge will be viscous and sticky—this is okay. Cover the bowl with a dinner plate or sheet pan for a lid and ferment overnight, or 8 to 10 hours, or until it doubles in size, is slightly domed, and smells fresh and apple-cider-like.

Make the candied ginger soaker Chop the ginger into pea-size bits and transfer to a 1-pint deli container (or similar container). Cover with the boiling water. Cover tightly with a lid and soak overnight or until needed.

DAY OF: MIXING THROUGH BAKING

Final mix Drain the candied ginger soaker. To the bowl with the sponge, add the whole-grain rye flour, whole wheat flour, water, candied ginger soaker, molasses, honey, salt, ground ginger, cinnamon, cloves, and black pepper and thoroughly mix by hand until there are no patches of dry flour. The dough will be viscous and sticky—this is normal.

Pop a digital thermometer into the dough to take its temperature—it should be between 79° and 85°F. (If the dough is above 85°F, stick it in a cool spot to proof—not the refrigerator—until it cools to between 82° and 85°F. If it is less than 79°F, place it in a warm location to proof until it reaches 79° to 82°F.)

Recipe and ingredients continue

FINAL DOUGH

300%	528g sponge
80%	141g whole-grain or dark rye flour
20%	35g whole wheat flour
75%	132g water
30%	100g candied ginger soaker
30%	53g molasses
30%	53g honey
4%	7g salt
2%	4g ginger, ground
2%	4g cinnamon, ground
2%	4g cloves, ground
2%	4g black pepper, ground

A handful of candied ginger, chopped, for the top

Shape Lightly spray a 9-inch springform pan with a light cooking oil and use a dough scraper to transfer the dough to the pan. Wet your hand and use it to gently pat the dough out so it reaches the rim in all directions.

Proof Coat a square of aluminum foil with a light cooking oil and cover the pan with it, oil-side down, loosely tenting it so the dough doesn't stick as it proofs or bakes. Crimp the edges of the foil on the pan so it stays put. Proof for 3 to 4 hours, or until it has almost doubled in size and feels full of air when gently pressed.

Preheat the oven to 500°F.

Bake Peel back the foil and sprinkle a handful of tiny candied ginger bits on top. Return the foil, crimping it onto the sides again. Bake for 10 minutes. Remove the foil and reduce the oven temperature to 450°F. Bake another 20 minutes, or until the bread has pulled away from the sides of the pan, is deeply browned, and has an internal temp of 205°F. Remove from the oven. Run a sharp knife between the edge of the pan and the bread. Pop open the springform sides and remove the ring, then remove the bread from the bottom disk of the pan.

Cure Wrap the bread in a kitchen towel while still warm and cure for 5 hours before cutting. (Or you can be naughty like me and cut into it early! Eeek!) Store for 3 to 4 days, cut-side down, in a paper bag tucked inside a cloth bag.

Refresh the rye starter 6 to 8 hours before mixing the leaven build one. Mix the leaven build
one and ferment 8 to 10 hours. The following morning, mix the leaven build two and ferment 24 hours.
Twenty-four hours later, mix the final dough and shape, proof, and bake the bread. Cure for 24 hours.

1 ROUND AT 1.2KG —— 9-INCH ROUND BANNETON —— DOUGH TEMP: 82°F —— LEVEL: ADVANCED

CHOCOLATE-CHERRY RYE

This is a decadent loaf with a robust, intense chocolate flavor. It's best eaten with
a glass of red wine and while wearing your favorite wool socks (trust me on this).

BAKER'S PERCENTAGES	WEIGHTS & INGREDIENTS
LEAVEN BUILD ONE	
100%	64g whole-grain rye flour
100%	64g water
20%	13g rye starter
CHERRY SOAKER	
100%	81g cherries, dried
100%	81g water, warm

THE AFTERNOON BEFORE: RYE STARTER REFRESH
Following the instructions on page 203, refresh your rye starter in the
afternoon, or 6 to 8 hours before mixing the leaven build one.

THE NIGHT BEFORE: MIX THE LEAVEN BUILD ONE, MAKE THE
CHERRY SOAKER, AND PREP THE CHOCOLATE
Mix the leaven build one In a large bowl, thoroughly mix together the
rye flour, water, and rye starter by hand until there are no patches
of dry flour. Cover the bowl with a dinner plate or sheet pan for a lid
and ferment overnight, or 8 to 10 hours, until it doubles in size, is slightly
domed, and smells fresh and apple-cider-like.

Make the cherry soaker Chop the cherries into pea-size bits, transfer
to a 1-pint deli container (or similar container), and add the warm water.
Cover tightly with a lid and soak overnight, or until needed.

Prep the chocolate Chop the semisweet chocolate into large pea-size
chunks and transfer to a 1-pint deli container (or similar container). Cover
with a lid and set aside until needed.

DAY ONE: MIX THE LEAVEN BUILD TWO
Mix the leaven build two Drain the excess water from the cherry soaker.
To the leaven build one, thoroughly mix in the dark rye flour, water,
cherries, chopped chocolate, cocoa powder, and salt by hand until there
are no patches of dry flour. You can squeeze the dough through your
hands, like extruding pasta between your fingers. The dough will be gluey
and cement-like—this is okay.

Recipe and ingredients continue

LEAVEN BUILD TWO

100%	234g dark rye flour
80%	187g water
60%	140g leaven build one
40%	93g chocolate, semisweet
35%	81g cherry soaker
5%	12g Dutch-process cocoa
4%	9g salt

FINAL DOUGH

300%	759g leaven build two
100%	253g medium rye flour
75%	190g water, warm

Pop a digital thermometer into the dough to take its temperature—it should be between 79° and 85°F. (If the dough is above 85°F, stick it in a cool spot—not the refrigerator—until it cools to between 82° and 85°F. If it is less than 79°F, place it in a warm location until it reaches 79° to 82°F.) Cover the bowl with a dinner plate or sheet pan for a lid and ferment for 24 hours.

DAY TWO: MIXING THROUGH BAKING

Mix the final dough To the bowl with the leaven build two, add the medium rye flour and water and thoroughly mix by hand until there are no patches of dry flour. You can squeeze it through your hands, like extruding pasta between your fingers. The dough will be gluey and cement-like—this is okay.

Shape Lightly flour a 9-inch round banneton and set aside. Sprinkle your work surface with flour. Use a dough scraper to turn the dough out onto the table. Knead the dough into a uniform mass and then knead it into a round with a smooth top and a seam on the bottom. Use a dough scraper to transfer it seam-side up into the floured banneton.

Proof Loosely cover the banneton with a kitchen towel and proof in a draft-free spot for 2 to 3 hours, or until it appears to have doubled in size and feels full of air when gently pressed.

Preheat the oven Set a combo cooker on a rack in the oven so the skillet is on the bottom and the pot is inverted as a lid. Preheat the oven (and the combo cooker) to 500°F.

Bake Wearing welding gloves, carefully remove the hot combo cooker from the oven and remove the lid. Turn out the dough onto the hot skillet (this bread has no score) and cover with the inverted pot. Return to the oven. Bake for 10 minutes at 500°F. Remove the combo cooker from the oven and set on the stovetop. Remove the lid (be careful of hot steam) and reduce the oven temperature to 450°F. Return the bread, still on the skillet portion of the combo cooker, to the oven and bake for another 30 minutes, or until the loaf is deeply browned and reaches an internal temperature of 205°F.

Cure Wrap the bread in a kitchen towel while still warm and cure for 24 hours before cutting. Store for 3 to 4 days, cut-side down, in a paper bag tucked inside a cloth bag.

Start the sprouted berries for the bread 3 days ahead of time (see Sprouting, page 46).
Refresh the rye starter 6 to 8 hours before mixing the leaven build one. Mix the leaven build one
and ferment 8 to 10 hours. Mix the leaven build two and ferment 24 hours. Twenty-four hours
later, mix the final dough and shape, proof, and bake the bread. Cure for 24 hours.

1 LOAF AT 1.2KG ——— **9-INCH PULLMAN PAN** ——— **DOUGH TEMP: 82°F** ——— **LEVEL: ADVANCED**

VOLLKORNBROT

Vollkornbrot means "whole-grain bread" in German and is a hearty
and robust 100% rye bread. Mildly sour (and yet surprisingly sweet), this loaf has
toasted seeds and sprouted rye berries in every bite. I love a slice smeared
with a thick coat of cultured butter and French breakfast radishes.

BAKER'S PERCENTAGES	WEIGHTS & INGREDIENTS
LEAVEN BUILD ONE	
100%	60g rye flour
100%	60g water
20%	10g rye starter
LEAVEN BUILD TWO	
128%	354g water
100%	277g whole-grain rye flour
47%	130g leaven build one
18%	50g sunflower seeds
18%	50g pumpkin seeds
18%	50g cracked rye
3%	8g salt

THE AFTERNOON BEFORE: RYE STARTER REFRESH
Following the instructions on page 203, refresh your rye starter in the
afternoon, or 6 to 8 hours before mixing the leaven build one.

THE NIGHT BEFORE: MIX THE LEAVEN BUILD ONE AND TOAST
THE SEEDS
Mix the leaven build one In a large bowl, mix the rye starter, rye flour,
and room temperature water. Cover with a lid and rest overnight,
or 8 to 10 hours.

Toast the seeds In a large skillet, toast the pumpkin seeds, sunflower
seeds, and cracked rye over medium-low heat, shaking the pan often,
until they are all fragrant, warmed, and lightly browned, 8 to 10 minutes.
Transfer the seeds to a plate to cool, then store in a 1-pint deli container
(or similar container). Cover with the lid slightly ajar and set aside
until needed.

DAY ONE: MIX THE LEAVEN BUILD TWO
Mix the leaven build two To the leaven build one, add the rye flour,
water, toasted seeds and cracked rye, salt, and thoroughly mix by hand
until there are no patches of dry flour. You can squeeze the dough
through your hands, like extruding pasta between your fingers. The
dough will be gluey and cement-like—this is okay.

Pop a digital thermometer into the dough to take its temperature—it
should be between 79° and 85°F. (If the dough is above 85°F, stick
it in a cool spot—not the refrigerator—until it cools to between 82° and

Recipe and ingredients continue

FINAL DOUGH

707%	919g leaven build two
100%	130g whole-grain rye flour
82%	106g water
15%	20g rye berries, sprouted
6%	8g molasses, blackstrap

85°F. If it is less than 79°F, place it in a warm location until it reaches 79° to 82°F.) Cover the bowl with a dinner plate or sheet pan for a lid and ferment for 24 hours.

DAY TWO: MIXING THE FINAL DOUGH THROUGH BAKING

Final mix To the leaven build two, add the rye flour, water, sprouted rye berries, and molasses and thoroughly mix by hand until there are no patches of dry flour. You can squeeze the dough through your hands, like extruding pasta between your fingers. The dough will be gluey and cement-like—this is okay.

Shape Lightly oil a 9-inch Pullman pan. Using a dough scraper dipped in water, scoop out and transfer the sticky dough to the pan. You can gently level it out with your palm (dip your hand in water first, and be careful not to degas the dough) or use the short side of the dough scraper to smooth it out.

Proof Cover the Pullman pan with the lid. Set aside in a warm draft-free spot (see Homemade Proof Box, page 56) for 3 hours, checking it periodically, about once an hour. (To check on the dough, pull back the lid and take a peek.) When fully proofed, the loaf will have risen to the top of the pan and may have a pockmarked surface, tiny holes, or cracks (this is all okay and normal) and when gently pressed will feel full of air.

Preheat the oven to 500°F.

Bake Transfer to the oven, with the lid on, and bake for 10 minutes. Wearing welding gloves, carefully remove the Pullman pan lid and reduce the oven temperature to 450°F. Bake another 30 to 40 minutes, or until the loaf is dark brown, pulls away from the sides of the pan, and reaches an internal temperature of 205°F.

Cure Carefully remove the loaf from the pan and wrap in heat-safe plastic, or keep it tightly wrapped in a kitchen towel, so it can steam itself as it sets. Cure for 24 hours. Thinly slice and enjoy! Store for up to 7 days, cut-side down, in a paper bag tucked inside a cloth bag.

Refresh the rye starter 6 to 8 hours before mixing the leaven build one. Mix the leaven build one and ferment 8 to 10 hours. Mix the leaven build two and ferment 24 hours. On the third morning, or 24 hours later, mix the final dough and shape, proof, and bake the bread. Cure for 24 hours.

1 LOAF AT 1.4KG ——— **9-INCH PULLMAN PAN** ——— **DOUGH TEMP: 82°F** ——— **LEVEL: ADVANCED**

RUGBROD

Rugbrod makes an excellent, sturdy, and flavorful base for *smørrebrød*, open-faced sandwiches. Try topping thinly sliced and toasted pieces with shrimp, lemon, shredded radicchio, and dill or salted butter, or with roast beef, kimchi, and spicy mayonnaise.

BAKER'S PERCENTAGES	WEIGHTS & INGREDIENTS
LEAVEN BUILD ONE	
100%	84g whole-grain rye flour
75%	63g water
10%	8g rye starter
SEED SOAKER	
300%	117g water, warm
100%	39g flaxseeds, golden or brown
100%	39g millet
100%	39g sunflower seeds

THE AFTERNOON BEFORE: RYE STARTER REFRESH
Following the instructions on page 203, refresh your rye starter in the afternoon, or 6 to 8 hours before mixing the leaven build one.

THE NIGHT BEFORE: MIX THE LEAVEN BUILD ONE AND THE SEED SOAKER
Mix the leaven build one In a large bowl, thoroughly mix the rye starter, rye flour, and water. Cover with a lid and rest overnight, or 8 to 10 hours.

Make the seed soaker Weigh out the flaxseeds, millet, and sunflower seeds and transfer to a quart-size deli container (or similar container). Cover with the warm water. Cover tightly with a lid and soak overnight or until needed.

DAY ONE: MIX THE LEAVEN BUILD TWO
Mix the leaven build two Drain the seeds of any excess water. To the leaven build one, add the rye flour, water, seeds, and salt and mix by hand until there are no patches of dry flour. You can squeeze the dough through your hands, like extruding pasta between your fingers. The dough will be gluey and cement-like—this is okay.

Pop a digital thermometer into the dough to take its temperature—it should be between 79° and 85°F. (If the dough is above 85°F, stick it in a cool spot—not the refrigerator—until it cools to between 82° and 85°F. If it is less than 79°F, place it in a warm location until it reaches 79° to 82°F.) Cover the bowl with a dinner plate or sheet pan for a lid and ferment for 24 hours.

Recipe and ingredients continue

LEAVEN BUILD TWO

100%	313g whole-grain rye flour
75%	235g water
50%	156g leaven build one
37%	117g seed soaker
3%	9g salt

FINAL DOUGH

300%	870g leaven build two
100%	290g whole wheat flour
80%	233g water
2%	7g molasses, blackstrap

DAY TWO: MIXING THE FINAL DOUGH THROUGH BAKING

Final mix To the leaven build two, add the whole wheat flour, water, and molasses and thoroughly mix by hand until there are no patches of dry flour. The dough will be gluey and cement-like—this is okay.

Shape Lightly oil a 9-inch Pullman pan. Using a dough scraper dipped in water, scoop out and transfer the sticky dough to the pan. You can gently level it out with your palm (dip your hand in water first, and be careful not to degas the dough) or use the short side of the dough scraper to smooth it out.

Proof Cover the Pullman pan with the lid. Set the dough aside in a warm draft-free spot (see Homemade Proof Box, page 56) for 2 to 3 hours, checking it periodically, about once an hour. (To check on the dough, pull back the lid and take a peek.) When fully proofed, the loaf will have risen to the top of the pan and may have a pockmarked surface, tiny holes, or cracks (this is all okay and normal) and when gently pressed will feel full of air.

Preheat the oven to 500°F.

Score Uncover the loaf and dust the top with flour, then gently press the metal edge of the bench knife into the top of the dough about ¼ inch deep to mark lines, triangles, or a diamond pattern. Lightly spray the top of the lid with a light cooking oil and re-cover the pan.

Bake Transfer to the oven and bake covered for 10 minutes. Wearing welding gloves, carefully remove the Pullman pan lid and reduce the oven temperature to 450°F. Bake another 30 to 40 minutes, or until the loaf is a dark brown, pulls away from the sides of the pan, and reaches an internal temperature of 205°F.

Cure Carefully remove the loaf from the pan and wrap in heat-safe plastic, or keep it tightly wrapped in a kitchen towel, so it can steam itself as it sets. Cure for 24 hours. Thinly slice and enjoy! Store for up to 7 days, cut-side down, in a paper bag tucked inside a cloth bag.

Refresh the rye starter 6 to 8 hours before mixing the leaven build one. Mix the leaven
build one and ferment 8 to 10 hours. Mix the leaven build two and rest 24 hours. Twenty-four
hours later, mix the final dough and shape, proof, and bake the bread. Cure for 24 hours.

1 LOAF AT 1.4KG ——— 9-INCH PULLMAN PAN ——— DOUGH TEMP: 82°F ——— LEVEL: ADVANCED

PUMPERNICKEL

Historically, these filling rye loaves were baked in the residual
heat of a wood-fired oven for hours on end, resulting
in a mahogany-colored crust and a pleasing cake-like interior.

BAKER'S PERCENTAGES	WEIGHTS & INGREDIENTS
LEAVEN BUILD ONE	
100%	76g whole-grain rye flour
75%	57g water
10%	8g rye starter
RYE CHOPS SOAKER	
100%	57g rye chops
100%	57g boiling water

THE AFTERNOON BEFORE: RYE STARTER REFRESH
Following the instructions on page 203, refresh your rye starter in the
afternoon, or 6 to 8 hours before mixing the leaven build one.

THE NIGHT BEFORE: MIX THE LEAVEN BUILD ONE, COOK THE RYE
BERRIES, AND MAKE THE RYE CHOPS SOAKER
Mix the leaven build one In a large bowl, mix the rye starter, whole-
grain rye flour, and water thoroughly by hand. Cover with a lid and rest
overnight, or 8 to 10 hours.

Cook the rye berries In a small saucepan, combine the rye berries with
water to cover. Bring to a gentle boil over medium heat, then reduce the
heat to low and continue cooking until the berries are chewy and plump
(they should be soft, not crunchy), 8 to 10 minutes. Remove from the heat
and drain. Transfer to a 1-pint deli container (or similar container), cover
loosely with a lid, and rest overnight, or until needed.

Make the rye chops soaker Weigh out the rye chops into a 1-pint deli
container (or similar container) and cover with the boiling water. Cover
loosely with a lid and soak overnight or until needed.

DAY ONE: MIX THE LEAVEN BUILD TWO
Mix the leaven build two Drain the rye chops of any excess water. To the
leaven build one, add the pumpernickel flour, medium rye flour, water, rye
chops soaker, cooked rye berries, and salt and mix by hand until there are
no patches of dry flour. You can squeeze the dough through your hands,
like extruding pasta between your fingers. The dough will be gluey and
cement-like—this is okay.

Recipe and ingredients continue

LEAVEN BUILD TWO

50%	141g pumpernickel flour
50%	141g medium rye flour
80%	228g water
50%	141g leaven build one
40%	113g rye berries, cooked
20%	57g rye chops soaker
3%	8g salt

FINAL DOUGH

300%	885g leaven build two
100%	295g light rye flour
75%	221g water

Pop a digital thermometer into the dough to take its temperature—it should be between 79° and 85°F. (If the dough is above 85°F, stick it in a cool spot—not the refrigerator—until it cools to between 82° and 85°F. If it is less than 79°F, place it in a warm location until it reaches 79° to 82°F.) Cover the bowl with a dinner plate or sheet pan for a lid and ferment for 24 hours.

DAY TWO: MIX THE FINAL DOUGH THROUGH BAKING
Final mix To the leaven build two, add the light rye flour and water and thoroughly mix by hand until there are no patches of dry flour.

Shape Lightly oil a 9-inch Pullman pan. Using a dough scraper dipped in water, scoop out and transfer the sticky dough to the pan. You can gently level it out with your palm (dip your hand in water first, and be careful not to degas the dough) or use the short side of the dough scraper to smooth it out.

Proof Cover the Pullman pan with the lid. Set the dough aside in a warm draft-free spot (see Homemade Proof Box, page 56) for 3 hours, checking it periodically, about once an hour. (To check on the dough, pull back the lid and take a peek.) When fully proofed, the loaf will have risen to the top of the pan and may have a pockmarked surface, tiny holes, or cracks (this is all okay and normal) and when gently pressed will feel full of air.

Preheat the oven to 500°F.

Score Uncover the loaf and dust the top with flour, then gently press the metal edge of the bench knife into the top of the dough about ¼ inch deep to mark lines, triangles, or a diamond pattern. Lightly spray the top of the lid with a light cooking oil and re-cover the pan.

Bake Transfer to the oven and bake covered for 10 minutes. Wearing welding gloves, carefully remove the Pullman pan lid and reduce the oven temperature to 450°F. Bake another 30 to 40 minutes, or until the loaf is dark brown, pulls away from the sides of the pan, and reaches an internal temperature of 205°F.

Cure Carefully remove the loaf from the pan and wrap in heat-safe plastic, or keep it tightly wrapped in a kitchen towel, so it can steam itself as it sets. Cure for 24 hours. Thinly slice and enjoy! Store for up to 7 days, cut-side down, in a paper bag tucked inside a cloth bag.

Extra Credit

CONGRATULATIONS! You've made a beautiful starter (or two or three) and now you're ready to explore its potential, am I right? In this chapter we will use the discarded portion of starters (see What Is Discard?, page 252) to add complex flavor and texture to familiar favorite treats, like Sourdough Piecrust (page 270) and the Cheddar and Black Pepper Biscuits (page 258). While the recipes in this chapter do require a healthy starter, unlike the planning required for bread, many of these goodies can be made on a whim.

WHAT IS DISCARD?

In a perfect world, all discard goes on to make bread or other baked goods.

STRICTLY SPEAKING, DISCARD IS the portion of the starter that is removed when you refresh your starter. In a perfect world, all discard goes on to make bread, and the portion left behind is given flour and water and left to ferment, a closed-loop ecosystem.

If you've been good to your starter with weekly refreshments and avidly baking bread, then there's really no difference between your starter and the discard in terms of activity and flavor. However, even the most attentive bakers sometimes slip up and forget to feed their starters. The dog runs off, your car breaks down, you get a cold (or—gasp—you take a break from bread!). Life just happens! Nursing a forgotten starter back to life is the most common place that you will encounter excess starter discard. This discard is going to be more pungent and less active than the discard from a routinely used starter, and it is not the kind of discard you will want to use in the following recipes.

The second place you're most likely to encounter a buildup of discarded starter is within the first two weeks of a new starter's life. When you start a starter from scratch, it needs to be fed daily, even sometimes twice a day in warm weather. Think about it like an infant. When a baby is born, it wants to eat a little bit around the clock. Your new mixture of flour and water is the same—it might get hungry and fussy and exhausted more easily because it's not biologically stabilized and robust. And that's the point: As you develop the starter, you train it to be predicable. (I would also argue that it trains you.) This training process leaves you with lots of discard! This is also not the kind of discard you will want to use in this chapter.

RULES FOR USING DISCARD

Rule 1: Do not use anything you wouldn't eat off your finger. This is helpful when you pull your starter out of the fridge and you think you might want to make some cookies (like Sourdough Chocolate Chip Cookies, page 262). Does it smell like rubbing alcohol and look stringy? If so, toss or compost the discard, then refresh your starter, wait 4 to 5 hours, and use *that* discard.

Rule 2: Don't use any discard from a young starter that is less than one week old, because, well, it's not really a starter yet! Those first few days—and really for about a month—your starter is in the process of becoming its adult self and doesn't have the proper acidity or balance of bacteria to be considered a true sourdough. It won't give you the rise or the flavor you expect. Any discard from the first week should head to the wastebasket or compost bin. Before this makes you too sad, you can rest assured knowing that the flour and water *did* serve a really important function: feeding your new baby!

Rule 3: If your starter ever has a pink or orange mold, toss the entire thing. If it's got some gray sludge or hooch on top, you'll need to refresh it. This is NOT the kind of discard you want in your coffee cake or banana bread. Shed a tear if you must, but that is just going to need to go to the compost or wastebasket.

For all of the starter discards used in this chapter, be they sourdough, desem, or rye, you want to begin with a healthy, bubbly starter that smells yogurt-like and fresh. Do not use discard starter that is pungent, vinegary, stringy, or flat. If your starter doesn't look happy, it may be necessary to refresh it, leave it out at room temperature, and use the discard from the well-fed starter 4 to 5 hours later.

ABOVE
Sourdough Chocolate Chip Cookies
(page 262)

MIX AND MATCH DISCARD—SORT OF

THE STARTER DISCARD CALLED for in each recipe is chosen for the overall flavor profile, just like how I match my white flour starter with bread dough calling for mostly white flour, my whole wheat starter with whole wheat flours, and my rye starter with doughs asking for a majority of rye flour. In this chapter, you have some wiggle room, but using a white flour starter where a rye flour starter is called for will give you a different flavor and overall texture. You may swap out a sourdough discard for a desem discard since both are wheat, but use only rye discard with the rye recipes.

OPPOSITE
Cheddar and Black Pepper Biscuits
(page 258)

MAKES ONE 9-INCH LOAF ———— DISCARDED STARTER: DESEM ———— LEVEL: BEGINNER

MONICA'S BANANA BREAD

My friend Monica Segovia-Welsh of Chicken Bridge
Bakery in Pittsboro, North Carolina, was kind enough to show
me this recipe a few years back. This is my favorite version!

WEIGHTS & INGREDIENTS

150g all-purpose flour

90g rye flour

2g cinnamon, ground

2g coriander, ground

2g baking soda

2g baking powder

2g salt

113g (1 stick) butter, unsalted, at room temp

150g granulated sugar

90g dark brown sugar

2 eggs, large

4g vanilla extract

4 ripe bananas, mashed

80g desem starter discard

100g walnuts, chopped (optional)

DAY ONE: MIXING THROUGH BAKING
Preheat the oven to 350°F.

Make a parchment sling Center a sheet of parchment over a 9-inch loaf pan so a few inches drape over each long side. Crease the parchment wherever there is an edge, so it sits nicely in the pan. Spray the parchment and exposed pan with a light cooking oil.

Prep the dry ingredients In a medium bowl, whisk together the all-purpose flour, rye flour, cinnamon, coriander, baking soda, baking powder, and salt. Set aside.

Mix In a stand mixer with a paddle attachment, cream the butter and both sugars on medium-high speed until fluffy, 2 to 3 minutes. Stop and scrape down the sides of the bowl with a flexible spatula as needed. When done creaming, the mixture will be light yellow, airy, and voluminous.

Add the eggs, one at a time, mixing on low after each addition until thoroughly blended. Stop as necessary to scrape down the batter from the sides of the bowl. The batter will be glossy and thick. Add the vanilla, the mashed bananas, and desem discard. Mix on low for another 30 seconds, until well combined.

Last, add the flour blend and mix on low until there is no visible dry flour. The batter will be loose and have chunks of banana throughout. If you're including walnuts, fold them in now. Pour the batter into the parchment-lined loaf pan.

Bake Transfer the bread to the oven and bake for 1 hour, or until a toothpick inserted in the center comes out clean. The banana bread will be deeply browned and pull away from the pan when done.

Cool Remove from the oven and let set for a few minutes in the pan. Use the parchment sling to transfer the bread from the pan to a wire rack. Fully cool to room temperature before serving. This bread is ultramoist and will keep, sealed in an airtight container, for up to 1 week.

MAKES TWELVE 2-INCH BISCUITS ——— **DISCARDED STARTER: SOURDOUGH** ——— **LEVEL: BEGINNER**

CHEDDAR AND BLACK PEPPER BISCUITS

This biscuit comes from my friend Ashley Capps, who wrote
it down almost a decade ago for me. It's a laminated dough filled with streaks
of butter; when the butter melts in the oven, steam is released and pulls
apart the alternating layers for the ultimate flaky bite!

WEIGHTS & INGREDIENTS

175g whole milk	6g black pepper, freshly ground
40g sourdough starter discard	4g salt
30g sour cream	45g cheddar cheese, grated
340g all-purpose flour	113g (1 stick) butter, unsalted, cut into cubes, very cold
16g sugar	
16g baking powder	

EGG WASH

1 egg, large	14g half-and-half

DAY OF: MIXING THROUGH BAKING

Prep In a medium bowl, whisk the milk, starter, and sour cream together into a slurry. Set aside.

Mix In a stand mixer fitted with a paddle attachment, mix the all-purpose flour, sugar, baking powder, black pepper, and salt on low speed until combined. Mix in the cheddar. Add the cold butter and mix on low until there are broken portions of butter in various sizes, some pea-size and others still large and chunky, about the size of a walnut half.

Stop the mixer and scrape down the sides and the bottom of the bowl, under the dough. Add the milk/sour cream slurry. Resume mixing on low, for about 1 minute, until there are no patches of dry flour. The dough may climb the paddle. If it does, stop the mixer and use your hand to push the dough off the paddle and back into the bowl, then resume mixing. Once the slurry is fully absorbed and the dough pulls together and away from the sides of the bowl, it's done. The dough should still be cold to the touch and you should still see chunks of butter (don't overmix).

Chill Turn the dough out onto a lightly floured surface and press into a rectangle. Wrap in plastic and refrigerate for at least 30 minutes or up to 24 hours (if you're worried the butter got too warm while mixing, leave it in for a solid hour and you'll be all set).

Roll out Sprinkle your work surface with flour. Remove the dough from the fridge and turn it out onto the floured work space with a short side facing you and the long sides on the left and right. Use a rolling pin to roll the dough into an 8 × 7-inch rectangle. Now imagine the dough is folded like a business letter into three equal portions. Fold the bottom of the dough over the center third, and the top of the dough down over the center, as you would fold a letter.

Chill again and prep the egg wash Wrap in plastic and return to the fridge for another 30-minute rest (or up to 24 hours). While you wait, in a small bowl, whisk together the egg and half-and-half. Set the egg wash aside.

Preheat the oven to 400°F. Line a sheet pan with parchment paper. Set aside.

Roll and cut Lightly dust your work surface with flour. Using a rolling pin and long, sweeping strokes, roll the dough into a 6 × 8-inch rectangle. Using a ruler and a pastry wheel, make a mark every 2 inches along each side. Use these marks and the ruler to create a grid on the dough, then use the grid to cut the biscuits with the pastry wheel. Transfer the biscuits to the prepared pan, spacing them 1 inch apart.

Egg wash and bake Use a pastry brush to brush the biscuits with egg wash before baking. Bake for 10 minutes, then reduce the heat to 350°F and bake for another 20 minutes, or until they are deeply browned on the top and golden on the sides. Use a spatula to transfer the biscuits to a wire rack and cool completely. These are best eaten warm, split with a fork and slathered with butter, or used to make an egg sandwich. Uneaten biscuits can be kept for up to 5 days in a paper bag tucked inside a cloth bag. Slice open and toast on a well-buttered griddle to refresh!

1 LOAF AT 840G ———— 9-INCH PULLMAN PAN ———— DISCARD: RYE ———— LEVEL: BEGINNER

RISE AND SHINE BREAD

This "bread" is my answer to a power bar. A slice topped with fruit or cheese makes
a great breakfast, or sliced thin it's a perfect addition to a cheese plate.

WEIGHTS & INGREDIENTS

100g rye starter discard	5g salt
100g cashews	120g dried apricots, chopped
100g almonds	50g golden raisins
100g macadamia nuts	50g bee pollen
100g rolled rye (or rolled oats)	5g eggs, large
50g golden flaxseeds	60g honey

DAY OF: MIXING THROUGH BAKING
Preheat the oven to 350°F.

Ready your pan Make a parchment sling for a 9-inch Pullman pan
by centering a sheet of parchment over the pan so a few inches drape
over each of the long sides. Crease the parchment wherever there
is an edge, so it sits nicely in the pan and doesn't slouch or slide down the
walls. Lightly spray the parchment and exposed pan with a light cooking
spray.

Toast the seeds and nuts In a large skillet, toast the cashews, almonds,
macadamia nuts, rolled rye, and flaxseeds over medium heat, stirring
frequently until browned and fragrant, 8 to 10 minutes. Remove from the
heat, spread out on a plate, and cool completely.

Mix In a large bowl, combine the apricots, raisins, bee pollen, nuts, rolled
rye, seeds, and salt. Set aside. In a medium bowl, beat together the eggs,
honey, and rye starter until well combined. Pour the eggy mix over the
nuts, seeds, oats, and dried fruit and stir together with a large spoon. Pour
into the parchment-lined pan.

Bake until the loaf is deeply browned and has pulled away from the sides
of the pan, about 1 hour. Allow to cool in the pan for up to 5 minutes.

Cool Wearing oven mitts, pull the bread out of the pan using the
parchment tabs on either side of the loaf. Cool on a wire rack for 1 hour
before thinly slicing. This loaf can be stored in an airtight container and
refrigerated for up to 2 weeks. I like to slice mine in half, keeping half
on the countertop and storing the other half, sliced, in the freezer, in a zip-
top plastic bag with the air pressed out of it, for up to a month.

SNAPSHOT
The dough is mixed before being rested in the fridge
overnight. The cookies are shaped and baked the following day.

MAKES 12 LARGE COOKIES ——— ——— DISCARDED STARTER: SOURDOUGH ——— ——— LEVEL: BEGINNER

SOURDOUGH CHOCOLATE CHIP COOKIES

This luscious dough is packed with chocolate chips and topped
with roughly chopped chocolate and large flakes of salt for bites that will
send you into heaven. Dunk into cold milk for the ultimate experience!

WEIGHTS & INGREDIENTS

COOKIE DOUGH

226g (2 sticks) butter, unsalted, at room temp	2 eggs
	14g vanilla extract
200g granulated sugar	75g sourdough starter discard
70g light brown sugar	275g all-purpose flour
2g baking soda	350g chocolate chips, semisweet
2g salt	

COOKIE TOPPINGS

226g bittersweet chocolate, roughly chopped into chunks the size of walnut halves and peas	15g flaky salt, such as Maldon

DAY ONE: MIXING AND CHILLING

Mix In a stand mixer fitted with a paddle attachment, cream the butter, granulated sugar, brown sugar, baking soda, and salt on low speed until light and fluffy, 2 to 3 minutes. Stop and scrape down the sides and the bottom of the bowl with a flexible spatula as needed.

Mix in the eggs, one at a time. Stop and scrape down the sides and bottom of the bowl as necessary. Add the vanilla and sourdough discard and mix on low until the batter is silky, shiny, and ultrasmooth.

Add half the flour (you can eyeball it) and mix on low for a few paddle strokes, then add the remaining flour and mix until there is no visible dry flour. Add the chocolate chips and mix until just combined. Use a dough scraper or flexible spatula to transfer the dough to an airtight container. (Try not to eat it all on the way!)

Chill Stick the dough in the fridge overnight or for up to 3 days!

DAY TWO: BAKING

Preheat the oven to 350°F. Line a sheet pan with parchment paper.

Divide Sprinkle your work surface with flour, remove the dough from the refrigerator, and use a dough scraper to transfer it to the table. Eyeball the dough into 12 equal portions.

Shape To shape the cookie dough, cup both of your hands in a C shape and put a chunk of dough in the middle. Move your hands in circular motions in opposite directions from each other, cupping the ball in the center. Roll into a ball. Repeat with the remaining portions to make

Recipe continues

12 cookies total. Set the dough balls on another parchment-lined sheet pan and refrigerate for 10 minutes.

Bake These cookies are baked 4 at a time. Remove 4 balls of dough from the fridge and place them staggered 2 inches apart on the parchment-lined sheet pan. Bake for 8 to 10 minutes, or until they are firm and dark brown on the edges and soft in the center. Remove from the oven to add the toppings. Press as many pieces of the rough-chopped chocolate into the tops as you like (get artsy), sprinkle with a pinch or two of flaky salt, and return to the oven to bake for another 8 to 10 minutes, or until they have a golden, firm edge, a slightly risen yet still soft center, and the rough-cut chocolate is slightly melted. Remove from the oven, cool for a moment on the pan, then use a spatula to transfer the cookies onto a wire rack to cool completely. Repeat with the remaining balls of dough until done. The baked cookies keep for up to 5 days sealed in an airtight container. You can also store them in a resealable bag in the freezer for up to 3 weeks.

SERVES 12 ———————— DISCARDED STARTER: DESEM ———————— LEVEL: BEGINNER

COFFEE CAKE

This coffee cake features a ribbon
of cinnamon in the center and crunchy crumble topping.

WEIGHTS & INGREDIENTS

CINNAMON FILLING

115g light brown sugar	6g cinnamon, ground
35g all-purpose flour	

CAKE BATTER

250g all-purpose flour	440g granulated sugar
3g salt	4 eggs, large
226g (2 sticks) butter, unsalted, at room temp	80g desem discard
	200g sour cream
	14g vanilla extract

CRUMBLE TOPPING

113g (1 stick) butter, unsalted, melted	50g light brown sugar
125g all-purpose flour	4g cinnamon, ground
50g granulated sugar	2g nutmeg, freshly grated
	2g salt

DAY OF: MIXING THROUGH BAKING
Preheat the oven to 350°F.

Make a parchment sling Center a long sheet of parchment paper over a 9 × 13-inch baking pan so a few inches drape over the long sides of the pan. Crease the parchment wherever there is an edge, so it doesn't slouch or slide down the walls. Lightly spray the parchment and exposed ends of the pan with a light cooking oil.

Make the cinnamon filling In a medium bowl, whisk together the brown sugar, all-purpose flour, and cinnamon. Set aside.

Prep the dry ingredients for the batter In a separate medium bowl, whisk together the all-purpose flour and the salt. Set aside.

Mix In a stand mixer fitted with the paddle attachment, cream the butter and sugar on medium until the mixture is light yellow, airy, and voluminous, 2 to 3 minutes. Use a flexible rubber spatula to scrape down the sides and bottom of the bowl as needed.

To the creamed butter and sugar, add the eggs, one at a time. Mix on low after each egg, stopping the mixer as necessary to scrape down the bottom and sides of the bowl, until all eggs are fully incorporated.

Next, add the desem discard, sour cream, and vanilla and mix on medium-low until blended, 1 to 2 minutes. Add the flour/salt mixture and mix until there are no visible ribbons of dry flour, about 2 minutes.

Layer the batter and filling Use a flexible spatula to scoop a little less than half of the batter into the center of the prepared pan. Use one hand to hold the parchment and one hand to guide the batter as you spread it as evenly as you can into all four corners of the pan. Sprinkle the cinnamon filling evenly over the batter. Scoop the remaining batter over the filling and use the spatula to smooth it out into all four corners, covering the filling.

Recipe continues

Make the crumble topping In a stand mixer fitted with a paddle attachment, combine the melted butter, all-purpose flour, granulated sugar, brown sugar, cinnamon, nutmeg, and salt. Mix on low speed. At first it will look dry, then sandy, and then pebble-size clumps and crumbles will form—which means you're done. Use your hands to sprinkle the topping evenly over the batter.

Bake Transfer to the oven and bake for 45 minutes, or until a toothpick inserted into the center of the cake comes out clean and the cake has risen, pulled away from the edges of the pan, and the topping is browned and crispy. (There might be a few large bumps where the cake expanded from a little air caught in the cinnamon ribbon layer—don't worry, the cake will settle as it cools.)

Cool Remove the cake from the oven and let it cool for a few minutes in the pan before using the parchment tabs to lift it out. Fully cool to room temp on a wire rack. Cut it into 12 or 24 portions, depending on how big of a slice you like. Eat the same day or place in an airtight container and serve within 3 days. You can also wrap and freeze individual portions for up to 3 weeks.

The batter is begun the night before and fermented
overnight before being finished and baked the following morning.

SERVES 4 ———————————— DISCARDED STARTER: SOURDOUGH ———————————— LEVEL: BEGINNER

OVERNIGHT WAFFLES

Darkened ridges and chewy, golden centers make these
Belgian-style waffles a standout, and that's not even mentioning
their cultured yogurt flavor thanks to the sourdough.

WEIGHTS & INGREDIENTS

OVERNIGHT BATTER

300g sourdough starter discard	100g all-purpose flour
300g yogurt, plain, whole-milk	100g whole white wheat flour
	100g water

FINAL BATTER

60g butter, unsalted, melted	2g baking soda
1 egg, large	2g salt
28g granulated sugar	(extra butter to grease the waffle iron)

THE NIGHT BEFORE: MIX THE OVERNIGHT BATTER
In a large bowl, whisk together the starter discard, yogurt, all-purpose flour, whole white wheat flour, and water. Whisk until all of the ingredients are blended and there are no patches of dry flour; don't overmix—you still want to see some lumps in the batter when you're done. Cover with a dinner plate or sheet pan for a lid and let it bubble away on the countertop overnight, or 8 to 10 hours.

DAY OF: FINAL MIX AND BAKE
Preheat a waffle iron to medium high. While the iron is heating up, finish the batter.

Mix the final batter Whisk the melted butter, egg, sugar, baking soda, and salt into the overnight batter until fully combined. (The batter will be thick and smell a little sour—this is normal.)

Cook Lightly spray the iron with cooking oil and pour the batter onto the hot iron by the ladleful, enough to fill the holes, but not so much that it runs over the edge. Quickly spread the batter to the edges of the iron with the back of the ladle, then close. Cook, following your waffle maker's instructions, until the waffles are firm and browned around the edges. Check the first waffle and adjust the temperature as needed. If the waffles are undercooked on the inside, reduce the temperature and prolong the bake. If they are taking a long time and staying pale, increase the heat. Enjoy the waffles hot; they're best eaten as they are made! Continue making more waffles with the rest of the batter.

Freeze extras (if there are any!) You can make a double batch and freeze the leftovers in a 1-gallon zip-top bag. Press all the air out and then double bag with another 1-gallon bag. Reheat the waffles at 250°F directly on the oven rack for 8 to 10 minutes.

MAKES ONE 9-INCH CRUST ———— DISCARDED STARTER: SOURDOUGH ———— LEVEL: BEGINNER

SOURDOUGH PIECRUST

The addition of sourdough starter in this classic pie dough
makes for a pliant crust that has a bold, cultured taste and, when
baked, complements any seasonal fruit filling perfectly.

WEIGHTS & INGREDIENTS

130g butter,
unsalted

80g sourdough
starter discard

20g +
2 tablespoons
ice cold water

180g all-purpose
flour

10g sugar

5g salt

DAY OF: MIXING THROUGH BAKING

Cube the butter into chunks the size of walnut halves, transfer to an airtight container, and store in the fridge while prepping everything else.

Prepare the sourdough slurry In a small bowl, whisk together the starter and 20g of the water until combined.

Mix In a food processor, pulse together the flour, sugar, and salt to combine. Add the cold butter and process until the butter is in pea-size pieces, about 5 seconds. Next, with the processor running on low, drizzle in the slurry. Let the processor run until there are no patches of dry flour, the dough becomes a uniform golden color, and you can still see little bits of pea-size butter. If you can squeeze the dough and it holds together without crumbling, you don't need any extra water. If your dough falls apart when pressed together, drizzle in the remaining 2 tablespoons ice water and process on low just a few seconds more.

Form into a disk Lightly dust your work surface with flour and turn out the dough. Work into a 4- to 5-inch disk. If cracks appear, and they will (cracks in pie dough are like wrinkles—I don't know how or why we ever started thinking they shouldn't, or wouldn't, be there), spritz with chilled water from a spray bottle or dip your fingers in cold water and smooth them out with your fingers. (Nine times out of ten, any imperfections will be resolved when the dough is rolled out—the cracks will be hidden with a beautiful, crimped edge!)

Chill Tightly wrap the dough in plastic and then roll over it with a rolling pin a few times. Transfer to the fridge for 1 hour, or up to 24 hours. Use to make Three Seasons Pie with Crumble Topping (page 272) or Roasted Veggie Galette (page 275).

HOW TO BLIND-BAKE A PIECRUST

A blind-baked piecrust is a bottom crust that is partially or fully baked before being filled. This ensures that the crust and filling are done baking in tandem and that the crust stays flaky and crisp.

Preheat the oven to 400°F. Remove the dough from the refrigerator and let it warm up for a few minutes so it's pliable.

Lightly dust your work surface with flour. Transfer the dough onto the table and begin to roll it out into a 10-inch round about ⅛ inch thick, using long sweeping motions. It's okay to sprinkle the dough with flour as needed to prevent it from sticking (brush off any excess with a pastry brush), but don't use handfuls of flour. Working in a cold environment, like a chilly kitchen, will help the dough roll out easily. I like to roll pie dough in the early morning with the windows open.

Make sure the dough is moving on the table! I'm constantly flipping the dough over and running my hand under it. If at any point you feel like you're fighting the dough, toss it on a sheet pan, cover it in plastic wrap, and chill for 10 minutes. If your kitchen is cold enough, then let it rest a little right on the table. Most shrinkage in blind-baking comes from an unrested dough contracting in the pie pan while it bakes.

To get the dough from the table into your pie pan, lay your rolling pin at the bottom edge of the circle of dough. Wind the dough around the pin as you roll up to the top. Hover the rolling pin over the top of the pie pan and unroll the dough into the pan. If you're off a little, simply shift the dough into place. If it gets any cracks, just pinch it back together.

Gently press the dough into the pie pan. Make sure it fills out any curves and is overhanging about 1 inch over the rim. Tuck the excess dough up and underneath itself on top of the rim of the pie pan, hiding the rough edges under a smooth top. Crimp with your fingers, or mark with the tines of a fork, all the way around the edge of the dough. Poke the dough with the tines of the fork on the bottom and sides, about 15 times.

Cut a 12-inch parchment round from a large sheet of parchment, crinkle it up, and lay it flat (this makes it fit better against the dough). Cover the dough with the parchment. Add 1 to 2 cups of pie weights or dried beans to the parchment-lined shell, taking care to get the weights all the way up the sides of the pan.

Transfer to a parchment-lined sheet pan and bake for 10 minutes, or until the dough is pale golden, firm, and risen but not fully baked. (You can use the exposed rim of the crust to help you tell how brown the dough is getting.)

Remove the sheet pan from the oven and lift out the parchment full of weights. Transfer the weights to a large bowl to cool. Reduce the oven temperature to 375°F and return the now-empty crust to the oven to bake for another 8 to 10 minutes, or until golden and firm to the touch. Now the crust is ready to be filled and fully baked.

This filling is flexible and easy to make. You'll need one Sourdough Piecrust (page 270), blind-baked.

MAKES ONE 9-INCH PIE ———————— DISCARDED STARTER: NONE ———————— LEVEL: BEGINNER

THREE SEASONS PIE WITH CRUMBLE TOPPING

Sometimes the best filling for a pie
is a mix! Mix and match one made of in-season fruit.

CRUMBLE TOPPING

113g (1 stick) butter, unsalted, cold, and cubed	80g light brown sugar
	80g almonds, sliced
125g whole wheat flour	8g cinnamon
	2g nutmeg, grated
100g granulated sugar	2g salt

FRUIT FILLING

2 Pink Lady apples, large, cored and chopped into bite-size pieces	28g water
	1 lemon, zested and juiced
168g blueberries	150g light brown sugar
680g strawberries, hulled and quartered	14g vanilla extract
100g granulated sugar	2g nutmeg, grated
35g cornstarch	4g salt

ASSEMBLY

1 Sourdough Piecrust (page 270), blind-baked

DAY OF: MIXING THE FILLING THROUGH BAKING

Make the crumble topping In a stand mixer fitted with the paddle attachment, beat together the butter, whole wheat flour, granulated sugar, light brown sugar, almonds, cinnamon, nutmeg, and salt on medium speed until pebble-size clumps begin to form, 2 to 3 minutes. Stop the mixer, scrape down the sides and bottom of the mixing bowl, and mix for another minute to incorporate any amount of remaining dry flour. When done, the topping will look like wet sand and hold together when squeezed in the palm of your hand. Set aside.

Preheat the oven to 375°F.

Make the fruit filling In a large mixing bowl, combine the apples and blueberries. Set aside.

In a medium saucepan, combine the strawberries, granulated sugar, cornstarch, and water. Bring to a boil over medium heat, stirring constantly. Use a large spoon to mash half of the strawberries, leaving the other half whole. Remove from the heat once the juices have reduced by half. (It will be a vibrant red, thick, jammy mixture.)

Pour the hot strawberry mixture over the apples and blueberries. Add the lemon zest and juice, light brown sugar, vanilla, nutmeg, and salt and stir together.

Assemble the pie Transfer the fruit filling to the blind-baked pie shell. Cover with the crumble topping and bake for 25 minutes, or until the crumble is golden brown and crisp and the juices are bubbling.

Cool Cool on a wire rack for 1 to 2 hours. Cut into 8 slices and serve. Keep any leftovers in an airtight container in the fridge for up to 3 days.

The veggies are roasted before being encased in a buttery sourdough crust.
You'll need the dough for one Sourdough Piecrust (page 270), chilled and ready to roll out.

MAKES ONE 9-INCH GALETTE ——— **DISCARDED STARTER: NONE** ——— **LEVEL: BEGINNER**

ROASTED VEGGIE GALETTE

I love making this for lunch during my bread making workshops!

WEIGHTS & INGREDIENTS

FILLING

½ onion, white, cut into ½-inch cubes	28g olive oil
2 carrots, cut into ½-inch cubes	Salt and freshly ground black pepper
1 beet, yellow or gold, cut into ½-inch cubes	2 to 3 kale leaves, lacinato
1 Yukon Gold potato, cut into ½-inch cubes	30g parmesan, shredded with a Microplane
1 fennel bulb, cut into ½-inch cubes	14g grated lemon zest
	4 cloves garlic, minced

GALETTE

1 egg yolk	1 Sourdough Piecrust (page 270), unbaked
28g half-and-half, heavy cream, or milk	

DAY OF: MAKING THE FILLING THROUGH BAKING
Preheat the oven to 400°F.

Make the filling In a large bowl, combine the onion, carrots, beet, potato, and fennel with the olive oil to taste and toss to lightly coat. Add salt and pepper to taste. Spread the cubed vegetables out over a sheet pan, loosely tent with foil, and bake for 40 minutes, or until the vegetables are easily pierced by the tines of a fork but not falling part.

Meanwhile, remove the kale ribs and tear up the leaves by hand. Toss into a large bowl. Add the parmesan, lemon zest, and garlic.

Remove the vegetables from the oven, leaving the oven at 400°F. Carefully remove the foil tent and allow them to cool. Once you can handle them, add the vegetables to the kale and toss. Set aside.

Prep the galette In a small bowl, whisk together the egg yolk and half-and-half with a fork. Set aside.

Lightly dust your work surface with flour. Remove the premade sourdough piecrust from the fridge and roll it out into a 12-inch round, about ⅛ inch thick (about the height of two stacked quarters). It's okay if the round is a bit uneven—that's the joy of a galette! Transfer the rolled dough to a parchment-lined sheet pan.

Pile the filling into the center of the dough, leaving a 3-inch border all around. Starting on one side, fold the border up halfway over the filling. Continue around the outer edge, bringing up the edge of the dough and folding it halfway over the filling. If you've mounded the veggies too high, then you can use your fingers, or a spoon, to gently push the filling into the inside edge of the crust.

Egg wash and bake Lightly brush the galette with the egg wash and bake for 45 minutes, or until the dough is deeply browned. Transfer to a wire rack and cool 30 minutes before slicing and serving.

Leftovers can be stored for up to 3 days in an airtight container in the fridge.

MAKES 6 TO 8 SMALL PANCAKES ———— DISCARDED STARTER: RYE ———— LEVEL: BEGINNER

RYE AND BUCKWHEAT PANCAKES

The combination of rye and buckwheat makes for a light
and tender pancake that still feels healthy, even when blanketed
by butter and syrup. Resting the batter overnight takes the rustic
flavor up a notch and gives the pancakes a bit of extra tang.

WEIGHTS & INGREDIENTS

OVERNIGHT BATTER

100g rye starter discard	100g whole-grain rye flour
300g yogurt, plain, whole-milk	100g buckwheat flour
	100g water

FINAL BATTER AND SERVING

2 eggs, large, separated	2g salt
60g butter, unsalted, melted	50g butter, unsalted, for greasing the skillet
28g sugar	Butter and maple syrup for serving
2g baking soda	

THE NIGHT BEFORE: MAKE THE OVERNIGHT BATTER
In a large bowl, combine the rye starter discard, yogurt, rye flour, buckwheat flour, and water. Whisk until all ingredients are combined. It's okay if the batter is lumpy—you just don't want to see strands of starter. Cover the mixing bowl with a dinner plate for a lid and let it bubble away on the countertop overnight. If your kitchen is especially warm (over 75°F), place the covered bowl in the fridge to rest.

DAY OF: MAKE THE FINAL BATTER, GRIDDLE, AND ENJOY
Make the final batter In a medium bowl, with a whisk or an electric mixer, whip the whites to soft peaks. (If you go a little too far, that's fine; folding them into the batter will just take a couple extra strokes!)

Add the yolks, melted butter, sugar, baking soda, and salt to the overnight batter and mix with a flexible spatula until combined. The batter will look a little lumpy and bubbly—this is normal. Dollop the egg whites onto the batter and fold in with sweeping strokes, bringing the top of the batter underneath itself and the bottom to the top. Once you don't see any streaks of egg whites, you're done.

Griddle Preheat a cast-iron skillet or griddle over medium-high heat. The skillet or griddle is ready when butter dropped on it sizzles and bubbles but stays bright yellow. If the skillet or griddle is too cool and the butter doesn't melt right away, up the heat. If the butter melts and burns immediately, reduce the heat, use tongs and a paper towel to wipe it out, and give the skillet or griddle a few minutes to cool before trying again with another tablespoon of butter. In general, it's better to have a warmer start temperature.

Recipe continues

Using a ladle or a ½-cup measure with a spout, add about ½ cup of batter to the center of the skillet or griddle. Cook until the edges are baked halfway up the side of the pancake, and the bubbles that have formed start to pop, 2 to 3 minutes. Shimmy a spatula underneath the pancake and flip it over. Use the first pancake to gauge the heat and adjust the temperature up or down accordingly. If the bottom of the pancake burns before the bubbles pop, then turn the heat down. If it's taking longer than 5 minutes per pancake and they remain quite pale, turn the heat up. After removing the first pancake, give your skillet or griddle a few moments to adjust to the corrected temperature. Continue ladling and cooking the batter until it's gone.

Serve the pancakes hot with plenty of butter and maple syrup. I often make a double batch on Sunday and freeze the leftovers in a 1-gallon zip-top bag. Reheat the pancakes from frozen directly on the oven rack for 10 to 15 minutes at 250°F.

MAKES ENOUGH FOR ONE BATCH OF BROWNIES —— **DISCARDED STARTER: NONE** —— **LEVEL: BEGINNER**

TAHINI BUTTERCREAM

I typically am not a frosting person, but once I stumbled upon
tahini in buttercream, I changed my tune. I love spreading it on the
Rye Brownies (page 280) and smearing it on the top of a baked
and cooled loaf of the Cardamom Bun Bread (page 129).

WEIGHTS & INGREDIENTS

226g (2 sticks)
butter, unsalted,
at room temp

240g tahini

340g confectioners'
sugar, plus
14g to 28g more
if needed

14g vanilla
extract

4g salt

14g to 28g
whole milk
if needed

DAY OF: MIXING THROUGH FROSTING

In a stand mixer fitted with the whisk attachment, cream the butter and
tahini on medium speed for 1 minute, or until fully combined, light, and
fluffy. Add the confectioners' sugar and mix until there are no visible
patches of sugar, stopping to scrape down the sides and bottom of the
bowl with a flexible spatula as needed.

Add the vanilla and salt. Whip on high until the frosting is voluminous,
3 to 4 minutes. If the tahini you're using is on the stiff side, add the
14g to 28g whole milk. If the tahini is thin, add 14g to 28g more of the
confectioners' sugar.

If using on the Rye Brownies (page 280), frost the cooled brownies right
away. Or transfer the buttercream to an airtight container and stick
it in the fridge for up to 24 hours. Bring to room temperature and stir
to soften before using.

RYE BROWNIES

These brownies are rich, chocolaty, and velvety and will take your flavor buds
on a magical journey. For an extra-fancy brownie, I finish the cooled pan with swoops
of Tahini Buttercream, drizzle with honey, and sprinkle with toasted sesame seeds.

WEIGHTS & INGREDIENTS

80g Dutch-process
cocoa powder

130g whole-grain
rye flour

4g salt

185g bittersweet
chocolate,
finely chopped

226g (2 sticks)
butter, unsalted,
at room temp

3 eggs, large

320g sugar

80g rye starter
discard

14g vanilla extract

28g vegetable oil

Tahini Buttercream
(optional;
page 279)

4g to 8g vegetable
oil (optional)

14g to 28g sesame
seeds (optional)

28g to 42g honey
(optional)

DAY OF: MIXING THROUGH BAKING
Preheat the oven to 350°F.

Make a parchment sling Center a sheet of parchment over a 9-inch
square pan, letting a few inches drape the sides. Fold the parchment
wherever there is an edge, so it sits nicely in the pan and doesn't slouch
or slide down.

Prep the dry ingredients for the batter In a medium bowl, whisk
together the cocoa powder, whole-grain rye flour, and salt and set aside.

Make a double boiler Fill a medium saucepan with 3 inches of water
and set it over high heat. Once the water comes to a simmer, turn
it down to low and set a medium metal bowl on top (the bottom of the
bowl shouldn't touch the hot water). Add the bittersweet chocolate and
butter to the bowl and stir occasionally until the butter and chocolate are
melted and completely combined. Remove the bowl from the saucepan
and set aside; reserve 28g of the hot water for the brownie batter.

Mix In a stand mixer fitted with the whisk attachment, cream the eggs
and sugar on medium speed. Once they become a thick, glossy batter,
increase the speed to high and whip for 5 minutes. The batter will turn
voluminous and climb the sides of the bowl. Stop the mixer and scrape
down the bowl as needed.

Reduce the mixer speed to low and add the hot water. Return the mixer
to high and whip the batter for an additional 1 minute.

With the speed on low, drizzle in the melted chocolate/butter and mix for
2 to 3 minutes, or until the batter is bubbly, and fully combined. Stop the
mixer and exchange the whisk for the paddle attachment. Add the rye
starter, vanilla, oil, and the cocoa/rye flour blend. Blend on low until the
batter is a uniform deep brown.

Recipe continues

Using a flexible spatula, scrape the batter into the prepared pan. Guide the batter into all four corners and smooth the top. (You may want to use one hand to hold the parchment and the other to hold the spatula.)

Bake Transfer the brownies to the oven and bake for 30 to 35 minutes, or until a toothpick inserted in the middle comes out clean. Remove from the oven and, using care, lift the brownies out of the pan using the tabs of exposed parchment.

Cool completely on a wire rack.

If desired, frost the brownies and make "sprinkles" Make the buttercream as directed on page 279. In a skillet, heat the oil on low and toast the sesame seeds until golden brown and crispy. Transfer to a paper towel with a spatula or spoon. Blot off the excess oil and cool to room temp. Frost the brownies, drizzle with honey, and sprinkle with the toasted sesame seeds.

Slice Mark 4 rows top to bottom and side to side and cut the brownies into sixteen 2¼-inch squares. Store the brownies for up to 5 days in an airtight container at room temperature. I like to freeze them for up to a month in 1-gallon zip-top bags.

A bright and intensely lemony tart filling. Make ahead one Double-Rye Tart Dough (opposite).

MAKES ONE 9-INCH TART ———— **DISCARDED STARTER: NONE** ———— **LEVEL: INTERMEDIATE**

MEYER LEMON TART

This filling is a riff on Shaker lemon pie filling, with even more lemon (I use floral Meyer lemons) and the addition of cornmeal. The cornmeal gives it a toothsome texture and lends an earthy sweetness to the intensity of the sugar.

WEIGHTS & INGREDIENTS

350g (about 5) lemons, Meyers if possible, thin-skinned

275g granulated sugar

3 eggs, large

28g butter, unsalted, melted

28g all-purpose flour

14g cornmeal, yellow

Confectioners' sugar and/or vanilla ice cream for serving

ASSEMBLING

Double-Rye Tart Dough (opposite), blind-baked

DAY ONE: MACERATE THE LEMONS

Macerate the lemons Slice the lemons crosswise into rounds as thinly as humanly possible—I use a mandoline. Pick out any seeds and discard. In a medium bowl, combine the lemon slices and granulated sugar and use a flexible spatula to stir the mixture, ensuring all the slices are well coated. Cover with a dinner plate for a lid and refrigerate for 24 hours.

DAY TWO: FINISH THE FILLING AND BAKE
Preheat the oven to 350°F.

Remove the lemon mixture from the fridge and stir well. Drain the lemons through a fine-mesh sieve set over a medium-size bowl. Reserve 175g (about 1½ cups) of the liquid. (Save any extra juice in an airtight container in the fridge and use it to add tart/sweetness to fruit-based pie fillings.) If the sugar gums up the sieve, scoop it out with a spoon and add it to the filling. Keep the lemon slices, set aside.

Mix In a stand mixer fitted with a paddle attachment, combine the juice, eggs, melted butter, flour, and cornmeal. Stir until combined. The filling will be a uniform golden color and thick.

Bake Pour the filling into the blind-baked tart shell. Working in a pattern from the outside in, layer the lemon slices in concentric circles. Bake the tart for 20 minutes, or until the filling is thick and bubbling and the rings of the lemon slices are deeply caramelized. The filling will turn jammy and your kitchen will smell amazing!

Cool Remove the tart from the oven and cool completely on a wire rack. Serve at room temperature dusted with confectioners' sugar and/or a scoop of vanilla ice cream. Refrigerate leftovers in an airtight container for up to 3 days.

The dough is mixed and chilled overnight before being shaped and baked the next day.

MAKES ONE 9-INCH TART CRUST ———— DISCARDED STARTER: RYE ———— LEVEL: INTERMEDIATE

DOUBLE-RYE TART DOUGH

From its stunning velvety darkness to the way it melts on your tongue, you'll make this dough once and wonder where it's been all your life. It's wonderful paired with the Meyer Lemon Tart (opposite) or the Three Seasons Pie with Crumble Topping filling (page 272).

WEIGHTS & INGREDIENTS

200g light rye flour

65g confectioners' sugar

14g coffee, finely ground

Salt

113g (1 stick) butter, unsalted, cold, cut into pea-size pieces

50g rye starter discard

1 egg yolk, large

14g half-and-half or heavy cream

6g vanilla extract

2 to 3 cups pie weights or dried beans (for blind-baking the crust)

DAY ONE: MAKE THE DOUGH AND CHILL

Mix In a food processor, pulse together the rye flour, confectioners' sugar, coffee, and salt. Add the butter and pulse until the mixture becomes crumbly, about ten 1-second bursts. Add the rye starter, egg yolk, half-and-half, and vanilla. Pulse until the mixture pulls away from the sides of the bowl, and the ingredients are fully incorporated, about three or four 1-second bursts. The dough should still be cold, and you should still see pea-size specks of butter throughout.

Lightly dust your work surface with flour and turn out the dough. Sprinkle the dough with flour and place inside a 1-gallon zip-top plastic bag. Use your rolling pin to flatten the dough and roll it to the size of a small 5-inch dinner plate. If you're averse to using plastic bags (I understand!), you can do the same motions between two pieces of parchment or between a folded pastry cloth.

Chill Transfer the rolled dough (still in the plastic bag) to the refrigerator to chill overnight (if the dough has cracks on the edges, don't worry—just pat/pinch the edge smooth).

DAY TWO: ROLL AND BLIND-BAKE

Preheat the oven to 350°F. Remove the dough from the refrigerator and let it warm up for a few minutes so it's pliable. Set a 9-inch tart pan, the kind with a removable bottom, on a parchment-lined sheet pan and cut a 12-inch round from a piece of parchment. Crinkle the parchment, then unfold it and set aside.

Roll out Lightly dust your work surface with flour. Remove the dough from the plastic bag and roll it out into a larger round with your rolling pin, using long sweeping motions. You're looking for an even 10-inch round that is ⅛ inch thick (about the height of two stacked quarters). Incorporate as little flour as possible as you roll.

Recipe continues

To get the dough from the table to the pan, lay your rolling pin at the bottom edge of the dough and wind the dough around it as you roll up to the top. Hover the rolling pin over the tart pan and unroll the dough, letting it gently fold off the rolling pin and into the pan. If you're off your mark a little, simply shift the dough into place with your hands. If you get any cracks, just pinch them back together.

Using your fingers, gently press the dough into the pan, making sure it fills out any curves and is flush with the rim. Use scissors to cut off any excess dough hanging over the edge. Poke the bottom and sides of the dough with the tines of a fork about 15 times.

Blind-bake Line the dough with the crinkled parchment. Fill with 1 to 2 cups of the pie weights or dried beans, adding more if needed so the weights go all the way up the sides. Transfer to the oven and bake for 15 minutes, or until the dough is firm, but not fully browned. (You can peek at the crust to see if it's firmed up by gently peeling back a corner of the parchment and looking.)

Wearing oven mitts, remove the tart from the oven and carefully lift the parchment full of weights out of the shell. Transfer the weights or beans to a large bowl to cool. Return the shell to the oven and bake for another 10 minutes, or until the crust is slightly risen and gently browned. The crust is now partially baked and, if filling it with something that needs more baking—such as the Meyer Lemon Tart on page 284—do so now, following the directions in the recipe for baking times.

To completely blind-bake the crust (if you're filling with pastry cream or a different filling that doesn't need baking), return the crust to the oven for another 5 to 10 minutes, or until it is deeply browned and firm. A fully baked shell can be stored in an airtight container overnight, or up to 24 hours, and filled the next day.

MAKES 32 CRACKERS ──────── DISCARDED STARTER: SOURDOUGH ──────── LEVEL: INTERMEDIATE

CHEESY CHEDDAR CRACKERS

The combination of cayenne, smoked paprika, and
sunflower seeds makes these cheddar-packed crackers a party hit!

WEIGHTS & INGREDIENTS

140g all-purpose flour

55g whole wheat flour

50g + 65g sunflower seeds

2g cayenne pepper

2g smoked paprika

2g salt

100g sourdough starter discard

226g cheddar cheese, shredded

113g (1 stick) butter, unsalted, cold, cut into pea-size pieces

14g to 28g ice water

DAY OF: MIXING THROUGH BAKING

Mix and shape In a food processor, combine the all-purpose flour, whole wheat flour, 50g of the sunflower seeds, cayenne, smoked paprika, and salt. Process for 10 seconds. Add the sourdough starter, cheddar, and butter and pulse until the mixture resembles coarse sand, about twenty 1-second bursts.

With the food processor running, drizzle in 14g of ice water. Pulse for 10 more seconds, or until the mixture pulls together and there are no patches of dry flour. (If the mixture hasn't come together, drizzle in another 14g ice water and continue pulsing.)

Sprinkle a sheet of parchment paper with flour. Position it with a long side facing you. Using a flexible spatula, turn out the dough onto the parchment. Now roll the parchment up over the pliable dough to compress the dough into a log. Gently roll the log back and forth, working the dough into a firm cylinder about 11 inches long and 1½ inches in diameter.

Open up the parchment and sprinkle the remaining 65g sunflower seeds over the dough. Fold the parchment back up and roll back and forth, pressing with enough force that the seeds embed themselves into the dough. Transfer to the refrigerator. (Fold up the ends of the parchment so the ends of the dough don't dry out.) Chill for 1 hour, or up to 24 hours.

Preheat the oven to 350°F. Line a sheet pan with parchment paper.

Remove the dough from the refrigerator and slice into sixteen ¼-inch-thick coins. Set the crackers on the prepared sheet pan in 4 rows with 4 rounds in each, spaced ½ inch apart. Return the log to the fridge, wrapped up in the parchment, until it's time to bake the next batch.

Bake Transfer to the oven and bake for 20 to 24 minutes, or until the crackers are puffed, golden, and slightly browned on the edges. Use a spatula to transfer them to a wire rack to cool completely. Slice and bake the remaining crackers. Store the crackers for up to 1 week in an airtight container (they will soften in the container and are really best eaten within 48 hours of baking).

MAKES 24 CRACKERS ———— DISCARDED STARTER: DESEM ———— LEVEL: INTERMEDIATE

SORGHUM GRAHAM CRACKERS

Graham crackers are named after Sylvester Graham, an American
Presbyterian minister who, in the mid-nineteenth century, advocated for
a strict vegetarian and whole grains diet. As a result, roughly milled,
whole-grain flour became known as graham flour. It's worth tracking down,
but if you can't find it, whole wheat works just as well.

WEIGHTS & INGREDIENTS

DOUGH

350g graham flour or whole wheat flour

40g all-purpose flour

60g dark brown sugar

2g salt

4g baking powder

2g baking soda

170g (1½ sticks) butter, unsalted, cut into pea-size pieces and frozen

80g desem starter discard

80g sorghum syrup or honey

1 egg, large

14g to 28g water, cold

EGG WASH

1 egg yolk, large

14g to 28g half-and-half

14g to 28g granulated sugar

DAY ONE: MIX THE DOUGH AND CHILL

Mix In a food processor, pulse together the graham flour, all-purpose flour, brown sugar, salt, baking powder, and baking soda until incorporated. Add the frozen butter and pulse for about 10 seconds, or until the mix resembles coarse sand. You still want to see flecks of unincorporated butter in the dough when done.

In a medium bowl, whisk together the desem starter, sorghum, egg, and 14g of cold water to make a slurry.

Turn on the food processor to low and drizzle in the starter/sorghum slurry. Continue mixing until the dough pulls into a rough ball, and is uniform in color and texture. This should take just under 1 minute. If the dough is dry and remains crumbly, add up to another 14g cold water. The dough is done when it will stick together when squeezed in your palm.

Chill Turn the dough out onto a lightly floured work surface. Sprinkle a little flour on top of the dough and gently pat into a rectangle. Wrap in plastic or transfer to an airtight container and chill for 1 hour or up to 24 hours.

DAY TWO: MAKE THE EGG WASH, SHAPE, AND BAKE

Preheat the oven to 375°F. Line a sheet pan with parchment paper. Set aside.

Make the egg wash In a small bowl, whisk together the egg yolk and half-and-half. Set aside.

Shape Remove the dough from the fridge and let it rest for about 5 minutes, or until pliable. Use a rolling pin to roll the dough into a 12 × 16-inch rectangle about ¼ inch thick. If you encounter cracks,

Recipe continues

dip your finger in a little water and smooth them over. Using a pastry wheel, trim along the edges for clean lines and remove any excess dough. Gather the scraps into a ball and set it aside for later. (If, after rolling the rectangle, the dough seems very dry and crumbly, fold it into thirds, like a business letter, sprinkle with flour, wrap in plastic or a non–terry cloth kitchen towel, and chill in the refrigerator for 10 minutes before again rolling into a 12 × 16-inch rectangle.)

With a long side of the rectangle facing you, use a ruler to nick the dough with the pastry wheel every 2 inches along the long edge. You'll have 8 "sections." Next, on one short side, using the ruler and pastry wheel, mark the dough every 4 inches so you have three "sections." Using the ruler, make a faint line with the pastry wheel from the bottom nicks to the top and from the side nicks to the opposite side. You'll now have a grid with 24 crackers. Use the pastry wheel to follow the lines and cut the dough all the way through.

Bake Use a spatula to transfer 12 crackers, one at a time, to the parchment-lined sheet pan, spacing them 1 inch apart. (You'll end up with 3 rows of 4 crackers each.) Brush the tops with the egg wash and sprinkle with granulated sugar. Bake for 15 to 20 minutes, or until puffed up, golden in the center, and dark brown on the edges. Remove from the oven and transfer to a wire rack using a spatula to cool completely.

Finish baking the remaining crackers, brushing each batch with egg wash and sprinkling with granulated sugar before baking. If you end up with a small ball of extra dough from trimming, roll it into a funky shape, brush with egg wash, and sprinkle with granulated sugar. Bake it last and crumble it over yogurt or dunk in some tea.

While the crackers will keep for up to 5 days in an airtight container at room temperature, they do soften as the days go on, so I prefer to eat them within the first 3 days after they're baked.

Resources

TOOLS AND EQUIPMENT

BREADTOPIA
BREADTOPIA.COM
In addition to their baking tools (this is where I get my bannetons) and tabletop mills, they are also an excellent source for mail-order grains and flours.

TMB BAKING
TMBBAKING.COM
The small wares and essentials page has excellent baskets, oven gloves, and dough cutters.

WEBSTAURANT STORE
WEBSTAURANTSTORE.COM
A commercial restaurant supply company that will deliver to anyone (you don't have to be a restaurant to order from them). This is where I buy my parchment paper, commercial-size spools of cling film, affordable sheet pans, and other essential equipment.

FLOUR

NORTHEAST

FARMER GROUND FLOUR
FARMERGROUNDFLOUR.COM
Find the flour in retail locations throughout New York and at GrowNYC greenmarkets.

KING ARTHUR
KINGARTHURBAKING.COM
Buy their flour in your supermarket or, better yet, visit the flagship store and take a class!

MAINE GRAINS
MAINEGRAINS.COM
Beautiful grains, flours, and wonderful baking tools.

SOUTH

ANSON MILLS
ANSONMILLS.COM
Absolutely stunning grits, rice, beans, and grains.

BELLEGARDE BAKERY
BELLEGARDEBAKERY.COM
Stone ground flour in retail
locations in New Orleans.

CAROLINA GROUND
CAROLINAGROUND.COM
Wonderful selection of Southern
flours and whole grains and
woman owned!

FARM & SPARROW
FARMANDSPARROW.COM
Order online or find in retail
locations in Asheville, North
Carolina. They specialize in
landrace grains.

GREAT BAGEL & BAKERY
EATGREATBAGEL.COM
Bagels, bread, and freshly milled
flour.

LINDLEY MILLS
LINDLEYMILLS.COM
Tenth-generation specialty flour
mill. Great sprouted flour and
mixes.

MIDWEST

**BAKER'S FIELD FLOUR &
BREAD**
BAKERSFIELDFLOUR.COM
Stone-milled, single-origin flour
available online and in person.

JANIE'S MILL
JANIESMILL.COM/
Stone ground, organic, artisan
flours.

SUNRISE FLOUR MILL
SUNRISEFLOURMILL.COM
Minnesota-milled, 100% organic
heritage grains and flour.

WEST/SOUTHWEST

BARTON SPRINGS MILLS
BARTONSPRINGSMILL.COM
Heirloom rye, wheat, corn, and
buckwheat flours.

CENTRAL MILLING
CENTRALMILLING.COM
This is where I order my roller
milled, white high-gluten and
bread flour.

GRIST & TOLL
GRISTANDTOLL.COM
Small-batch, whole-grain, regional
flours.

HAYDEN FLOUR MILLS
HAYDENFLOURMILLS.COM
Family owned and family grown—
the best white wheat flour I've ever
used.

NORTHWEST

CAIRNSPRING MILLS
CAIRNSPRING.COM
Fresh flours with state-of-the-art
milling.

CAMAS COUNTRY MILL
CAMASCOUNTRYMILL.COM
Whole grains and artisanal flours
of very high quality.

Acknowledgments

THANK YOU to Leslie Stoker for bringing this book to the table; and to Raquel Pelzel, you allowed me to find my voice with patience and humor. I'd also like to thank Patricia and the entire team at Potter who planted this book, watered it, and watched it grow. We have done something amazing together. A big thank-you to Claire Saffitz for a warm foreword, and to Jan Buchczik for the cutest grain I've ever seen. To Melissa Martin, you were my book doula; thank you for answering every early-morning phone call. My deepest gratitude to Keia Mastrianni, who not only tested each recipe and provided honest feedback but also baked many of the breads for the photo shoot, along with Ashley Capps, Gus Trout, and Stevie Mangum. Johnny Autry, you added the vibrancy to this book; and Charlotte Autry, what can I say? Not only did you style it perfectly but you also helped me find my own style, too. Thank you to my husband, Marley Green, who took our newborn outside to walk in the forest so I could work. And to my parents, Barry and Joan Jensen, who took Violet to the beach and put her down for countless naps so I could finish; and to Al and Nancy Fox, who generously let me stay in their house so I could have a quiet space to write. And to all those who I have stood beside in bakeries over the years, you taught me about family and friendship in a world that is often tough and thorny—I wish each of you good bread.

Index

Published in the United States by Clarkson Potter/ Publishers, an imprint of Random House, a division of Penguin Random House LLC, New York.
ClarksonPotter.com
RandomHouseBooks.com

CLARKSON POTTER is a trademark and POTTER with colophon is a registered trademark of Penguin Random House LLC.

Library of Congress Cataloging-in-Publication Data is available upon request

ISBN: 978-0-593-23246-0
eBook ISBN: 978-0-593-23247-7

Printed in China

Photographer: Johnny Autry
Food and Prop Stylist: Charlotte Autry
Editor: Raquel Pelzel
Editorial Assistant: Bianca Cruz
Designer: Robert Diaz
Production Editor: Patricia Shaw
Production Managers: Heather Williamson and Kim Tyner
Compositors: Merri Ann Morrell and Hannah Hunt
Copy Editor: Kate Slate
Indexer: Elizabeth T. Parson
Marketer: Allison Renzulli
Publicist: Erica Gelbard

10 9 8 7 6 5 4 3 2 1

First Edition

Clarkson Potter/Publishers
New York
ClarksonPotter.com
RandomHouseBooks.com

Cover design: Robert Diaz
Cover photographs: Johnny Autry
Endpaper illustration: Jan Buchczik